Unstable Ideas

Unstable Ideas

Temperament, Cognition, and Self

Jerome Kagan

Harvard University Press
Cambridge, Massachusetts
London, England

Copyright © 1989 by Jerome Kagan
All rights reserved
Printed in the United States of America
10 9 8 7 6 5 4 3 2

First Harvard University Press paperback edition, 1992

Library of Congress Cataloging-in-Publication Data

Kagan, Jerome.
  Unstable ideas.

  Bibliography: p.
  Includes index.
    1. Self.   2. Temperament.   3. Cognition.
4. Developmental psychology.   I. Title.
[DNLM: 1. Cognition.   2. Human Development.
3. Personality.   4. Self Concept.   BF 713 K11u]
BF697.K26   1989   155.2   88-28376
ISBN 0-674-93038-X (alk. paper) (cloth)
ISBN 0-674-93039-8 (paper)

A word is not a crystal, transparent and unchanged, it is the skin of a living thought and may vary greatly in color and content according to the circumstances and the time in which it is used.

—Oliver Wendell Holmes

I have steadily endeavored to keep my mind free so as to give up any hypothesis, however much beloved, as soon as facts are shown to be opposed to it.

—Charles Darwin

Contents

Unstable Ideas

Introduction

Ten years ago when I last prepared a set of essays for publication, I was preoccupied with the themes of connectedness in development and the sequence of maturing cognitive functions. These ideas seemed to me to be among the central questions in human ontogeny; and preliminary, but less than satisfying, answers are contained in the books *Birth to Maturity, Change and Continuity in Infancy, Infancy,* and *The Second Year,* as well as in a number of shorter technical reports.

Rereading those texts in later years, I realized, to my embarrassment, that I had assumed fixed meanings for ideas like maturation, memory, and continuity of mood and habit. While writing a draft of an essay critical of that assumption during the summer of 1985, I began to treat seriously one feature of the philosophical movement of logical positivism—or logical empiricism—which has fallen into disfavor during the last two decades, especially in the behavioral sciences. The critical idea is that the meanings of terms in empirical science are influenced by their specific source of evidence—or, as philosophers would put it, their conditions of justification. Even provisional acceptance of this suggestion changes our view of empirical social science in a serious way.

A concrete illustration may be helpful. Most of us assume that the state we call fear, like the pen I am holding or the far side of the moon, exists. We have felt afraid and are convinced that we can tell when our friends are experiencing that state. But when scientists try to measure the experience of fear, they confront the surprising and frustrating fact that different procedures lead to different diagnoses.

One person who answers affirmatively to our inquiry about a feeling of fear fails to show any biological signs of that state, while another who denies feeling fear shows all of the expected biological signs. This inconsistency is so common that psychologists are faced with a dilemma with two resolutions. The one most prefer claims that fear exists; we have just been unable to find the correct way to measure it. After all, before microscopes were invented no one could see the bacteria that cause illnesses. A person who felt perfectly well might harbor tubercle bacilli, while someone who felt fatigued might harbor none. There is no epistemological problem; we will have to wait until someone very smart invents a powerful method that will reveal fear's essence. This eminently reasonable position reflected my views a decade ago.

Today, instead of regarding nature as a forest full of hidden treasures to be discovered through clever use of the proper techniques, it has become a series of brief memoranda written in different languages, delivered on an irregular schedule, telling the scientist where next to search. Upon arriving at each new secret location, the investigator finds only another note. It took me too long to realize that the treasures did not easily fit into the small box that I had brought, although the pile of notes fit perfectly. Gerald Holton phrases it gracefully: "The study of nature is a study of artifacts that appear during an engagement between the scientist and the world in which he finds himself. And these artifacts themselves are seen through the lens of theory. Thus, different experimental conditions give different views of nature" (Holton, 1988, p. 156).

I now favor a resolution that is both counterintuitive and inefficient and, therefore, less satisfying. The new construction portrays nature as a set of entities together with the processes in which those entities participate. Most entities are slow to change and retain a relatively delineated existence that can be sensed directly—rocks and flowers—or indirectly with proper aids, like bacteria and neurons. Many of the processes that the entities enter into change quickly and seamlessly. As a consequence, it is not possible, or at least extremely difficult, to freeze them in time. Further, any method used to detect the processes reveals only a part of the whole phenomenon as we believe it exists in nature.

When a different method reveals different evidence, we have the problem of selecting names for the dissimilar information produced by the two procedures. Should we use two different names because the phenomena observed are dissimilar, or the same name because we are relatively certain the data reflect the same invisible process? Most scientists favor the latter solution, on the assumption that the scientist should always try to name the whole process as it is assumed to exist in nature. Even though each investigation captures only a part of the whole, we want our term to refer to the entire event. One physician may use a body temperature of 101 degrees and another may note the patient's chronic fatigue, but both may conclude that the patient has a bacterial infection. The problem is that both symptoms might be present because the patient was poisoned rather than infected. Remember that when fifteenth-century clergy decided that a person was bewitched, they sometimes used as evidence a rash of bad luck, sometimes illness, sometimes the premonition of a misfortune. Despite the different signs, they were confident that each was a valid index of the state of being bewitched.

This argument has led me to side with those, like Frege, who insist that we must differentiate between the validity of a scientific statement, on the one hand, and its sense meaning, on the other. Meaning, for Frege, assumes two forms—referential and sense meaning. The referential meaning is the event in the world to which the word refers—the old woman to whom a Puritan housewife points as she declares, "She is a witch." On the other hand, words and propositions have a sense meaning that is derived from the family of ideas the word or proposition generates. If I write, "Beauty is eternal," most readers will extract a relatively consensual sense meaning, even though one may think of Beethoven's "Eroica" and another "Mont Blanc in Winter."

The *theoretical* meaning of a proposition combines sense and reference. The sentence, "Infants who are loved by their mothers will grow up to be happy adults" has one referential and, therefore, one theoretical meaning if asking the mother about her feelings for the child provides the evidence of maternal love, but a very different referential meaning if an observer watches the mother play with her infant. The theoretical proposition could be true or false with either referential meaning of maternal love. When a scientific proposition has been shown to be true with a particular source of evidence, other scientists will begin to adopt that procedure and there soon will be agreement as to the theoretical meaning of the statement. But if there is little agreement on validity, there will be minimal consensus on theoretical meaning. That is the state of large parts of the behavioral and social sciences today. Because many parts of psychology have too few true statements, it is often the case that no single theoretical meaning of a term wins out in the competition. We work with the unfortunate burden of a small number of concepts used repeatedly to refer to a large number of very different phenomena; hence, the same word may not have the same theoretical meaning. Texts in psychology contain too many sentences of the type, "Infants who are loved by their mothers grow up to be happy adults," whose truth or falsity depends upon their referential meaning. Every chapter in this volume engages, directly or indirectly, this issue. Chapter 1, "Meaning and Procedure," elaborates this theme and provides a frame for the remaining essays, especially those on cognitive development and the concept of self.

Contemporary Preconceptions

Each scientist holds a small set of preconceptions—not always articulated—to which conscious speculations are referred for manipulation and elaboration. These assumptions can be likened to a program language which, after accepting ideas written with specific symbols and syntax, permits the operator to write commands that will produce new, and we hope correct, propositions.

Most psychologists writing between the two World Wars relied on the assumption that feeling states of pleasure and displeasure were central (Chapter 2). A psychologist studying hungry animals running in mazes assumed that the animals learned the correct turns because mastery led to the pleasures of the reinforcement of food. Developmental psychologists observing the emergence of stranger anxiety in infants assumed that infants cried because the unfamiliar people had been associated with prior displeasure.

The extraordinary attractiveness of the conceptual frame provided by the conditioning process is contained in the image of stimulus-response bonds being altered by a punishment, disappointment, kiss, or gift. Although no one knew how such molar events might cause a person to acquire a new response or substitute one action for another, one could always point to the robust examples of salivary conditioning in dogs, and later, bar pressing and maze running in hungry rats. Hence, it was reasonable to assume that the conditioning principles, like Kant's categorical imperative, should be universalized. Producing a change in behavior through contingent reinforcement met every important criterion for a satisfying explanation; it was logical, simple, and mechanical, and it made the environment omnipotent.

As a result, there was resistance to complicating the story by awarding influence to the biology of the learning organism. Adding caveats to conditioning principles stained their beautiful parsimony. I confess to being so persuaded by the coherence of learning theory that I told my first class in child psychology in 1954 how these principles could explain the symptoms of autism—they, too, were convinced.

The history of subsequent investigations which, in Huxley's words, "slayed the beautiful idea with an ugly fact" is well known. Two of the more important findings were Harlow's demonstration that monkeys would spend less time on a wire surrogate that provided food than on a terry-cloth object that would not—a clear violation of conditioning principles—and Garcia's demonstration that rats could not be conditioned to avoid drinking a solution that was followed by illness if the drinking were accompanied by a visual conditioned stimulus but would learn to avoid drinking if the conditioned stimulus was a distinct taste. This fact meant that the conditioning principles had to accommodate to the biology of the animal.

During the last decade two very different preconceptions have gained access to popular psychological discourse. One is characteristic of scholars in artificial intelligence, whose computer programs simulating human cognitive functioning trace their way back to electrical impulses arriving at specific locations in a machine. I suspect that programmers who think about an infant's fear of a stranger imagine propositions with inconsistent commands arriving simultaneously at the same point. The ideas of pleasure and pain are irrelevant.

The other preconception is a product of dramatic advances in our knowledge of the central nervous system, especially the circuits involving sensory association areas, limbic structures, and the prefrontal cortex. Neurobiologists assume that when a stranger appears in front of an eight-month-old infant, the central nervous system's representation of that event is transmitted to the hippocampus and amygdala which, when activated, send messages to the prefrontal cortex and back to sensory-association areas indicating whether or not the stranger resembles a stored representation. If it does not, the amygdala innervates the corpus striatum, hypothalamus, and autonomic nervous system and the infant may cry. None of these interrelated neural structures experiences comfort or discomfort.

The new biological frame that is becoming ascendant can impose a conception as extreme as conditioning. When I now look at a shy two-year-old, I envision an excitable amygdala; twenty years ago I saw a child who had been punished for particular social behaviors or had experienced discomfort in peer or adult interaction. This change in perspective has altered my attitude toward the small number of adults whom I know well who have a very short fuse. I used to invent a history of life events that created their temper, and I privately blamed them for not using their will to prevent their past history from influencing them. Currently, I am more forgiving; after all, it is not their fault that they were born with a reactive limbic circuit. I realize the logical flaws in this new view but it does not seem to help.

I recall a discussion with a biologist who called me aside after I had presented a colloquium on our work on temperamental inhibition. In the introduction to the talk I said I had not anticipated my new allegiance to biology when I was a younger scholar. He replied that he was surprised at my confession, for when he was young and reflected on the behavioral differences among strains of dogs it seemed to him that the same genetic processes should apply to differences among humans. I said that when I had reflected on the same genetic variation among dog breeds, I concluded that the same mechanisms could not apply to humans, adding that each scientist's political views and philosophy exert a strong influence on his or her willingness to acknowledge the power of biology.

An analogous contrast between the two frames is contained in a comparison of the views toward infectious disease in the period before viruses and bacilli were discovered and the period following Koch and Pasteur. During the earlier era citizens were persuaded that the quality of the air, diet, climate, and earlier, sorcery and witchcraft, could cause epidemics. Indeed, the city of Hamburg suffered many more deaths in its 1892 cholera epidemic than was necessary because the medical advisor to the city refused to acknowledge the new ideas and failed to tell the government to be careful with its water supply. However, we should remain on guard against a biological determinism that is so extreme it ignores the contributions of experience.

Thus, one pair of complementary preconceptions, which guides theory, balances the malleability of the child's behavior to the viscissitudes of experience with the realization, now well documented, that some qualities are inherent consequences of the maturation of the central nervous system, as long as a child lives in a world of people, plants, and pebbles. A second, less clearly articulated pair of complementary premises, which is ethical, contrasts the child who is attracted to autonomy with one who seeks supportive social relations. The developmental scholar, therefore, must balance two opposing conceptions—an infinitely malleable versus a biologically constrained child and an autonomous versus a social child. As I note in Chapter 2, the history of developmental psychology is a tale of the attempts to balance these two pairs of claims. During the half-century following the dissemination of Pavlov's ideas, the balance favored the infinite plasticity of young children, who were to be trained to value autonomy. But during the last decade, investigators have acknowledged biological limitations on what can be taught and a preparedness for social relationships. As we adopt either extreme, we move away from what is likely to be true.

One of the social dangers of an unreflective allegiance to the omnipotence of biological forces is an uncritical acceptance of the attitude that since humans are animals, they may have difficulty controlling their "animal-like" behavior. As a result, society must become more tolerant of violence, greed, and unbridled sexuality. This attitude is beginning to permeate our novels, plays, and television dramas. During prime time on a January evening several years ago I watched a highly publicized two-hour television drama on incest entitled, "Something about Amelia." Because the play was about a fundamentally psychological theme, and intended to be of high quality, an examination of its two central premises might reveal the view of human nature that the writers believed was held by the audience of 60 million Americans—premises, I might add, that are also present in the less well crafted dramas that fill the after-dinner hours.

The most profound assumption, which was made explicit after the father's molesting of his daughter had been discovered, is that humans are vulnerable to such overpowering, animal-like impulses that no person can be held totally responsible for his or her behavior when passion grows strong. The central figure in the play is a middle-class Caucasian man in his late thirties who holds a responsible white-collar job, drives his car within the speed limit, tends his garden conscientiously, and presumably, has never struck, murdered, or raped anyone. Yet, he becomes so overwhelmed by sexual impulses toward his daughter he is unable to control them. Although such a characterization of human nature is not shared universally—neither

sixteenth-century Puritans nor contemporary Javanese would understand the father's behavior—I suspect it provoked, along with revul-
sion, a private nod of comprehension from most Americans who
watched the play. Americans are prepared to believe that humans are
so closely related to animals that their biological drives can, on occasion, subdue their sense of what is right.

In the century following the American revolution, European and
American scholars held the opposite view: Every human being inherited a moral sense, with will as its executive. As a result, incest, rape,
homicide, and excessive greed for power and wealth, in an otherwise
sane person, reflected a failure of the will, not the push of irresistibly
powerful passions. Even though nineteenth-century writers acknowledged that humans shared some characteristics with primates, men
and women were unique because they commanded an ability to
choose between morally proper and improper behavior. The ideological revolution sparked by Darwin and continued, initially, by biologists and later by psychologists rejected a discontinuity between
humans and apes, declaring that a continuum between man and animals was the more correct description. Human beings were, with
reference to emotionally based actions, hairless versions of silver
backed gorillas.

This conception of human behavior has some appeal because it is in
accord with the overwhelmingly popular philosophy of materialistic
determinism. This perspective maintains that most of our actions are
controlled, in part, by biological forces over which we have little
control because *Homo sapiens,* like savannah baboons, must give
precedence to hunger, territorial aggression, and sexual drive in order
to survive. The last unsuccessful defense against that view occurred at
the turn of the century when some biologists, threatened by a rigid
determinism they read into the mechanism of natural selection, promoted a Puritan Lamarckianism that made each organism's efforts at
self-improvement the basis for the biological qualities of its heirs. The
new science of genetics effectively destroyed that argument, leaving
humans once again helpless in the face of invisible forces they could
not oppose.

Another reason for the appeal of this view is traceable to our need
to rationalize the conditions of our daily lives. The philosopher A. C.
Danto has noted that the ethics of a society must bend a little to
accommodate to the factual conditions of existence; if not, each person will be vulnerable to terrible tensions during every day. A major-

ity of Americans live and work in large metropolitan areas, far from family and childhood friends, and in frequent encounter with strangers who they suspect will exploit or frustrate them. These strangers will block access at crowded highway intersections, push ahead in long queues, and some may even cheat them when their roof leaks or when they elect surgery for a possibly infected gall bladder. It seems necessary that each of us be continually ready to resist exploitation and to display anger if threatened or forced to defend our property or dignity. Each person must have quick and easy access to the biological emotion of anger.

Most television dramas depict vividly how easy it is for anger to well up and to force otherwise reasonable people to behave in ways they will regret, even though they will eventually be forgiven if their intentions were not unredeemably evil. In order to rationalize the blizzard of cruelty and aggression in contemporary society, it is helpful, and occasionally therapeutic, to believe that it is not always possible to control open anger, rivalry, and jealousy. This rationalization mutes feelings of guilt and dilutes a continuing sense of personal responsibility for hurting others. The Japanese, by contrast, believe that each person can control his or her anger, and the differential frequency of violence in Tokyo and New York implies that if people believe they can tame their aggressive impulses they often do.

The belief that anger, jealousy, and competitiveness are natural emotions that must be expressed has obvious advantages in a society in which a large number of strangers must compete for a small number of positions of dignity, status, and economic security. Under these conditions, it helps to be self-interested, and it is disadvantageous to be too cooperative, too loyal, too altruistic, or too reluctant to protest frustration or unjust advantage by another. In the film *El Norte*, a young Guatemalan who fled his Indian village for a job in a Los Angeles restaurant is advised by a Mexican coworker that, in America, it is best to look out for yourself first. But rather than acknowledge that the structure and philosophy of our society invite each of us to accept self-interest as the first rule, many Americans find it more attractive to believe that this mood, along with jealousy, hatred, violence, and incest, is the inevitable remnant of our animal heritage and so we must learn to accept it.

A second premise in contemporary drama, also present in "Something about Amelia," is revealed when the therapist treating Amelia's father tells the mother that what the father actually needed was love, not a slaking of his sexual desire. The assumption that all humans possess a biologically based need to love and to be loved, which is given form by the child's early relationships with its parents, is basic to Freud's hypothesis regarding the transformation of libidinal energy from infancy to adulthood, at the core of John Bowlby's ideas on the consequences of secure and insecure attachments, and central to Erik Erikson's suggestion that an infant's trust of its mother will eventually become the adult's ability to love another.

Although sexuality has never been unimportant in any culture, romantic love in our society has come to be regarded not only as a source of special pleasure but also as an experience of great beauty and a major source of self-enhancement. Americans treat love as a uniquely intimate, spiritual experience in a world perceived to be isolated, impersonal, and amoral. The anger toward pornography held by many Americans is based, in part, on the threat it poses to the idea of faithful, sacred, romantic love. While watching Bunuel's 1950 film *Wuthering Heights,* I was struck with the similarity between the final scene in which the hero tenderly kisses the face of his dead beloved lying in silk in her ornate coffin and my memory of a lone Guatemalan peasant in a cathedral gently touching the feet of a Christ figure.

I share the belief that love for another is a vital source of satisfaction and élan, but I also believe that a few other special activities can be accompanied by pleasurable psychological states with benevolent consequences. Although I do not understand all the historical events that permitted loving and being loved to crowd out these other candidates, one possible basis for its prominence lies with the attenuation of the pleasures to be had from community service. Gaining the recognition of respective members of the larger community through benevolent acts has become sullied—reminiscent of Groucho Marx's remark that he would not join any club that would accept him. Moreover, because many of us feel relatively impotent to create a safer and more just world, we turn from these sources of gratification to a close relationship with one other person. Such an intimate bond mutes the empty feelings of anonymity that are endemic in large cities of strangers and permits each of us to fall into the relaxing trust of at least one other human being.

The emphasis on a love relation with another is due also to the increased dignity Western society has awarded to women since the middle of the seventeenth century. As symbols of care, affection, and love, women are regarded by both sexes as transcending the meanness of life. Love is regarded as such a sacred feeling that if one truly loves another almost anything can be forgiven. In a popular European film *The Return of Martin Guerre*, a sixteenth-century French Catholic peasant woman knowingly accepts a stranger as her husband and has his child. But at the end of the film, after the imposter is hung, the woman's adultery is forgiven by the clerical judge because she declares her strong sexual attraction to and love for the stranger. During the summer of 1982 I saw a documentary movie made by the National Film Board of Canada describing a marriage between a prostitute and a truck driver whose mutual love was so strong that the husband regarded his wife's work as an honest trade, simply a way for her to "pull her weight."

Make love, not war, was not just a protest against the indifference and lack of humaneness in Vietnam; it was also a positive statement that love between parent and child, teacher and pupil, fiance and fiancée, and husband and wife was an activity all of us should try to pursue in the hours when work is not necessary. Most psychiatrists, pediatricians, or psychologists believe, with Bowlby, that an unloved child is doomed and that "loss of a loved person is one of the most intensely painful experiences any human being can suffer." Yet, I suspect that very few philosophers or naturalists writing before the eighteenth century would have made such a statement, because the essence of each person's vitality, virtue, and happiness was based not only on having a close relation with another but also on the feeling that one had come close to meeting private standards of kindness, talent, restraint, and religious faith. These standards were met with the help of a resolute will that acted on benevolent impulses and withstood totally self-interested temptations.

The contemporary receptivity to the twin ideas that humans are reservoirs of lust, anger, greed, and ambition and that love, not will, is the source of our salvation has profound implications for the laws that are written in congressional committees and upheld in county courtrooms. Every time a judge excuses a violent act of aggression by a sane adolescent of average intelligence because the boy grew up without caring parents, the court, speaking for all of us, declares that to be unloved is so debilitating a disease no person subject to this experience should be required to use the universal knowledge that maliciousness is wrong and the human ability to control malevolence. Although I do not doubt the essential correctness of modern evolutionary theory, some Americans have become too accepting of Darwin's view that "man still bears in his bodily frame the indelible stamp of his lowly origin." An uncritical attitude toward that assumption could make it a self-fulfilling prophecy.[1]

Temperament and Cognition

The pair of essays in Part Two on temperamental differences among children should not be interpreted as a brief for biological determinism in human personality. Temperamental factors impose a slight initial bias for certain moods and behavioral profiles to which the social environment reacts. But the final behavior we observe at age 3, 13, or 33 years is a product of the experiences to which the changing temperamental surfaces have accommodated.

Infants vary on a large number of physiological and psychological dimensions. The small set of temperamental qualities that have been studied, like activity or fearfulness, were selected because they are relatively easy to observe and seemed to be related to the child's future adaptation. However, the words chosen to name an infant's temperamental qualities, as Chapter 3 argues, are partly a function of the investigator's methods. If scientists use interviews and questionnaires with parents, which is a typical strategy, they are likely to invent dimensions that describe behaviors of concern to parents—fussiness, ease of feeding, regularity of sleep, and fearfulness. If Linneaus had asked informed people to describe the animals they knew, the informants probably would have put roosters and turkeys correctly into the same taxonomic category but would have incorrectly placed whales and sharks in the same class and squirrels and seals in different ones. Thus, parents' descriptions of children, although useful initially, should be replaced with sources of evidence that are less seriously colored by the language and preoccupations of adults, for there is only a modest relation between a child's degree of shyness in social settings as observed by psychologists and parents' ratings of that quality.

1. An article entitled "Why mothers kill their babies" in the June 20, 1988, issue of *Time* magazine implies that because women experience unusual changes in hormones at the time of child birth, and because caring for a baby is a demanding task "many women are ill prepared for," it is not fair to hold a mother responsible for murdering her infant. And some judges have agreed with that evaluation.

When Howard Moss and I were analyzing the data for *Birth to Maturity* in the late 1950s, we found a small group of extremely fearful and timid infants who became anxious adolescents and, later, shy, cautious adults. But the doctrine of environmentalism was strong at the time, and so we did not pursue the study of a temperamental quality to explain the preservation of this family of characteristics. Today, thanks to the pioneering work of Alexander Thomas and Stella Chess, most scholars acknowledge the importance of two temperamental dispositions, one related to restraint and the other to spontaneity when young children are in unfamiliar situations. Of the many temperamental qualities that have been studied, these two seem to be preserved for the longest time.

My collaborative studies with Steven Reznick and Nancy Snidman (Chapter 4) reveal that both qualities are preserved from the second to the eighth year of life. There are several possible reasons for this. Unlike most behaviors, the conditions that elicit inhibited or uninhibited behavior toward other people are present continually. Almost every day is punctuated with social interactions that require a decision to withdraw or to participate. Each time a person chooses one or the other of these strategies, the relevant disposition is strengthened, making this quality an intimate part of each person's character. Moreover, the tendency to display either an initial inhibition or lack of inhibition to the unfamiliar is tolerated by adults and other children, unlike extreme aggressiveness or nonconformity to authority. A few parents are pleased with their child's initial caution because they assume it means the child will not rush impulsively into dangerous situations. And because a shy child from a middle-class family is likely to devote more time to academic mastery than to group activities, he may develop the intellectual skills that invite adult approval.

The two classes of children—each makes up about 10 to 15 percent of a random sample of two-to-three-year-olds—will not be treated similarly; each will interpret and react to some experiences differently. Because each child's temperament leads him or her to impose a special frame on encounters, it is difficult to predict the consequences of particular rearing environments. Hence, there can be no purely environmental explanations of human development, as there can be no purely biological ones.

The temperamental qualities of inhibition and lack of inhibition to the unfamiliar engage the issue of qualitative categories versus quantitative dimensions, which is considered in Chapter 3. The tension between a quality and a quantity has persisted since Aristotle's insistence on discrete qualities and Plato's view that the surface characteristics that comprise experience derive from continuities of more basic elements. I believe that the status and power of mathematics, which were enhanced in the subsequent two millennia, persuaded most Enlightenment scholars to side with Plato and to assume that God used mathematics as the language of nature; hence, the continuum became the preferred premise.

Most psychologists, too, prefer variables that are quantified as continuous. If they discover a relation between two variables, say, between stress and health, they assume that the quality implied by the relations is a graded dimension, with each subject assignable to a position on a continuum. But it would be a mistake to assume an underlying continuum for the relation between these two qualities, as it is unwise to assume a continuous relation between body temperature and changes in the circulatory system. For special processes generated when body temperature falls below 95 degrees are silent when the temperature is between 96 and 99 degrees. So it is likely that children with extreme values on a particular temperamental dimension are qualitatively different from those with average or very low values. The research on inhibited and uninhibited children supports that view; the two groups seem to be qualitatively different from each other and from the average child.

Part Three contains two papers on cognitive functioning. The first essay applies the ideas in Chapter 1 by claiming that many of our current terms for mental functions are too broad and do not specify sufficiently the context of the cognitive process. Memory, for example, refers to a family of processes with different ontogenetic schedules and functional laws. The three-month-old can recognize a visual pattern after a twenty-second delay but cannot recall the location of the same toy with a one-second delay. One reason for the resistance to analysis in cognitive theory is that the basic processes are described with predicates for events, rather than nouns for things. Analysis of entities into finer classes is more common in science than the parsing of processes, and therefore cognitive constructs for intellectual functioning remain overly abstract. That is why I argue that cognitive processes must be parsed into smaller, more unitary components that are activated in specific contexts. Terms like memory and perception should be replaced with phrases like recognition memory for the shapes of objects or the perception of motion. Further, a construct representing a cognitive process should refer explicitly to the type of cognitive unit that participates in that process. Thus, generalizations about the processes of recognition or transformation of information when applied to schemata will be different from the generalizations that involve concepts.

The short, informal essay on creativity in science (Chapter 6) tries to make three points with persuasion but without the help of firm empirical facts, because the evidence is missing. The first is that a creative product requires both a specific talent and a motivation to generate a novel idea. Second, chance, often in the form of setting, plays an important role in the uniting of talent and motivation. Finally, I suggest that among creative scientists one can see a division between two groups, those who celebrate mind and those who celebrate nature.

The speculative quality of this essay should reassure those who may misinterpret Chapter 1 as a plea to return to the positivism characteristic of psychology just after World War II. The orthodox version insisted that statements without empirical support were without any meaning and, therefore, of no value. Although persuasive evidential support is lacking, I distinguish among the different meanings of creativity and point to the kinds of information that can affirm or refute these ideas.

Concepts of the Self

Many years ago while watching toddlers react to a woman who modeled some acts in front of them, my staff and I noted that many children between 18 and 22 months would cry after the model finished her demonstration. We wondered why they became upset and presumed that uncertainty was the origin of the distress. When we asked why toddlers might be uncertain in such a setting, a reasonable reply was uncertainty over their competence to duplicate what the model had done, yet an obligation to do so. That idea led to the hypothesis, discussed in Chapter 7, that an initial sense of right and wrong and of self-awareness develop during the second year.

Chapter 8, on the measurement of self, criticizes the psychologists' excessive reliance on self-report evidence because it represents a very special phenomenon supplying a theoretically weak referent for what most scholars mean by self. Very few psychologists or psychiatrists writing about the self before 1960 expected self-report information to supply the primary evidence. But because they were unable to invent more powerful procedures, the next generation of psychologists took the road of least resistance. It is very easy to gather, code, and analyze checks on a piece of paper. As that method gained popularity, the obvious theoretical problems with the procedure were repressed. As a result, contemporary scientists exchange results which, like Confederate money, have legitimacy only for the group that uses them. A person's report that she is confident or free of anxiety is not without value, but other more dynamic meanings of these ideas are not being measured through self-report. Most psychologists wish to understand a different set of phenomena.

The final essay, in the form of a dialogue, presents my frustration at the complexity and ambiguity surrounding the ideas of self and consciousness. Because humans probably are the only objects in nature who can represent their experiences, every term has two meanings—a subjective and an objective one—and that idea returns us to the original essay.

The popularity of ideas related to self represents a renewed celebration of human consciousness, resembling the mood in the nineteenth-century laboratory. It is not clear to whom we should ascribe responsibility for this change. Cognitive science has played some role; hermeneutics, a larger one. I also suspect a role for the shared premises of economics and decision theory, which have made self-interest a primary component in human behavior. Self-interest, as used in most reports, seems to require an awareness of one's feelings, rather than structures and processes that lie beyond conscious articulation. However, few scientists adhering to this premise ask their readers to put down their journal to ask themselves privately what they would say if an interviewer asked them, "How are you feeling? Are you happy? Sad? Mad?" The long pause most informants would display implies that the contents of consciousness are not always a useful guide to the forces that monitor behavior and mood. Thus, we might ask: How did explorations of consciousness come to dominate psychological research?

When each domain in contemporary science began its growth, scholars first tried to explain puzzling phenomena that were available to everyone using methods most could understand and some could implement. Natural philosophers' initial attempts to understand the movements of the stars, planets, and moon required only observation. Newton's insights into the light spectra originated in data requiring only a prism and sunlight passing through a window. Physics is different today. The concepts of quantum mechanics are not intuitively obvious—Feynman says some of these ideas are absurd—and the methods are complex, expensive, and available to a select few. The same can be said of biology, whose practitioners began by examining plants and animals but today create clones and synthesize interferon using concepts that are abstruse and procedures that cannot be implemented in one's basement.

The much younger discipline of psychology initially took perception, hunger, and the learning of new skills as some obvious problems to understand and employed methods that were relatively simple and easy to comprehend. When humans were the targets of study, investigators talked with them, and each person's consciousness of his feelings, perceptions, thoughts, and intentions was given primary emphasis. When learning theory became ascendant, scholars talked of the pleasure or displeasure following positive reinforcement or punishment. They shared the presumption that people avoided initiating acts that led them to feel consciously unpleasant emotions but eagerly implemented actions that made them feel consciously pleasant. Although Freud is known for awarding causal power to the unconscious, most of his evidence came from the statements of his patients and searching introspections of his own conscious experience. Perhaps that is why he gave to the unconscious the feature of aim or goal direction, which is, of course, a primary characteristic of consciousness.

But as I hinted earlier, consciousness is a less important idea in both artificial intelligence and neuroscience. A currently popular program for human thought, called parallel distributive processing, accounts for aspects of perception and memory without the use of any concept that resembles consciousness. Neuroscientists also explain the conditioning of new habits, eating behavior, and even aspects of perception without any reference to consciousness. Their reports and essays describe the circuits in the brain that mediate a child's reaching for a hidden toy, a monkey's recognizing the shape of a piece of wood under which a raisin was hidden, or a cat's acquiring a classically conditioned response. The concept of consciousness does not appear in any of these descriptions because it does not seem necessary.

The young children who are born with a bias to be easily aroused and irritable in the first year, shy in the second year, and introverted during the school years were born with a lower threshold of arousal in the limbic circuits. As a result of the lower threshold, of which they are unaware, they behave as described. There is no need to posit the concept of consciousness to explain their irritability and sleeplessness as infants or their tendency, as two-year-olds, to seek their mother when they suddenly confront an unfamiliar child. Further, as I note in Chapter 8, there is no relation between reports of conscious feelings of anxiety, sadness, or anger and biological signs of these emotional states, like cortisol or norepinephrine level. Richard Nisbett tells us that adults are unaware of how they arrive at a solution to a problem, and when I am lecturing I am unaware of selecting strings of sentences.

Consider a more dramatic example. There is a rare group of patients, called prosopagnosics, who have bilateral lesions of the occipital and temporal lobes. If these patients view photographs of familiar people—spouse, sweetheart, and children—along with unfamiliar photos, the patients report that they do not recognize any of the familiar faces in the photographs. However, if one repeats the experiment but this time measures the patients' galvanic skin reactions, they show increased skin conductance to the familiar photos, but not to the unfamiliar ones. Thus, some circuits in brain/mind recognize the familiar photos, even though the patients are consciously unaware of that fact.

The historian Frank Sulloway has found that later-born scientists of eminence, when compared with first-borns, whether living in the fifteenth or twentieth century, were more likely to promote revolutionary ideas, like those of Copernicus, Freud, and Darwin, because of unconscious dispositions established as a consequence of being a later- rather than a first-born child. We might say of psychology what E. H. Carr said of history, "What the historian is called on to investigate is what lies behind the acts; and to this the conscious thought or motive of the individual actor may be quite irrelevant" (p. 65).

But we do need the construct of consciousness when an individual has a choice to make or is in a state of uncertainty because of a discrepant or challenging event. When a person encounters an event that is outside of routine and cannot be handled automatically, he or she becomes aware of the necessity of a decision. If an atypical feeling of sadness, anger, or joy interrupts the habitual tone, there is awareness of a need to explain the unexpected feeling and, possibly, to take action. Consciousness can be likened to the staff of a fire department.

Most of the time, it is quietly playing pinochle in the back room; it performs when the alarm sounds.

Facts and Ethics

Of what use are these philosophical essays and summaries of new facts? Some would say to guide action. But I am not sure. Every community needs protection against a small set of potential dangers, one of which is the disquiet that grows when there is too great a disagreement on values among the legitimate members of a society. One protection against this threat is to impose a common set of standards on the community; Plato, Hobbes, and Mao Tse-tung argued forcefully for that strategy. Our own society, committed to egalitarianism, tolerance, and liberty, rejects that temptation. We believe that one way to combat that peril is to gather knowledge, hoping that when the community learns the facts, their respect for reason will lead to a shared perspective and a resolution of quarrels. A second danger lies with the uncertainty of the future. Here, too, our society believes that facts are useful; by providing a preview of future perils, they give us time to prepare for or prevent them. Although facts are not without utility, they are not as effective as guides for action on issues that are primarily ethical as many believe. It is of interest that some shy children began life with a special biological state, but this fact does not imply that we should try to change such children. That is an ethical decision not contained in the facts.

We need a corrective to the popular belief that the results of scientific research are to be used not only to enhance understanding but also as the primary basis for deciding issues that are touched deeply by personal values. We would like to believe, with the Greeks, that reason reveals morality. The Greeks assumed that beyond the sensory world of diversity were enduring substances that comprised reality. Thales thought it was water; Anaximander treated it as a boundless entity; Heraclitus insisted it was fire; and Plato supposed it to be a set of geometric forms. But despite the variability in the form of the answer, they agreed that there was a small number of abstract, enduring substances that were the essential bases of natural experience. Since the motion of these entities gave rise to all natural phenomena, including man's thoughts and actions, in principle, man's values and beliefs could be derived from natural laws. Plato then added a critical assumption. The substances in motion were ideal forms with a natural disposition to move toward the good. Since man's thoughts were the product of the motion of these ideal forms, knowledge of what was good would inevitably lead to morally proper behavior. By attributing value to nature's elemental substances, Plato provided ethics with a foundation in natural law. Faith in the power of intellect to reveal proper conduct was subdued during Christianity's high period, when morality was given by God's word and faith in authority replaced reason as the procedure to discover virtue. But when post-Renaissance science emerged, it insisted again that the facts of nature were to be the basis for ethics.

Each historical era holds a few primary assumptions which have to be defended against the attacks that inevitably result from the roll of social events. And each period awards differential status and power to the particular intellectual weaponry selected to defend the presuppositions, whether logic, appeal to authority, phenomenology, or empirical fact. The quintessential enigma in fourteenth-century Europe was whether God existed. Thomas Aquinas defended God's existence by logical argument; he would have chosen a different strategy today. The two central uncertainties of modern society are whether there is a priority of significance that can be assigned to our actions and whether there are any absolute moral truths? Because science, which has been given the responsibility of answering the first of those questions, depends on objective evidence, facts have become the most potent method of persuasion and the preferred basis for decisions. Although the significance of an action is quite different from its moral standing, some scientists have tried to reduce these two quite separate issues to one by tacitly assuming that significance is to be judged by adaptive value and by subtly promoting the idea that the morality of an action could be decided by its adaptive significance. Konrad Lorenz, for example, suggests that aggression is a significant act because it permits the animal to survive; he allows the uncritical reader to conclude that a behavior that is in such accord with nature cannot be totally immoral. Others award significance to sexual behavior since it leads to an increase in the population of a species.

The publication of E. O. Wilson's *Sociobiology* (1975) stimulated scholarly discussions aimed at determining what ethical principles, if any, could be deduced from present knowledge of the biological bases of behavior. Such inquiries are motivated, in part, by a desire to find some nonrelativistic basis for moral propositions. Since biology is a strong discipline, it is hoped that information on man's inherited dispositions can provide a guide to an ethical code. Wilson wrote, "Scientists and humanists should consider together the possibility that the time has come for ethics to be removed temporarily from the hands of the philosophers and biologicized" (p. 562). But as a biologist he was wary of the responsibility he had just advocated, so a few pages later, he added, "It should also be clear that no single set of moral standards can be applied to all human populations . . . to impose a uniform code is therefore to create complex intractable moral dilemmas—those, of course, are the current condition of mankind" (p. 564). I. Eibl-Eibesfeldt had voiced a similar objection to the notion of relying on biological predispositions to rationalize man's actions when he wrote that there is "no doubt that ethologists do not intend to accept aggression as inevitable . . . there is no reason to accept behavioral dispositions as inevitable and uncontrollable" (1974, p. 53).

Roger Sperry, who has written forcefully and elegantly on this theme, has tried to link a person's value decisions to his neurophysiology by making consciousness an emergent property of neural events that has the capacity to influence the very processes that sustain its existence. The assumption of a richly reciprocal relation between human decision and neural processes led Sperry to declare that "objective facts and subjective values become parts of the same universe of discourse . . . Human values are inherently properties of brain activity, and we invite logical confusion in trying to treat them as if they had independent existence artificially separated from the functioning brain" (1977, pp. 240-241). For Sperry, the criteria for final value decisions, when all the facts are in, is our guess as to nature's intention: "What is good, right, or to be valued is defined very broadly to be that which accords with, sustains, and enhances the orderly design of evolving nature" (1977, p. 243). But even Sperry, who sees scientific fact as the very best guide to values, recognized, with Wilson, that science cannot deliver final absolute answers to moral dilemmas, only better informed ones: "The question is not whether science can provide final, complete or perfect answers but whether there is any alternative that does as well, by long term, future generation standards" (1977, p. 243).

Thus, even those natural scientists who argue most forcefully for viewing man's behavior in an evolutionary or biological perspective do not go so far as to suggest that our moral evaluations of human behavior should accommodate only to what is known about man's biology or the actions of animals. They stop short of stating that what is true in nature should form the sole basis of what should be good for man.

Many adults are forced to be more competitive or aggressive than they wish to be, and they brood about the morality of those actions and related motives. When the biologist declares that competitiveness and aggression are natural responses (perhaps a true statement), his readers are prone to interpret that statement as meaning that such behavior is also morally proper. The press of everyday affairs demands certain behavioral accommodations, and we try as best we can to cover them with a veil of morality so that we can say that our actions are not only necessary but virtuous. Each adult needs guides for action in times of uncertainty, and it is reasonable that each looks to facts for that guidance. But we should not confuse such information with moral evaluation.

The procedures of science provide one of the most powerful—some might say the most effective—ways to illuminate the nature of the world. The propositions that are constructed from the mysterious marriage of the concrete and the imagined are capable of bringing clarity, comprehension, and, on occasion, a feeling that combines delight, awe, wonder, and serenity into an emotion for which we have no name. Science is to be celebrated! But we still ask for more. Not satisfied with the gift of understanding, we demand that the fruits of empirical effort also tell us what we ought to do when alternative actions require choice.

Knowledge and morality are, of course, not independent. There is a relation between what is and what ought to be, between an empirically based belief and an ethical one. Facts can eliminate incorrect bases for holding a moral conviction, and conditions in nature or society can lead to actions that become linked to moral imperatives. In a society with no married couples there can be no adultery; in a community with no centralized state there can be no treason.

Our moral concepts are not completely independent of our factual beliefs. Moral statements are seriously influenced by beliefs assumed to be true. Hence what ought to be true is not independent of what one believes to be true.

If eighteenth-century Americans had not been so keen on basing ethics and legislation on natural phenomena, a great deal of conflict might have been avoided. During the century prior to the Civil War, many of the arguments for and against the morality of slavery hinged on whether the negro was of the same species as the white. If he was, he had to be awarded freedom; if he was not, slave owners were justified in denying him liberty. Empirical fact was used as the basis for deciding an essentially ethical issue. Why wasn't the eighteenth-century American more friendly to a different defense of ethics, either adherence to some absolute principle (like equality) or even the word of authority? Why did they and why do we regard empirical fact as the most potent defense of a moral proposition?

One reason is that empirical fact is supposedly objective. It resides in nature rather than opinion. It therefore seems impartial, and, by implication, just. Additionally, science, which is the coherent organization of fact, has gained the respect of the community through marvelously useful inventions that have permitted humanitarian advances, technical feats that magnify man's sense of potency, and the ability to predict a few brief moments in the future. As a result of these real victories, science and a rational approach to experience have acquired a secular power that makes it easy for citizens to expect that the knowledge generated by scientists is the best guide to morals.

Consider three ethical issues being debated in contemporary America—abortion, homosexuality, and racial segregation in educational institutions. Proponents and opponents of all three themes are responsive to arguments of fact. Those concerned with abortion want scientists to tell them when life begins, as if that question had an empirical answer of the same order as, "At what time will the next solar eclipse occur?" Those who want more liberal legislation on homosexuality applaud when research shows that homosexuals have not inherited an anomalous disposition, and assume that the resolution voted by the members of the American Psychiatric Association that homosexuality was not a disease had scientific content. Opinions on segregation are influenced by published reports on the academic achievement of black children bused to integrated school settings. But such factual information is secondary to the quintessence of the ethical issue. The decision on abortion turns on whether a woman has the right to decide what to do with her body. The value conflict pits the woman's right to autonomy of personal choice against the fetus' right to life. These are transcendental themes which cannot be decided by an appeal to evidence. Since Western society currently holds individual freedom sacred, the Supreme Court's 1976 ruling sided with the woman.

Legislation on homosexuality also turns on whether adults are free to behave as they choose, and recent court rulings have used this premise in arriving at decisions. Attitudes toward busing to achieve racial integration in schools are also influenced by facts, for data on the academic achievement of children in integrated settings is always part of the argument. The moral dilemma involves the sacredness of each family's liberty set against the society's need to move more quickly toward an integrated community. The courts, being pragmatic, have waffled between the two positions, but consistent with their recent decisions on abortion and homosexuality, have leaned toward self-determination. There is, of course, little in natural law that affirms or refutes either ethical stance.

Western nations face a major decision regarding the primacy of individual freedom when it conflicts with the harmony of the larger community. Resolution of that dilemma should be made on the basis of a commitment to a particular set of values. We members of Western society cannot evade that responsibility by pretending that facts will make the proper choice obvious and save us the agony of having to choose between two of our most beloved ideals.

Although since the time of Galileo we have become accustomed to referring to the empirical sciences most matters of truth as well as of ethics, we have forgotten that the natural sciences confessed, at the beginning of this century, that their knowledge had no implications for morality, since nature had no values. Science, we were told, was "value free" and the citizenry would have to look elsewhere for ethical guidance. As the nineteenth century came to a close, many European intellectuals—scientists, philosophers, and novelists—were elaborating Immanuel Kant's distinction between knowledge and values and assenting to Sören Kierkegaard's plea that we recognize the unbridgeable chasm between what is known and what is good. Ethics was not to be found in reason, Kierkegaard claimed, but in each person's faith.

Despite the arguments of Kant, Kierkegaard, and others, the increasing power of science intimidated citizen and scholar, and in the years prior to World War I there was a need for an elegant philosophical statement that used the procedures of science, in this case logic, to justify the separation of fact and value. Allan Janik and Stephen Toulmin (1973) have suggested that Ludwig Wittgenstein's *Tractatus Logico-Philosophicus* was written, in part, to accomplish that mission. "Wittgenstein's radical separation of facts from values can be regarded as the terminus of a series of efforts to distinguish the sphere of natural science from the sphere of morality, which had begun with Kant, had been sharpened up by Schopenhauer, and had been made absolute by Kierkegaard" (p. 197). Wittgenstein's intention for the Tractatus was not only to write a critique of language but also to argue for the transcendent quality of ethics—to celebrate morality's permanent independence from objective knowledge. Trying to find a compromise between the physics of Hertz and Boltzmann and the ethics of Kierkegaard, Wittgenstein wrote, "It is impossible for there to be propositions of ethics . . . propositions express no theory that is higher—ethics is transcendental—ethics and aesthetics are one and the same" (1922). But the society was not receptive to such a declaration. It had been persuaded for over several centuries that the natural sciences could provide guides to moral imperatives. Since neither the Church nor philosophy was able to fill the void (unfortunately, many twentieth-century philosophers lost interest in metaphysics and the problems of truth and morality and left the society more emotionally dependent on science than ever), the social sciences stepped forward to fill the breach. Psychology, sociology, and anthropology occupied the space abandoned by philosophy, the Church, and the physical sciences and implicitly promised to solve the problem of ethical guidance by gathering objective information on issues that were of concern to the community.

It is not clear that the social sciences can keep their promise. It is commonly believed, by scientists and nonscientists alike, that investigations of nonmodern cultures will reveal man's basic nature and that such knowledge will tell us how to adjust our ethics so that they are consonant with nature's wish rather than in opposition to it. It is unlikely that ethnographies can serve that function. Middle-class Americans allow their children to express anger and mild aggression because they believe it is in accord with nature. Many parents tell their children to defend themselves if coerced because they have been told that if anger is suppressed a child may develop psychosomatic symptoms or even depression, since empirical data have suggested that repression of anger and excessive control of aggression can lead to unhealthy somatic tension and psychic disquiet. But Jean Briggs (1970) challenged the universality of the principle. Among the Utku Eskimo of Hudson Bay, with whom Briggs spent twenty months, every display of anger in a child after age two is followed by a "silent treatment." Initially the child is upset, but after several years there are no more tantrums and little interpersonal aggression. However, colitis, migraine headaches, and the other psychological symptoms that are presumed to result from suppressed anger are absent. Hence it is reasonable to ask: Is it basic to human nature to express anger or to suppress it? The answer seems to be "Neither." The consequences of suppression of anger are a function of the social context in which the child is adapting. In our own culture, where children can leave the home to play with friends and where the social norm is to defend oneself when attacked, it is adaptive to permit children some public display of hostility. But for a family living in an igloo nine months of the year, it is maladaptive to allow family members to live with anger for three-quarters of every year. Should they do so, it is highly likely that they would develop somatic symptoms.

Robert Edgerton (1971) evaluated personality traits like autonomy, independence, aggression, and sexuality in several African tribes, some of whom were pastoral and some agricultural. Within the same tribe, he found the pastoralists to be more likely to express anger and autonomy, while the agriculturalists were more likely to suppress interpersonal aggression. Edgerton argued that when two pastoralists developed mutual resentment they could separate and wander off with their property, while the settled agriculturalists could not. Both clusters of personality traits are natural, as are both modes of sustenance, and each economy carries with it a model set of traits. Neither the agriculturalists nor the pastoralists are closer to human nature.

Comparative psychologists would like to make inferences about the essence of human nature from studies of animal behavior. Jane Goodall has commented that day care centers are not healthy for infants because nature intended mothers to be with their children during the first three years of life; Goodall bases her advice on the fact that chimpanzee mothers behave this way. But closely related species of macaque monkeys behave differently with their infants—the bonnet macaque relinquishes her infants to almost any other female in the living area, whereas the stubtail macaque ferociously protects her infant from the curious. Since there is so much variability of behavior among related species of our nearest subhuman kin, it is difficult to argue that the behavior of any one of them informs us of nature's intention for the human species.

Moreover, our selection of the behavior and species to study is often guided by current social preoccupations. The contemporary Western world requires competitiveness, a capacity for aggression and dominance, access to one's sexual passions, and an ability to be alone. Hence, scientists are tempted to investigate those qualities in animals rather than their opposites. There are many more studies of the effect of brain stimulation or ablation on aggression than on passive withdrawal. Yet one can probably alter passive behavior in a rhesus monkey as easily as aggression by destroying or stimulating parts of the brain. The comparative psychologist, who cannot help but be influenced by the unresolved issues in his society, may investigate mother-infant separation in primates because that topic is currently a node of uncertainty in the human community, not because it happens frequently among primates in natural contexts. Or he may investigate the influence of early social isolation on later development, because some scientists have claimed that educationally retarded children lack sufficient physical stimulation during the early years.

The plea for "relevant research" by congressmen and citizens is based on the assumption that such knowledge can guide ethical decisions about the education and socialization of children. Science can suggest the mechanisms by which individuals decide whether an action or thought is good or bad and point to invalid bases for ethical positions; but it cannot supply the constructive basis for a moral proposition. Moral propositions imply that one action is better than another, and it is rarely the case that a particular action is good for all of the potential beneficiaries. The person at risk, his family, and the society in which the individual lives are three major social beneficiaries in our society; few acts are good for all three. Each moral decision carries with it an implied beneficiary; abstract moral principles rarely map across all situations. Classic Chinese society accepted this limitation on law; western society resists it because of an affection for simplicity and abstract rules that subdue local perturbations.

The results of empirical research cannot be the sole guide for judging what is psychologically good for children or families. Regardless of the facts, each individual must make a value decision, for one cannot rely on evidence to rank the degree of benevolence associated with all possible outcomes for all possible targets. Hence, ethical decisions must be informed by a priori assumptions.

During the first three decades of this century a strong eugenics movement in the United States looked to the science of genetics as a basis for legislation on sterilization of immigrant populations (Ludmerer 1972). Supporters of this movement urged restriction of marriage and sterilization in order to reduce the occurrence of epilepsy, criminality, mental retardation, and insanity. Sixty years later, when the scientific bases for a genetic component to schizophrenia and certain forms of mental retardation were even stronger than they were in 1910, fewer Americans were receptive to the suggestion that individuals afflicted with these disorders be sterilized because our moral attitudes toward sterilization had become less permissive, not because science had shown the original idea to be faulty.

Facts are, of course, not irrelevant and at times are critically useful. As psychologists came to discover that most forms of criminality and alcoholism were not inherited, the position of the eugenicist became more difficult to defend. Prior to World War I eugenicists had spread the idea that there was a large increase in feeble-minded persons in the population and that these genetically tainted individuals were responsible for most forms of antisocial behavior (a fear reminiscent of the recent concern over lower scholastic aptitude test scores among contemporary high school graduates). This fallacious idea was weakened in 1919 when the results of intelligence tests on 1.7 million recruits were published. The IQ data indicated that 47 percent of American whites were feeble-minded. Since this proportion was so high it made the eugenicist's position appear foolish, an instance of knowledge making a moral position less tenable. Nonetheless, many still held the old belief (Ludmerer, 1972). Although scientific information had weakened the rational basis for the ethical view on sterilization, it did not, and, of course, could not, help Americans decide whether sterilization is a good or bad action to impose on any individual.

A final example of the necessity for a priori assumptions is more recent. Since World War II, federal and state legislators have been generous in support of educational functions and special instructional programs for children, especially those from poor families and those from ethnic minorities. Indeed, one of the rationales for such aid was that it would lead to greater economic equality in the nation. Christopher Jencks' controversial book *Inequality* (1972) challenged that premise. He used facts to argue that the decision to invest money in education in order to equalize income was ill founded. Although one could argue with some of the facts, even if they are valid, their utility lies in their power to refute those who want to base educational funding on a desire to reduce diversity in income. The facts do not imply that the community cannot decide, a priori, that it is still good to invest in education—for self-actualization, for appreciation of science and art, or for general enlightenment.

Where are the *a priori* assumptions necessary for ethical decisions to come from? If our ethics cannot originate in either facts or the opinions of a benevolent authority, where does the community find a basis for generating moral propositions? One source lies in consensual sentiment, which will change over time. Most Americans regard aggression, violence, dishonesty, and coercion as morally indefensible, and a referendum on each would reflect that deeply held belief. Indeed on each election day more and more moral issues are placed on the local ballot, indicating the community's receptivity to using public sentiment as a guide to ethical dilemmas. When the Supreme Court recognized how difficult it was to define pornography in an objective and logically consistent manner, it declared that local attitudes should determine which books and movies violated sensibilities. The court legitimized the individual's private, emotional reaction as a participant in the creation and maintenance of values. It is extremely difficult to implement that strategy more broadly in our society because of the extraordinary diversity of opinion on critical issues and a deep resistance to having legally binding propositions rest, in any way, on nonrational grounds. That is one reason why science has been placed in the position of moral arbiter. Although science can help in this role by supplying factual evidence which disconfirms the invalid foundations of ethical premises, it cannot supply the basis for a moral proposition. Facts prune the tree of morality; they cannot be the seedbed.

Many of America's nineteenth-century philosophers, including Emerson, Peirce, and James, also rejected Locke's rationalist approach to ethics. Each held, with different degrees of conviction, that a person's feelings about an issue, even though unsupportable by logical argument or a coherent corpus of established fact, should be respected in matters of ethics. This attitude was present early in American history. James Wilson, a colonial philosopher of law, defended a phenomenological contribution to moral commitment: "If I am asked—why do you obey the will of God? I answer—because it is my duty so to do. If I am asked again—how do you know this to be your duty? I answer again—because I am told so by my moral sense of conscience. If I am asked a third time—how do you know that you ought to do that, of which your conscience enjoins the performance? I can only say, I feel that such is my duty. Here investigation must stop; reasoning can go no further" (in McCloskey, 1967).

Jefferson held similar views, in part, because he wanted to ensure that the farmer without access to training in logic, rhetoric, and science would still be able to construct a valid moral code. In a letter to a nephew he wrote,

> Moral philosophy. I think it lost time to attend lectures in this branch. He who made us would have been a pitiful bungler if he had made the rules of our moral conduct a matter of science. For one man of science there are thousands who are not. What would have become of them? Man was destined for society. His morality, therefore, was to be formed to this object. He was endowed with a sense of right and wrong nearly relative to this. This sense is as much a part of his nature as the sense of hearing, seeing, and feeling; it is the true foundation of morality . . . the moral sense or conscience is as much a part of man as his leg or arm. It is given to all human beings in a stronger or weaker degree, as force of members is given them in a greater or less degree . . . State a moral case to a ploughman and a professor. The former will decide it as well and often better than the latter because he has not been led astray by artificial rules. [In Boyd, 1955]

Even though Jefferson's apparent anti-intellectualism was influenced by the desire to celebrate the common sense of the average citizen, such a prejudice does not necessarily indicate that the use of sentiment to help decide moral issues is either incorrect or, for that matter, dangerous. But as I have indicated, this view lost adherents in the years after the Civil War as science gained more respect and greater persuasive power. In the decade before the turn of the century W. K. Clifford wrote,

> Belief is desecrated when given to unproved and unquestioned statements for the solace and private pleasure of the believer . . . whoso would deserve well of his fellows in this matter will guard the purity of his belief with a very fanaticism of jealous care, lest at any time it should rest on an unworthy object and catch a stain which can never be wiped away . . . If a belief has been accepted on insufficient evidence the pleasure is a stolen one . . . it is sinful because it is stolen in defiance of our duty to mankind. That duty is to guard ourselves from such beliefs as from a pestilence which may shortly master our own body and then spread to the rest of the town . . . it is wrong

always, everywhere, and for everyone to believe anything upon insufficient evidence. [In White, 1972, pp. 188-189]

William James answered Clifford and insisted, with Jefferson, that a moral belief was not governed solely by scientific evidence: "A moral question is a question not of what sensibly exists but of what is good or would be good if it did exist. Science can tell us what exists, but to compare the worths both of what exists and what does not exist we consult not science, but what Pascal calls our heart" (1898, p. 2).

We could name many instances in which knowledge catalyzed alterations in beliefs or practices that fall within the sphere we classify as moral. But in all of these cases the evidence was maximally effective when a critical proportion of the community had already decided, before the evidence was available, what outcome was more virtuous, so that they were receptive to rational support for the new view or to factual bases for undermining the old one. It is a tribute to man's respect and need for rationality that Darwin's thesis on the evolution of animal forms led many to question further their faith in creationism. But had they not been psychologically prepared to believe the data and argument Darwin organized, his evidence would have been ignored. Ernst Mayr (1977) has suggested that if Darwin himself had not begun to lose his Christian faith in the mid-1830s, he might not have had the illumination in September of 1838 that formed the essence of his theory.

Thus data, presupposition, and logic mix in a mysterious way to influence the values of a person or a community. As Morton White noted, "Sentiment is not enough, logic is not enough, and experience is not enough, if we wish to know and to know what to do. Each should be given its due by the intelligent man as he tests his stock of beliefs and actions" (1972, p. 310).

This volume is critical of a number of popular practices in contemporary social science while presenting some new information on temperamental qualities and cognitive development. No commanding ethical implication flows from any of the essays. But I do hope readers will gain a richer understanding of the unstable relation between the meanings of propositions in the literature on human behavior and the invisible events each imagines to be their true source.

Part One

On Meaning

1

Meaning and Procedure

Scientists recognize that empirical facts gain their meaning from the theoretical network in which they are embedded. But because each theory is linked to special procedures, the meaning of the propositions that summarize empirical data is also affected by the specific sources of evidence produced by those procedures. When a discipline enjoys strong theory, as psychology did from the early 1930s to the late 1960s, scholars agree on the meaning of propositions, in part, because a theory is linked to methods that tie the abstract meaning of a construct to empirically realizable referents. For example, when psychologists committed to traditional learning theory used terms like *drive* and *learning,* their colleagues understood that the referent for drive was deprivation of food or water and learning referred to improvement in the performance of an operant response, like running a maze or pressing a lever. During the same era, when investigators committed to psychoanalytic theory used words like *anxiety* and *defense,* their colleagues knew that the evidence included a person's verbal statements (in an interview or to a projective stimulus) and a specific profile of symptoms.

However, the recognition that the meaning of a theoretical proposition is dependent, in part, on the source of evidence for that proposition has been challenged recently by some philosophers who argue that the meaning of a construct is determined only by the theoretical network in which it participates (Thomas, 1979), and by some members of the new generation of social scientists who write as if all the assumptions of logical empiricism have been found to be invalid and inimical to scientific progress. The purpose of this essay is to argue that one of the tenets of the philosophical movement called logical empiricism—namely, that the meaning of a theoretical construct may change when the referent changes—is still useful and that indifference to this idea is creating theoretical mischief in contemporary psychology.

Sense and Referential Meanings

The meaning of words intended to describe relations among events is a central problem in all domains of scholarship but especially in the social and behavioral sciences, where many terms have their origin in folk language rather than in new observations. An important insight articulated during the last century is the recognition that words which serve as concepts have two different types of meaning. One is contained in the network of symbolic dimensions associated with the word. The other is comprised of the events in the world to which the word refers. A word can have the first type of meaning without the second—ghost and angel being two examples (Hayakawa, 1941; Putnam, 1975). Although many scholars have written on this general theme, including Russell (1962), who opposed the distinction, Frege's (1892) description of the *sense* and *referential* meanings of words seems to capture the central idea behind the two kinds of meaning.

The sense of a word, according to Frege, is the thought it expresses. The referential meaning is contained in the events to which the word points. Both the *morning star* and the *evening star,* which have different senses but the same referent, is a favorite illustration among philosophers. The words *intelligent* and *clever,* on the other hand, have a similar sense but different referents. The sense of these two terms includes the ideas of an alert state, ability to learn new skills, exploitation of novel opportunities, efficient problem solving, and reasoning talents; there is also the disguised presumption that these abstract properties are correlated. However, the referential meaning of *intelligent* in contemporary America is a score on a standardized intelligence test, while a primary referent for *clever* is vocational and financial success. A correlation among referential meanings is always hoped for but is not always realized.

There is a general consensus among scientists that the meaning of a word that is intended as a theoretical construct combines both sense and referential meanings. The theoretical meaning of anxiety among psychoanalysts combines the ideas of childhood conflict and repression of sexual motives with specific symptoms. If an analyst used the score on a group-administered questionnaire as the referent for anxiety, instead of the relevant symptoms, the theoretical meaning of anxiety would be altered. Any change in the source of evidence always has the potential to change the theoretical meaning of the construct (Dyson, 1979).

Even the familiar concept of the unconscious fails to possess a univocal theoretical meaning. The referents in Freud's essays—spontaneous dreams, symptoms, and slips of the tongue—are used as evidence for aims or motives that are not available to consciousness. The referents in cognitive explanations of unconscious inference are answers to direct questions involving perception or reasoning. Further, the two different sources of information are used in different theoretical structures.

Contemporary physicists and biologists are more sensitive to this possibility than are behavioral scientists; in part because the latter are far less certain than their colleagues in biology or chemistry that the evidence that provides the rationale for a construct captures the desired meaning. Hence, behavioral scientists often treat serious changes in reference as having a minimal effect on the meaning of the theoretical construct. The problem with this attitude, as Frege noted, is that the truth value of a statement in empirical science applies to the referential, not the sense, meanings of its terms. "It is the striving for truth that drives us always to advance from the sense to the reference" (p. 63).

This issue prompted MacCorquodale and Meehl in 1948 to publish an argument for a distinction between intervening variables (which emphasize the referential meaning of a term) and hypothetical constructs (which emphasize sense). The essay achieved a deserved fame because it provided psychologists with a solution to the serious and obstructive problems raised by logical positivism, which had become popular in a relatively short period of time (Carnap, 1956; Feigl, 1956; Kraft, 1953; Schlick, 1979). This philosophical movement, at least in its early orthodox form, declared that the only meaningful and, therefore, scientifically acceptable propositions are those whose concepts are traceable to observables so that every statement is potentially vulnerable to refutation. A concept without any possible referent is inadmissible to scientific discourse because the proposition of which it is a part is not verifiable. The stricture implied by this principle of verifiability may have seemed reasonable for late nineteenth-century physics, but it was much too stringent a demand for a young psychology concerned with great themes but methodologically impoverished. Adherence to the letter of logical empiricism would have meant not only elimination of many popular, important constructs with a sense meaning, including Hull's anticipatory goal response, Allport's traits, and Freud's libido, but also a loss of legitimacy for creative, inductive research that was guided initially by concepts that could not be verified.

MacCorquodale and Meehl freed psychologists from the constraints of the orthodox operationism inherent in the new philosophy by urging them to define their concepts in terms of laboratory procedures, as Bridgman (1927) advised, and to call these ideas *intervening variables*. But if that failed, psychologists could use a concept that represents a quality or process that would account for a robust covariation among different events, even though no defining procedure for that concept exists at that time; these ideas were to be called *hypothetical constructs*.[1] MacCorquodale and Meehl's compromise with logical positivism permitted behavioral scientists to feel confident that they were practicing good science, even though they were not accommodating completely to a positivistic philosophy. However, three relatively independent and continuing historical processes, which have been accelerating since the 1948 essay, make it necessary to readdress the problem of meaning in the use of scientific language that they tried to solve.

Historical Changes in Psychology

After 1960 a large number of experimental psychologists turned from the study of animal learning, where the referents for the constructs of

1. Although an intervening variable was supposed to be no more than a name for data produced by a particular procedure, careful examination revealed that it, too, functioned as a hypothetical construct. For example, on a 40-item scale intended to measure anxiety as an intervening variable, the investigator was actually regarding different magnitudes of correlations among the 40 items as reflecting high, moderate, or low anxiety. This logic does not differ from inventing another term, say *Anxiety 2*, as a hypothetical construct to explain the correlations between two different anxiety scales. In the first case, the correlation is among the answers on a particular scale and, in the second, between the answers on two scales. In both cases, the term *anxiety* is intended to name the covariation among responses and implies a hypothetical process that is responsible for the correlated events.

operant, drive, punishment, and reward are relatively easy to specify, to investigations of human cognitive processes, which rely on terms like schema, deep structure, and stage of short-term memory that do not have standard measurement operations. Hence, behavioral scientists wished to be freed from all of the restrictions of logical empiricism. Escape was made easy by philosophical critiques that eroded faith in two of the three central premises of logical positivism: the obligation to favor parsimony in explanation and, especially, the warning to avoid propositions that could not be tested and, therefore, refuted. These two tenets became obsolete as modern physics and biology were forced by their data and elegant mathematical arguments to create explanations that were not immediately verifiable. The third tenet, which holds that the meanings of terms in a proposition reside in the data generated by relevant procedures, has not suffered as serious a defeat, but some psychologists became indifferent to this principle, too, as part of a general rejection of the first two assumptions.

A second change since 1960 is an increase in the number of investigations of children and adults that use self-report procedures to evaluate a person's emotional states, beliefs, motives, and cognitive processes. These procedures rely either on a person's verbal statements or affirmation/refutation of sentences invented by the investigator. Such methods are widely used to assess parental practices, attitudes, and evaluations of the child's behaviors and moods. In both cases, however, the information used for theoretical inference is based on linguistic descriptions of psychological qualities that have first been evaluated by the subject's consciousness. This method is legitimate, but many investigators continue to use the same theoretical terms that had been, or are being, used by investigators who implement very different procedures.

A third historical change is the consensus among physicists, chemists, and biologists that the meaning of all constructs in empirical generalizations is derived, in part, from the evidence produced by specific procedures (Whitehead, 1928; Dyson, 1979). In quantum physics, for example, one cannot combine information about a system that comes from two different measurement procedures (Petersen, 1985). A contemporary physical chemist notes that with respect to the concepts *heat* and *work*, "The most important contribution of nineteenth-century thermodynamics . . . has been the discovery that they are names of methods, not names of things . . . To heat an object means to transfer energy to it in a special way. The same is true of work" (Atkins, 1984, pp. 23–24). Le Douarain (1982) begins the opening chapter of her monograph on the embryology of the neural crest by describing the methods she uses to trace migrating neurons. Such an introduction is rare in technical monographs written by behavioral scientists. Weisblat and Stent (1982) tell their fellow biologists that the validity of their conclusions about cell lineages in the leech are totally dependent on the assumption that the tracer chemicals injected into the cells do not pass through the junctions linking them. Such a caveat is usually missing in the procedural sections of technical papers in psychology, sociology, and anthropology.

The acceptance of this contextual view of the meaning of propositions by physical and biological scientists was made easy by stunning advances in machines and methods that produced information, some of which demanded the creation of new theoretical terms. Perception of the tiny space between the axons of one neuron and the dendrites of another, made possible by new, powerful microscopes, participates in the theoretical meaning of synapse. The invention of the EEG permitted the recording of changing brain voltages from the scalp. The concepts used to describe these phenomena participate in the meaning of the phrase *paradoxical sleep*. One reason particle physicists invent novel terms like *charm* and *quark* is because they wish to avoid generating the misleading connotations that are often implied by familiar words, and to emphasize the potential referent for the new concept.

But scientists do not always invent new words, despite the fact that a new procedure has produced a unique class of evidence. Video recorders and stop-frame players permit psychologists to code very brief changes in the muscles of the face (not perceptible under ordinary conditions) to which they have given familiar names like fear, anger, and sadness (Ekman, Friesen, and Ellsworth, 1972). But these terms for human emotions refer specifically to the transient changes in facial muscles and not to the more coherent set of changes in limbic structures, autonomic nervous system, muscle tone, and voice that other scientists, and most nonscientists, intend when they use the very same words.

Before there were scientific disciplines with apparatus and special strategies of inquiry, the two major sources of information for statements about the world were ordinary sensory experience and communication from others. Therefore, all members of a community knew implicitly the source of the evidence for a proposition and were able to judge, perhaps unconsciously, first its meaning and subsequently its validity in light of its evidential origin. But because modern science has invented novel sources of information, it is necessary to attend closely to the meanings of those terms intended to describe new information but applied to the older classes of evidence. That is why Dyson (1979) has written that the meaning of a descriptive statement is always dependent on its procedural origins.

Over a century earlier Flourens intended the same idea when he wrote, "Everything in experimental research depends upon the method, for it is the method which gives the results" (1842, p. 502). Whitehead (1928) explained why physical theory was outrunning common sense: "The reason why we are on a higher imaginative level is not because we have a finer imagination, but because we have better instruments" (p. 166). Holton's (1973) commentary on Bohr's famous 1927 lecture on complementarity highlights the importance of the source of data for comprehension of the summarizing descriptions. "As soon as he sets up the observation tools on his workbench, the system he has chosen to put under observation and his measuring instruments for doing the job form one inseparable whole" (p. 119).

These three historical changes during the last forty years invite a reexamination of some of the themes that MacCorquodale and Meehl addressed, for their solution, which had been helpful, has led to an indifference to the relation between method and meaning. This chapter is not concerned, as logical positivists were, with whether a statement does or does not have meaning—all statements have a sense meaning. Rather, this essay is concerned with the different meanings a proposition can assume as a function of the referential foundations of its terms.

Meaning and the Source of Evidence

Natural scientists use words to describe events that have been or will be observed and to account for covariation among events. Most words, whether used as descriptors ("The child's intelligence is in the top quartile") or as theoretical constructs ("Intelligence is an inherited quality"), have a large number of defining features that differ in their salience, or centrality, in a given context (some readers may prefer the phrase *critical dimensions* or *primary qualities* to *defining features;* Churchland, 1979, uses the phrase *informational function*). The intention to harm another is usually a salient feature of the term *hostile.* But the salient features of the words *desire, talent,* and *spirit,* like most scientific terms, are less obvious and often change with time as theoretical conceptions change. Francis Galton regarded sensory acuity as a salient feature of intelligence; David Wechsler believed size of vocabulary was primary. These two features are typically uncorrelated.

When the construct *motive* in traditional learning theory emphasized an acquired link to primary drives like hunger, an animal's speed of response was a salient feature of the concept. But when psychologists found that animals would work for events that had no relation to hunger, the theoretical meaning of motive was altered to make cognitive features important. As a result, behavior produced by other methods, like TAT stories, became more popular referents for motives. When Descartes used the word *corps* in sentences discussing the body-mind problem, the primary defining quality he intended was not, as it is for modern neurophysiologists, the columnar organization of neurons in the cerebral cortex. The phrase *sex of a person* can refer in contemporary essays on gender to an individual's chromosomes, gonads, or external genitals; in the eighteenth century the phrase referred only to the latter.

Thus, the specific source of empirical information—the referent—that contributes to the theoretical meaning of a scientific term is associated with a particular hierarchy of salient, defining features. These features represent select aspects of the events—usually called the dependent variable—that are quantified in a particular investigation. Each dependent variable is mediated by specific hypothetical processes, or mechanisms, linked to a procedure. Often the same process can mediate different phenomena. But when the processes mediating two phenotypically different dependent variables presumed to bear on the same construct are different, the propositions summarizing the evidence have different theoretical meanings.

In measurement theory, this principle states that if two procedures do not lead to the same numerical assignments to the same entities, then the scales are not the same (Ellis, 1966). If, on the other hand, it can be argued, or better yet demonstrated, that the processes mediating the observed events are the same, it is proper to treat the two sources of evidence as representative of the same construct. When an outside thermometer reads 90 degrees Fahrenheit and many people are perspiring while walking on the sidewalk, we believe both observations are mediated by the kinetic energy of the molecules in the air. Hence, each observation reflects the same salient feature that gives meaning to the proposition "The day is hot." But it is less obvious that the processes which mediate precocious attainment of the object concept during the first year of an infant's life are the same as those that mediate precocious attainment of a large vocabulary in the tenth year. Hence, it may be an error to regard both referents as having the same meaning with respect to the theoretical construct of intelligence.

Many comparative psychologists who study aggressive behavior in rodents assume that the forces producing behavioral variation among different strains of mice in the tendency to lunge at and bite another animal are similar to the forces that make some ten-year-olds strike a peer on a playground. But Cairns, MacCombie, and Hood (1983), who held that assumption in the past, have now concluded that the variation in attack behavior in mice is due to differences in restraint in an unfamiliar context, not differences in aggressive drive. Hence, lunging and biting in mice probably do not belong to the same theoretical category as striking another among humans.

When two observations do not share a common process, they should not be regarded as signs of the same construct, no matter what the intuitions of an investigator may be. The theoretical meaning of "mentally retarded with an IQ of 75" when early family experience is presumed to be the process causing the low IQ is different from the meaning when phenylketonuria is the presumed mediator, even though the referent—an IQ score of 75—remains unchanged. Because each class of method generates evidence that is mediated by particular processes, the meaning of a scientific term is always affected by procedure. The imprinting process in a duckling appears to be gradual when distress calls are the evidence. But it appears to be all-or-none when the evidence is the duckling's following behavior. The theoretical meaning of *imprinting* is not the same in these two informational contexts (Hoffman, Eiserer, Ratner, and Pickering, 1974). Similarly, evolution appears to be gradual if soft tissue and biochemistry supply the evidence, but seems more abrupt when fossilized bones are the primary data. The truth value of a proposition claiming that a state of fear is conditioned in an animal when a light signal is followed by electric shock depends on whether a change in behavior or a change in heart rate to the light is the reaction quantified (Campbell and Ampuero, 1985).

Although the position argued here is similar in spirit, but not letter, to the proposals of Bridgman (1927) and the writings of the scholars who comprised the Vienna circle during the early 1930s, it is more permissive and I believe avoids their more serious counterintuitive flaws. The philosophy of logical empiricism was a reaction to the metaphysical excesses of philosophers like Hegel and Heidegger, as well as an attempt to rescue the importance of empirical definitions following Russell and Whitehead's stunning feat of deducing mathematics from the propositions of logic without reference to experiential data (Kraft, 1953). The primary mission of this philosophical movement was the construction of rules for deciding which propositions have meaning in empirical science; they were less concerned with the specific meaning a proposition might assume.

The most abstract proposition has a sense meaning and may have a referential one (Putnam, 1975). The task is to discern the meaning by determining the salient features the author intended. In Bridgman's view, each concept's central feature is represented by the procedure used to produce the relevant data: "the concept is synonymous to the corresponding set of operations" (1927, p. 5). Because the meaning of a term is synonymous with the procedure, any change in method implies a change in meaning. Thus, an orthodox interpretation of Bridgman holds that the meaning of the word *hot* in the proposition "This day is hot" changes if two different types of thermometers are used. But most scholars agree that Bridgman went too far in demanding that every change in procedure implies a new theoretical meaning. If different methods produce information referring to the same defining features of a term (because they are linked to the same mediating processes), its meaning remains unchanged. Thus, the meaning of *hot* to describe the temperature of the air is the same with any form of thermometer because the defining feature of *hot* (the kinetic energy of molecules in the air) remains constant. But the meaning of *hotter* in the sentence "The piece of iron is hotter than the piece of wood" has one meaning if it refers to the ability of each of the objects to warm a third body but a different meaning if it refers to a person's sensation of heat upon touching each of the objects; the defining features of *hotter* are not identical in the two instances (Churchland, 1979).

Similarly, the proposition "The tree (as I see it) is smooth (as I feel it)" could have the same meaning as "The tree (as I feel it) is smooth (as I see it)" if, despite the different sources of information, the same defining features of *tree* and *smooth* were intended. However, the proposition "The forest (as I see it) is sensuous (as I smell it)" has a meaning different from "The forest (as I smell it) is sensuous (as I see it)" because the salient features of *forest* and *sensuous* are likely to be different for the two sources, or methods, of knowing. Imagine each of three people who say of the same gold harp, "This object is beautiful," but one only sees it, one only touches it, and a third only hears it being played by an expert. The statement has three meanings because each person is using a different source of information as evidence for the declaration.

Do Words Name Essences?

Many social scientists begin their work by assuming the existence in nature of an event they have named and subsequently searching for the procedure that will reveal its essence in purest form. The search by some for the essence of language provides an example. The concept of sleep provides another. Investigators who study sleep often write as though there were a most essential form of this state in nature—a unique set of events that is more basically sleep than any other—rather than assume a family of different sleep states, each characterized by a set of correlated qualities. The state defined by eyes closed, slow waves in the EEG, no rapid eye movements, and no awareness of being awake when aroused by an experimenter comprises one profile. The state defined by eyes closed, slow waves in the EEG, but rapid eye movements and a consciousness of being awake is another. Each is an equally legitimate example of *sleep*. The state that particular investigators select as primary will be a function of their theoretical interests. Some features of sleep—dreaming, for example—occur more often in one profile than another. The fact that our language contains the word *sleep* tempts us, as it did Aquinas, to posit an essence; at least in the Western mind, words invite the idea of a most fundamental referent in nature for the event named.

Contemporary technical reports on maternal love, stress, or risk status at birth, which rely on one particular feature as referent, read as though a description of that feature not only captured the meaning of the concept but also proved its reality. Imagine four different investigators studying five-year-old children in separate laboratories who each find positive correlations among four variables: withdrawal to the mother following encounter with an unfamiliar peer, a rise and

stabilization of heart rate to cognitive stress, large pupil size in anticipation of cognitive stress, and high cortisol levels in the saliva. However, each investigator awards the covariation among the four qualities a different name because each awards salience to a different
source of data. The investigator who emphasizes the behavioral evidence calls the coherence *shyness;* the one who emphasizes the cardiac data calls it *fear;* the one who treats the pupil data as special calls
it *sympathetic arousal;* and the one who regards the cortisol level as
primary names the coherence *anxiety.* A fifth scholar who reads
about the replicated coherence names it *vulnerability to uncertainty.*
But the meaning of this phrase, too, is derived from the information
produced by the procedures (Kagan, Reznick, Clarke, Snidman, and
Garcia-Coll, 1984).

This example is not hypothetical. We have found such covariation
in two longitudinal samples in young children, but only about one
third of the children show all four qualities. Some children show
consistent behavioral withdrawal to unfamiliar children and adults
over a period of six years but have never shown a high and stable
heart rate; a few children have always shown a high and stable heart
rate but have never displayed behavioral withdrawal to unfamiliar
persons. This example illustrates the conceptual problem that follows
the assumption of an essence like anxiety or shyness.

Early nineteenth-century British naturalists, like Robert Knox and
Richard Owen, who posited the law of the unity of type, were
friendly toward essences. They assumed that there was a best member
of each animal and plant species which represented not only the most
frequently occurring type but also the essential one. Darwin's revolutionary insight was that a modern animal species, say a lion, was not
simply an heir of some original essential lion from the deep past but
the result of transformations that traced their way back to small
plant-eating mammals, and before that to reptiles and worms. There
is no essential lion.

Darwin's insight is relevant to contemporary discussions of the
preservation of individual differences in human qualities, for current
opinion resembles the pre-Darwinian assumption of unity of type. A
person's intelligence at twenty years of age, as manifested in grades,
academic prizes, or IQ scores, is regarded by some psychologists as
different manifestations of the same essential characteristic that could
have been observed at six months of age, albeit in an altered phenotypic form (see Fagan, 1984). However, I suggest that facility in
reasoning with words and numbers at age twenty is a product of a

series of transformations upon very different infant qualities, perhaps alertness to subtle discrepancy or a sturdier stage of short-term memory. These early qualities may have participated in the transformations that eventually resulted in the profile of cognitive skills classified as intelligent in the adult. But there is no hidden essence of intelligence that has been preserved over the twenty years, only a history of transformations on early qualities that were not part of the adult.

Many psychologists assume that when there is statistical evidence for preservation of individual differences in a quality, say vulnerability to fearfulness, some core quality must have been preserved. However, if the procedures that assess the quality emphasize different features over the period of study, as they often do, the meaning of the term that describes the quality is changed. That counterintuitive statement creates a problem, for it implies that a particular human quality was not preserved, despite statistical evidence for its continuity. But this may not be as serious a problem as it seems to be on the surface.

Consider an analogy from evolutionary biology. The quality a biologist might call "the cyclicity of female receptivity to mating" has continuously differentiated between mammals and reptiles over the last 30 million years. Differences between the two groups of animals in this quality have been preserved over this long epoch despite major changes in behavior and physiology from ancient mammals and reptiles to modern ones. Thus, although the specific features that define "cyclic qualities of receptivity to mating" have changed, through transformations in both groups, the differences between reptiles and mammals that existed earlier are present today.

A better example involves the changes in a person's face from infancy to adulthood. The size, shape, and relative distances of the parts of a person's face from the first birthday to age forty are transformed seriously. Yet it is possible to detect the faces that belong to particular infants and adults because the pattern of differences between the faces has been preserved over the intervening years. Perhaps the same conclusion holds for personality characteristics like vulnerability to fearfulness or schizophrenia (Zubin and Spring, 1977). What is preserved is a set of transformations on some original set of qualities.

Essences and the Form of the Evidence

The existence of essences was the source of a deep controversy between Einstein and Bohr regarding the nature of reality. The basis for the controversy, which resembles Helmholtz's disagreement with Mach several decades earlier, rests, in part, on the specific evidence used to describe a phenomenon. Einstein believed that reality consisted of substances whose properties were unaffected by their relation with other substances. Bohr conceptualized reality as consisting of relations between substances; hence, each measurement procedure always uncovered an intrinsic aspect of that relation, but always in relation to other phenomena (Hubner, 1983). Bohr wrote, "Nothing is necessarily true, but rather, that every position is dependent upon the particular conditions of its origin" (cited in Hubner, 1983, p. 89).

An observer can describe a fir tree in a forest as an object with an essence or as sets of relations among molecules that are under continuous, dynamic change. These two descriptive frames can also be imposed on mental and physiological processes. But there seems to be a relation between the source of the information about an event and the tendency to treat it either as an entity with an essence or as a set of relations. When the evidence for the tree originates in vision, it appears discrete and unchanging and we are tempted to regard it as an object with an essence. But if the evidence about the tree comes from a summary of a week's measurements of the amounts of oxygen and carbon dioxide exchanged with the air, it will seem that the tree consists of sets of relations.

There is a different way to state this idea. Reality is composed of objects and events that change at dramatically different rates. Most objects in the perceptible world—rocks, trees, and cups—change very slowly. Others—ripples on the water, clouds, and the invisible events we name neutrino and synaptic potential—change rapidly. Most events have both rapidly and slowly changing components. The shape of a hippocampal neuron changes slowly, but its post-synaptic potentials change quickly. When the rate of change of the quality selected to be a salient part of an event is very slow, it seems heuristically useful to regard the event as a stable essence, as we do for the neuron. It is intuitively less compelling to regard a rapidly changing event, like a synaptic potential, as a stable essence. However, whenever a mathematical argument predicts a quantity in nature with certainty—like the energy of an atomic particle—some mathematicians are prone to assume, with Einstein, that there must be an element in reality corresponding to that quantity. A set of mathematical equations and their predicted quantities written on a piece of paper are unchanging—like my perception of a sturdy tree in the forest. However, the primary data for Bohr consisted of patterns of physical measurements. Hence, like the changing values of carbon dioxide and oxygen within the tree, it seemed more reasonable to Bohr to treat reality as sets of coherent relations inferred from the experimental evidence.

I suspect some psychologists, especially those who study humans, prefer Einstein's view because of the procedures used in their experiments. Much current research on human behavior relies on verbal responses—whether answers in an interview, responses to a test probe, or marks on a printed questionnaire. These signs, like Einstein's equations, do not change. When a college student in a study of emotion says, "I am sad," or checks *yes* to ten questions enquiring about feelings of anxiety, the primary data are static, discrete signs. Hence, it is tempting to treat as essences the psychological processes that are presumed to have produced these data. But suppose these scientists had measured the subjects' heart rate, galvanic skin response, and EEG while they listened to and answered the same questions. Because the data would now consist of changing relations among the three measurements, I suspect they would have sided with Bohr and denied this emotional state essential status.[2]

The problem that no philosopher has been able to solve satisfactorily is the invention of a rational defense of a middle position between, on the one hand, a Platonic idealism that assumes an ontologically real essence behind each theoretically useful construct and, on the other, a skeptical materialism that declares that all any investigator ever has are clusters of correlated events. A century ago Mach wrote, "All that is valuable to us is the discovery of functional relations and that what we want to know is merely the dependence of experiences on one another" (Mach, 1959, p. 35)—a statement that the fourteenth-century Oxford skeptics would have applauded. More recently, Putnam (1983) captured the same idea:

> It begins to look as if Kant was right, and science only gives us relations between objects and not the objects themselves (p. 44) . . . Not only has modern physics failed to reveal to us any ready-made

2. Most historians also write as if it were possible to know the essence of a past event through brilliant inferences made from qualitatively different sources of evidence—diaries, demographic statistics, or laws. But, as with natural science, conclusions drawn from different sources of information may have very different meanings.

objects, any objects with a built-in and unique description, but the objects it does postulate are intimately connected with the observer and his ways of observing them (p. 178).

Perhaps all scientists can do is to work toward discovering and conceptualizing more robust coherences among dimensions in order to approach, but, of course, never reach, the least adulterated form of the phenomena whose understanding is being pursued.

"There is no quantum world," Bohr wrote, "there is only an abstract quantum physical description. It is wrong to think that the task of physics is to find out how nature is. Physics concerns what we can say about nature" (cited in Petersen, 1985 p. 305).

The Use of Animal Models

The strategy of using animal models to illuminate human behavior tacitly assumes an essential process that is common to both the animal species being studied and human beings. Eighteenth-century naturalists selected animals as the best models for understanding plants, regarding the bark of trees as serving the same function as an animal's skin and the sap as similar in function to blood (Delaporte, 1982). There is often similarity between processes in different families, genera, or species, but not all of the time. Hence, one is always at risk in generalizing across species.

The use of one species to illustrate a process in another is, of course, analogous to using a special laboratory procedure, for each species is likely to highlight a different dimension of the profile of correlated events that is of theoretical interest, a point made effectively by Henderson (1967) in investigations of emotionality in four inbred mice strains. Consider the work of Sackett and his colleagues as an example (Sackett, Ruppenthal, Fahrenbruch, Holm, and Greenough, 1981). Harlow had assumed a coherent set of consequences that followed from imposed isolation of an infant monkey during the first six months of life, called the *isolation syndrome*. It was presumed that all primate species, including human infants, would show the same behavioral profiles following early and prolonged isolation. However, closely related species of macaque monkeys placed in isolation for the opening months of life are not affected in a similar way. Isolated crabeaters do not show any important change in social behavior when compared with nonisolated animals, while rhesus show major impairment in social behavior. Hence, *isolation syndrome* has a different meaning in these two species. Similarly, an unknown number of conclusions generated from biological and psychological research on albino rats may not generalize to other species, for albino rats may have less neuromelanin in the central nervous system than pigmented rats, and melanin, which is a semiconductor, plays an important role in the biochemical functioning of the brain (Creel, 1980).

Some of the work in sociobiology raises serious problems of meaning equivalence (Wilson, 1975). The word *altruism,* for example, has been used traditionally to name a person's conscious attempt to help another person. Choice and intention are central dimensions of the concept of altruism in humans. A salesman who made a buyer happy because he accidentally sold a customer a car for a low price would not be called altruistic. However, when sociobiologists write about altruism in birds or bees, the ideas of conscious intention and choice are absent. Rather, the dimension highlighted pertains to the reproductive consequences for both the agent and the target of the agent's action. Because this is not the central feature of altruism when it is applied to humans, the two uses of the word are seriously different in meaning. Indeed, comparing the behavior of bees in a hive with that of a volunteer in a hospital comes close to meeting the criterion for metaphor, where a salient feature of the vehicle is a secondary feature of the topic (Ortony, 1979). Much of the writing in sociobiology is flawed by the use of words that refer to an agent's feelings and intentions when applied to humans but refer to reproductive consequences when they are applied to animals. Thus, Washburn and Dolhinow (1983) urge that "those who would compare human behaviors with those of other animals might start with a rich understanding of human behavior" (1983, p. 28). However, just as it is possible for different procedures to reflect the same features of a concept (the vocabulary tests on the Stanford-Binet and the Wechsler emphasize the same features), so, too, is it possible for different species to share central features of a psychological process. But we cannot know that fact *a priori*. It is an assumption to be affirmed through careful empirical work and tight reasoning—a prize to be won rather than a gift given before the journey.

The Reliance on Self-Report

Psychologists who study personality and attitudes have come to rely, in some cases almost exclusively, on self-report information to make statements about emotional states, beliefs, self-esteem, motivation, and even cognitive processes. Some investigators write as though the most valid meaning of a term resides with the information produced by this method, or that information gathered with other procedures must be in accord with the self-report data. In some cases, all of the evidence for a complex construct is based on self-report information (Watson and Clark, 1984). However, there is often no relation between an index of "high self-esteem" based on self-report, on the one hand, and display of empathic identification with a figure symbolic of someone with high esteem, on the other (Kagan, Hans, Markowitz, Lopez, and Sigal, 1982; see Chapter 8).

In one study, middle-class preadolescent academically competent children, rated by their teachers as having a high self-concept with respect to academic skill, rated themselves significantly lower in academic ability than did working-class children who had been rated by their teacher as having a low self-concept (Marsh and Parker, 1984). Similarly, there is no relation between an adult's self-report of anxiety, on the one hand, and changes in finger pulse volume to a stressful situation, on the other (Smith, Houston, and Zurawiski, 1984), between adolescent self-reports of aggressive behavior and objective indexes (Cairns and Cairns, in press), or between women's ratings of sexual arousal and a physiological index of that arousal (vaginal blood volume pulse amplitude) while listening to an erotic narration (Adams, Haynes, and Brayer, 1985; see also Knight and Borden, 1979; Lang, Levin, Miller, and Kozak, 1983). Indeed, a person will report that he was not sleeping when his EEG at the time he was awakened indicated Stage 2 sleep (Sewitch, 1984). The author notes, "Whatever the underlying internal signals that are detected and used by subjects to report whether they had been awake or asleep, they are not necessarily the same signals that are indexed by polygraphic data" (p. 258).

The term *hurt* provides a particularly persuasive example of the special qualities of self-report information (Wall, 1974). When adults are administered low levels of electric shock just below or at threshold and are asked to say when they "feel a sensation," they display remarkable consensus, both across different laboratories and across time, in the shock level associated with the first report of a sensation. Hence, the concept of "sensory threshold for feeling shock" has a stable and clear meaning in this procedural context. However, when the shock level is increased and the subjects are asked to report when they "feel that the stimulus hurts," there is far less agreement, both within and across subjects. Why is there consensus, in this context, for the meaning of the term *feel,* but not for the word *hurt?* One possibility is that *feel* involves only one judgment made over a short period of time, namely, whether there is a difference between one's conscious feelings of a sensation before and after the stimulus. But *hurt* involves more than one judgment. In deciding if a stimulus *hurts,* the person implicitly asks other questions, like "Is the shock tolerable?" or "Is this feeling similar to other pains I have known?" The answers to these questions are less reliable—or less consistent—because of these additional evaluations.

These additional evaluations are inherent in most, if not all, self-report instruments. Every question, whether printed on a scale or asked by an interviewer, forces a subject, unconsciously, to decide on the meaning of the terms; the investigator cannot assume highly similar understandings of the meanings of questions. The meaning inferred is based on the features of the terms the subject selects as salient, and those features may not be the ones the investigator intended. After discerning meaning, but before answering, the subject relates the comprehended meaning to a larger frame to judge its coherence. For example, suppose a questionnaire asks a mother, "Is your child active—yes or no?" The mother must first decide on the meaning of *active.* The meaning chosen will be influenced by her associations and by the larger frame to which she relates these associations, especially her understanding of her child. If the mother regards her child as intelligent, she may select as a salient feature of *active* the qualities of being curious and exploratory, and so answer yes. But, if she selects the quality of restlessness as a salient dimension of *active,* she may answer no if she views restlessness as inconsistent with high intelligence. Not all parents discern the same meaning in a question, in part because of idiosyncratic associations to the words and in part because of the larger frame to which the question is referred, even after its meaning is comprehended. Thus, the theoretical meaning of a term applied to self-report data is likely to change when the same term is applied to other referents (Plomin and Foch, 1980; Rothbart and Derryberry, 1981).

Subjective and Objective Frames

The meaning of self-report information on private states and beliefs returns us to the differences between sense and referential meaning and engages the contrast between subjective and objective frames.

These two frames resemble Popper's (1972) World 2 and World 3 and Strawson's (1985) participant and objective perspectives. The information from each of the two frames is complementary and need not be consistent because each has a different source. Because we cannot know the private states of animals, they are ignored in objectively framed descriptions and explanations of animal behavior. If all the pigeons generating data affirming the principle of scheduled reinforcement were able to communicate to their investigators that they did not peck at the key in order to get food, such a confession would not weaken the validity of the objectively framed theoretical statements that link the occurrence of operant responses to the schedule of food delivery.

Human beings have an awareness of their intentions, beliefs, and feeling states, although cultures name this quality with different terms. Although these states have primacy in the conduct of each person's daily life, an objectively framed explanation need not be consistent with the subjective frame nor with the terms particular individuals may use to describe their beliefs, emotions, or self-consciousness. Nisbett and Wilson (1977) have argued persuasively that people do not have access to their mental processes when they solve problems, and there is often no relation between a person's report of a motive state and an objective index of that motive. "The accuracy of subjective reports is so poor as to suggest that any introspective access that may exist is not sufficient to produce generally correct or reliable reports" (p. 233).

Astronomers are legitimately unconcerned over the fact that each person's subjective experience that the sun moves around the earth is not in accord with the scientists' objective frame. But many social scientists are concerned over the discrepancy between the popular and intuitively reasonable belief that television violence enhances aggressive behavior and objective empirical data that fail to support the subjective impression. Freedman (1984) writes, "The available literature does not support the hypothesis that viewing violence on television causes an increase in subsequent aggression in the real world" (p. 244). Self-report of a belief, idea, or state should be viewed in the objective frame of the investigator as a source of data that is no different in kind from a galvanic skin response, a facial expression, or a score on a test. As Churchland (1979) notes, our private judgments, when used as data for objectively framed propositions, have no special epistemic clout; as measuring instruments, "humans stand rather badly in need of wholesale recalibration" (p. 41).

No serious epistemological consequences follow from the suggestion that the subjective meaning of a self-report is often, but not always, different from the meaning ascribed to the same information in the objective frame. A patient who believes dead ancestors can cause illness says: "I am ill because I lied to my brother." That statement has a meaning for the speaker in the subjective frame, but probably has a different meaning in the objective frame of a western physician. This conclusion contains no logical difficulties. The statement "I am ill because I lied to my brother" assumes a causal force that produced the illness. If the physician, after examining the patient, also concludes that the person is ill because he told a lie to his brother, the doctor's proposition would also assume a process that made the person ill. But the defining features of the implied cause of the illness would be different in the two statements. In the subjective frame of the patient, the cause is the action of deceased ancestors. In the objective frame of the physician, the cause is likely to be an altered physiology that involves changes in the hypothalamic-pituitary-adrenal-autonomic system following chronic guilt over the violation of a personal standard on lying. Hence, the two statements have different implied meanings, despite identical surface meaning. If an entire community believes that dead ancestors can cause illness, that statement, too, is in the objective frame, but, as is characteristic of controversy in science, two statements in the objective frame need not be in accord. Thus, both the sense and referential meanings of a term can, on occasion, have a different interpretation in the subjective and objective frames.

A nice example of the different meanings that emanate from the subjective and objective frames involves mothers' attitudes over the importance of giving physical affection to infants and the balance of restriction or permissiveness to be imposed on older children. When we asked over 100 working and middle-class mothers, as defined by education and vocation, whether they thought a great deal of physical affection was good for infants and children or potentially harmful because it might make them too dependent, over 90 percent insisted, with feeling, that infants needed physical affection for future mental health. We then asked 30 mothers from working-class backgrounds and 30 from middle-class backgrounds to listen to two tape-recorded essays—each about 300 words long—and to recall as many words as they could after they heard each essay. The first essay dealt with the importance of giving infants a great deal of physical affection. The arguments favorable to affection claimed that kissing and hugging would make the child more secure and that close physical proximity between mother and infant was natural among mammals. The opposing arguments in the essay stated that caring mothers in some societies do not always display physical affection because too much physical affection can spoil a child and make him or her too dependent upon the parents for approval.

More working-class mothers recalled and elaborated more of the argument claiming that excessive affection was harmful, while more of the middle-class mothers recalled and elaborated the opposite theme. Two key phrases in the essay, which occurred in different places, were as follows:

> Those who favor affection point to the fact that infants, puppies, and kittens are always physically close to their mothers for the opening weeks of life and for this reason it is likely that children, too, need physical warmth.

And,

> Too much physical affection can spoil a child and make him or her too dependent upon the parents for love and approval.

One-third of the middle-class mothers recalled the first theme but not the second, while only 7 percent of middle-class mothers recalled the second but not the first idea. By contrast, only 13 percent of working-class mothers recalled the puppy-kitten theme but not the theme about spoiling, while 45 percent of working-class mothers showed the reverse pattern.

In the objective frame, a mother's attitude about child rearing is not a unified, coherent cognitive structure that is measured with varying sensitivity by different procedures. Rather, an attitude is part of a family of related structures, and each member of the family is revealed by different empirical procedures.

It is not necessary to decide whether the subjective or objective meaning is the more valid, or whether one should judge both meanings with reference to some third, ideal frame, as we do with inconsistent statements in the objective frame.[3] A belief that is valid for a

3. Churchland (1979) seems to regard an individual's beliefs in the subjective frame as a competitor for beliefs phrased in the objective frame; therefore, issues regarding the relative validity of the two beliefs become relevant. Strawson (1985), however, does not see them as inconsistent. Schlick (1979) provides a clue to the intended targets of his severe criticisms of the philosophical practice of

person in the subjective frame need not be valid in the objective frame of another, and vice versa. When I drive home from my laboratory, my subjective experience is that the earth is flat. But an observer who asks me why the hours of daylight increase in Spring would, in agreement with modern physics, conclude in the objective frame that I believe the earth is round. Each belief is correct with respect to its frame (Kagan, 1984).

The differences in meaning between information in the subjective and objective frames are analogous to the differences between the classical wave and particle features of light. Physicists treat the light that comes from a candle as a wave but treat the light from x-ray sources as composed of discrete particles. Wave and particle are different defining features of the construct *light,* and one cannot invent an experiment that "simultaneously exhibits the wave and particle aspects of atomic matter" (Holton, 1973, p. 119). The two descriptions are not inconsistent, and each has a useful purpose. Bohr believed that because quantum phenomena were always affected by measurement, one could not combine propositions about waves with propositions about particles because the evidence came from different experimental procedures.

Application of this premise to human behavior implies that an investigator may not always be able to combine self-report statements with information from domains that have different metrics, like facial expressions, heart rate, or EEG voltages. One reason is that logical inconsistency is rare in the language of self-report. A sane person does not say to an interviewer, "I am afraid and I am happy," because these concepts refer to two inconsistent ideas. And if a subject made such a statement, the interviewer would not know what to do with it. However, patterns of facial muscles can contain some components presumed to signify fear as well as some components signifying joy. Thus, it is possible for the face to yield information that suggests a combination of fear and joy, while such a combination is not usually permissible in self-report descriptions.

---

his period by explicitly chastising those scholars who claimed that private, transcendental states of consciousness do not have to be tied to real experience. I believe that one source of the intellectual energy behind the establishment of logical empiricism was a desire to delegitimize a person's private experience as a basis for truth and to force all members of a community to agree that the truth of a statement must rest with information that is available to all, so that disputes can be settled with consensus.

Additionally, the scientist who measures a person's heart rate variability or alpha waves in the EEG will use descriptive terms with no obvious synonym in the language subjects might use to describe their emotional state. Perhaps that is why there is typically a poor relation between self-report indexes of an emotional state and indexes of accompanying biological processes. The two sets of data can have a functional relation to each other, but they may not have the same theoretical meaning because they do not reflect the same process. One might even say that the two sets of data were incommensurable, in the same sense that the high-energy physicist uses the term to compare the results of the 1960's with contemporary results in linear accelerators. J. J. Thomson invented the poetic metaphor of a conflict between a tiger and a shark to capture such a state of affairs; each is potent in its own territory but impotent in the territory of the other. In a similar vein, self-reports of mood, attitude, and motive have a meaning and validity in the subjective frame of the agent that need not be consistent with those in the objective frame of the investigator.

Implications

Recent philosophical essays have begun to argue that the meaning of a construct is influenced primarily by the theoretical network in which it participates (Thomas, 1979). As a result of this trend, many scholars have begun to place less emphasis, or no emphasis at all, on the referential meanings of a concept. In the extreme, this movement has led some students of human behavior to declare that propositions that seek to describe or explain human behavior are qualitatively different from those in the natural sciences. This claim is accompanied by a willingness to decide theoretical controversies by decree, without recourse to evidence. Crews (1986) notes, "Today we are surrounded by theoreticism—frank recourse to unsubstantiated theory, not just as a tool of investigation but as anti-empirical knowledge in its own right . . . The empiricism that stands in some jeopardy today is simply a regard for evidence—a disposition to consult ascertainable facts when choosing between rival ideas . . . What antipositivism really comes down to is a feeling of nonobligation towards empiricism in a broad sense—that is, towards the community that expects theory to stay at least somewhat responsive to demonstrable findings" (p. 37).

Each theoretical network consists of its own concepts and sources of evidence. In psychometric theories of differential intelligence, for example, terms like heredity and spatial ability are theoretically linked, while in Piagetian theory the linked terms are equilibration, assimilation, accommodation, sensorimotor coordination, and concrete and formal operations. The referents that specify the terms in the two theoretical networks are also different. In the first they include the IQ scores of monozygotic and dizygotic twins; in the second network they include behavior on the procedures for object permanence and conservation. Hence, the meaning of intelligence is very different in the two networks. Indeed, it is rare for a term present in two different theoretical networks to involve the same empirical procedures.

A different way to state this conclusion borrows from Tversky's (1977) theoretical essay on the similarity between ideas. Tversky notes that the degree of similarity between two linguistic concepts, say England and France, depends upon the context of inquiry, or cognitive frame, imposed by an agent. In the context of a discussion of world history, the two countries will be judged much more similar than they will in the context of a discussion of philosophy or cuisine. Different empirical procedures can be viewed as analogous to different contexts in which the similarity between a specific corpus of data and a theoretical construct is being judged. In the context of a quiet laboratory, the simultaneous occurrence, in a majority of subjects, of a rise in heart rate and a decrease in skin resistance to the greeting of a white-coated experimenter will be judged by most psychologists as indicating a theoretical similarity between the propositions that summarize the autonomic reactions of the subjects and the construct of anxiety. The occurrence of the same two autonomic reactions in the same subjects when each has just received an affectionate embrace from a friend on a city street will not be so judged because, as noted earlier, the processes that produce the changes in heart rate and skin resistance are different in the two contexts. Thus, the use of a particular empirical procedure, species, or age cohort represents a specific context in which information related to a theoretical idea is gathered and so supplies a specific referential meaning to the term. Although a change in context need not necessarily alter the degree of similarity between the terms used to summarize the empirical evidence and the theoretical construct, there is no guarantee of this happy circumstance (see Stich, 1983, for a similar argument).

Because the salient features of words change with time, due partly to a change in theoretical conception, partly to the introduction of new methods, and partly to historical events in the larger society, both sense and referential meanings are altered. Hence, investigators should specify the primary dimensions they intend when they use a word in scientific prose.[4] In empirical work, that means either specifying the procedural source or inventing a new word when a procedure produces data that imply a change in defining features. Psychologists might append to theoretical constructs a symbol that informed the reader of the procedural source of the information for that term. As an example, investigators might note when the concept *secure attachment* refers to a child's behavior in the Ainsworth Strange Situation and when it refers to a history of parental abuse. The two referential meanings need not be correlated (Schneider-Rosen, 1984).

Physical scientists argue less about the meanings of terms because they have greater consensus on referential meanings. There is, after all, an accepted way to measure wavelength, electrical resistance, and the velocity of protons in an accelerator. But physicists do argue, for a while at least, when new concepts are first introduced and it is not yet obvious which procedure is best for a given theoretical idea. For example, a current controversy in astrophysics involves dark matter, presumed to be an invisible ectoplasm that fills the universe (Newton's ether has returned). If the relevant data come from observations on the cosmic abundance of light elements, like deuterium and helium-3, one meaning of dark matter is implied. But a different meaning is implied if the defining features are based on galactic red shifts (Waldrop, 1984). However, physicists seem to settle their definitional differences more quickly than do behavioral scientists.

Behavioral scientists and philosophers eventually rejected Bridgman's orthodox version of operationism because it was both counter-

---

4. In a general sense, many philosophers have assumed the responsibility for detecting a historically induced change in the meaning of a term and attempting to reconcile the old and emergent meanings. Churchland (1984), for example, attempts to find an accord between the community's traditional understanding of conscious psychological states and the new meanings implied by neurophysiologists and scholars writing about artificial intelligence. Pears (1984) legitimizes the role of emotion in human judgment as part of an accommodation to new empirical findings and historical events since the Second World War. It is probably not a coincidence that the formal discipline of philosophy plays a more central role in societies with a great deal of ideological pluralism, as in the West, than in societies with far less variability in the understanding of the community's central ideas; classic Japan is one example.

intuitive and inimical to empirical progress to assume that use of two different rulers changed the meaning of length. But I believe that some social scientists have gone too far in completely ignoring the deeper message Wittgenstein, Bridgman, Schlick, and Carnap intended. A new procedure can produce information that alters the salient defining features of a popular, summarizing concept. As a result, the concept is infused with a fresh life. "A fresh instrument," Whitehead wrote, "serves the same purpose as foreign travel; it shows things in unusual combinations" (Whitehead, 1928, p. 167). The microscope changed the meaning of *basic body unit* from organ to cell, although prior to the invention of high-power lenses observers saw only globules under the microscope and concluded that they were the basic life units. The ability to fertilize an ovum in a laboratory dish with sperm from a deceased father has seriously changed the meaning of *human reproduction.* Chromatography, by providing a way to measure blood proteins in different families of animals, has changed the meaning of *biological similarity among animal groups.* Indeed, the estimated age of the first human ancestors varies by about ten million years, depending upon whether one uses bone fragments or biochemistry as the index of the relation between apes and hominids (Ciochon and Corruccini, 1983). In psychology, the tachistoscope produced data that altered the meaning of *perception;* the polygraph and its amplifiers generated evidence that changed the meanings of *attention, arousal, effort,* and *stress;* and the modern computer has altered the meanings of *intelligence* and *knowledge.*

Sometimes a new method introduces a new feature; sometimes it merely changes the hierarchical position of an existing one. New features are added more often in the physical sciences; in the social sciences it is more common for the existing features of a concept to change their position in the hierarchy. The invention of the PET scan has not led to new psychological terms, only to an enhancement of the salience of changes in brain states that are components of the meanings of cognitive processes and emotional states. I believe that behavioral scientists should be more friendly to those who work toward the invention of new apparatus and procedures. Biologists are generous in their support of colleagues who are willing to work on a new stain for a part of the central nervous system or a new method for cloning cells. Sherrington's discoveries would not have been possible without the prior advances in microsurgery of the neuron, the method of spinal sections, and the vacuum tube amplifier. There is, unfortunately, insufficient enthusiasm for methodological invention among psychologists. Perhaps that is why Ackermann (1985) notes, "What the human sciences require for more dramatic progress is not simply more data . . . but new instrumentation for obtaining data . . . so that more exhaustive explanatory possibilities can be tried" (p. 169).

Instrumental bases for theoretical progress are the rule in the physical sciences. The regular march of progress in our understanding of the constituents of matter depended upon increasingly complex machines, from Oersted's use of an electrified compass needle to Rubbia's access to the accelerator at CERN. In some cases the information produced by the apparatus became a major incentive for a new conceptualization; for example, Heisenberg invented new mathematical functions in order to explain the atomic spectra new apparatus made possible. These mathematical ideas led to the replacement of the traditional concept of continuous energy with the discrete, discontinuous quantum.

The story told to psychology students, however, is that one morning a brilliant theorist thought of a concept that suddenly explained a set of puzzling phenomena. Darwin's invention of natural selection and Freud's notion of the repressed wish are among the most popular examples of this script for intellectual progress. The romantic element in this script is that the evidence Darwin and Freud used—fossils and anatomical variation in related species or hysterical paralyses and recall of childhood sexual experiences—were available to a great many discerning minds. But because these men were creative, they saw a meaning in these phenomena that other minds missed. The conception of theoretical advance in the social sciences is so dominated by the examples of Darwin and Freud that most sociologists, anthropologists, and psychologists ignore, or in some cases are hostile to, the utility of machines. I use the term *machine* generically to refer to any manufactured object that permits the observation of events not available to the unaided human senses. The construction of the vacuum tube and induction coil by men without advanced degrees in physics led to the discovery of x-rays, which became the incentive for inquiry into atomic particles. The rest of the story, which is now well known, changed the basic nineteenth-century premises regarding the essence of matter.

Some of the concepts that form the scaffolding for the major areas of contemporary psychology (including learning, motivation, perception, memory, social behavior, personality, and development) have been altered by methodological innovations, even though the two deeper premises—that the elemental structures of mind are acquired through sensory experience and that goal-oriented behaviors are composed of chains of smaller sensory-motor units established as a result of contingent reward and punishment—often remain unchanged.

Work in the neurosciences supports the claim that machines have contributed to changes in theory. A half-century ago the domain called *learning* relied on the twin concepts of biological drive and primary reinforcement to explain changes in the goal-directed behavior of animals learning to master a maze or press a lever. The invention of amplifiers and microelectrodes permitted quantification of changes in electrical potentials in single neurons to the pairing of neutral and biologically relevant signals. The resulting evidence has led to the replacement of drive and reinforcement with physiological concepts. For example, changes in the discharge of cerebellar neurons to the pairing of a puff of air to a rabbit's eye with a tone or light is now described with biological words like stimulation of sensory neurons, synaptic potential, and movement of calcium ions.

New methods to diagnose brain states could change the meaning of memory trace. Most psychologists assume that the mind/brain contains a structured representation of a past event and that a probe stimulus activates the trace with different probabilities—the presumed metric is continuous. But suppose future perfection of magnetic resonance imaging techniques permits the quantification of brain changes that accompany the introduction of a probe. Suppose also that the data reveal an "all or none principle," rather than a probabilistic continuum. Such a finding would change our theory of knowledge representation and recognition memory. Further, if there were no differences between the magnetic resonance profiles produced by a probe that required the subject to define the word *peso* (semantic memory) and a probe that required the subject to recall a word that was placed third in a list heard a minute earlier (episodic memory), the current distinction between semantic and episodic memory would be challenged.

The study of personality in the years after the Second World War explored a person's verbal interpretations of TAT and Rorschach cards using the constructs conflict, stress, motive, anxiety, and defense. The invention of chemical assays for norepinephrine, epinephrine, and cortisol, as well as instruments to evaluate heart rate, vagal tone, blood pressure, and, more recently, glucose utilization in the brain yielded data that changed both the sense and referential meaning of these constructs, without altering the traditional assumption that individual differences in emotions are an important basis for psychological symptoms.

Because the theoretical meaning of *anxiety* when cortisol level is the source of evidence is very different from the meaning when TAT stories are the relevant information, propositions about the consequences or antecedents of anxiety based on the biological evidence contain novel ideas. Further, the meaning of changes in norepinephrine, cortisol levels, heart rate, and other signs of emotional arousal are usually independent and often unrelated to self-reports of anxiety. This fact implies that the concept of general emotional arousal, which was central to the theories of Clark Hull and Kenneth Spence, is deeply flawed.

During the early decades of this century, students of human development relied on naturalistic observations of children and summarized their data with concepts that referred to molar, goal-directed acts like mastery, autonomy, dependency, and aggression. The video camera and cassette recorder permit contemporary scholars to record and later code events so brief they could not have been noted reliably by a human observer (for example, profile of change in facial expression, limb movement, and quality of vocalization to the entrance of an unfamiliar adult). The new information has produced new concepts, like discrete emotions, behavioral inhibition, and insecure attachment, as well as constructs that combine affective states with cognitive structures. The discovery that limbic structures participate in both the generation of emotion as well as the acquisition and retrieval of schemata renders the distinction between hot and cold cognition obsolete. This victory is to be celebrated by all.

Unknown Worlds

If the machines now in use had not been invented, many of the constructs generated to explain the data the machines produced would not be part of our current vocabulary. Had different apparatus been invented, the observations would have been of a different kind and the constructs may have had different theoretical meanings—as is true of wave and particle. Suppose that instead of the apparatus that permitted measurement of the electrical activity of neurons, nineteenth-century engineers had invented an apparatus permitting quantification of very small changes in temperature (in nano degrees) on the surface of the skull or cortex. The recent invention of thermography cameras makes this example less hypothetical.

It is likely that the profile of temperature changes following the pairing of a puff of air to a rabbit's eye with a light signal would require constructs different from those used by Richard Thompson and his colleagues to explain the conditioned nictitating membrane reflex. And the resulting explanation might be as logically coherent and aesthetically satisfying as the current one. If someone had invented a machine that measured simultaneously plasma epinephrine and norepinephrine, blood pressure, and heart rate while the person was solving mental tasks, it is likely that cognitive theorists would have been differentiating between difficult and easy tasks rather than between verbal and spatial ones. As a result, theory in individual differences would have been more concerned with differential motivation than with variation in competences. Both constructs are useful, but historical accidents awarded priority to the latter over the former.

Or suppose a machine quantifying the velocity and acceleration of movements of head, limbs, and trunk had been invented rather than the video camera and cassette recorder. The motor patterns of a child encountering both strangers and separation from the mother in an unfamiliar room would differ from the rapid changes in facial expression that are now coded from video tapes. It is likely that the constructs required to explain the motor evidence might not resemble the emotional concepts of fear and surprise that are now used.

Nature contains alternative coherences; we discover only those that our procedures permit. I do not claim that the phenomena that have been discovered and their associated explanations are invalid. Rather, I suggest only that our current knowledge represents only one of many corpora that could have been described.

Many domains in contemporary psychology do not contain a large number of concepts that were demanded by evidence resulting from new apparatus. A large number of investigations of animal and human behavior in our best journals—*Behavioral Neuroscience* is an obvious exception—gathered data "the old-fashioned way." The scientists relied on careful observations of behavior and answers to tests and questionnaires. Even though investigators place animals or humans in unusual situations (a harness for an animal being conditioned, a testing room for a child), the primary evidence is overt behavior. As a result, the most popular constructs refer to events close to the surface that are assimilable to the intuitions of the educated citizen. Is this state of affairs necessarily inimical to progress? The answer, unfortunately, is yes, if the history of our sister sciences is taken as a useful guide. If psychology is to arrive at a more generative set of units, it is likely that it, too, will need new procedures that will reveal what has been invisible.

There are good reasons to resist the implications of this essay. There is an understandable reluctance to have to relate every proposition to a larger frame in order to evaluate its truth value. Thus, many social scientists have sided with philosophers who claim a proposition derives both its meaning and validity from the network of related ideas of which it is a part (Stich, 1983; Churchland, 1984).[5] The greater the empirical and logical coherence of the related propositions, the more valid an individual proposition in the network. Thus, the enterprise of science is analogous to building a house of bricks, with each investigator checking each brick to see if its color and shape blend well with the entire structure. One cannot judge a single, isolated brick as good or bad intrinsically. Similarly, there is no simple criterion that permits one to decide if the isolated statement "Introverts are anxious in social situations" is true or false.

Some readers may regard this essay as empty of significance for, after all, an investigator usually does not know the processes that

5. This conclusion assumes, incidentally, that the meanings of terms that retain some tie to observables—the philosophical position called *foundationalism*—are different from the meanings that derive solely from a coherent network of propositions that has no link to experience, sometimes called *epistemological holism*. Thus, the meaning of the proposition "Water causes iron to rust," when held by a person who has experienced the rusting of metal, is different from the meaning of the same proposition stored in a computer program that holds in memory all of the propositions of inorganic chemistry. "The purpose of words," Russell (1962) noted, "is to deal with matters other than words" (p. 141). But because rapid advances in technology and theory in the physical sciences have produced short half-lives for what seemed to be true propositions, a mood of skepticism regarding empirical truth has risen. As a counter-reaction to this skepticism, some philosophers have claimed that logical coherence alone can be a criterion for truth. A few, like Richard Foley (1986), have become unusually permissive, claiming that if a proposition seems likely to be true following reflection upon its premises, the person should allow himself to be persuaded by that proposition and its accompanying argument.

mediate a new, interesting phenomenon. If the scientist errs by incorrectly assuming similar processes for two different events and giving them the same name, future research will make the correction. Hence, it would seem that there is little harm in ignoring the arguments in this essay. However, effort, time, and funds are limited resources, and a self-consciousness about this problem will lead to savings in all three. During the period from 1930 to 1960 a large number of psychologists interpreted evidence from experiments with albino rats running mazes as providing information about processes of learning that were assumed to be similar to, if not identical with, learning in humans. Beach's (1950) famous paper, "The Snark Is a Boojum," criticized this broad extrapolation from rodents to primates and implied that if psychologists had reflected more on the sense and referential meanings of *learning* in their experiments, much time and money could have been saved.

An important change in the philosophy of language that began with the Enlightenment, but has accelerated during this century, is a shift from a preoccupation with the existence or nonexistence of the entities propositions describe to a concern with the meaning of the words in those propositions. Pari passu, this shift entails an acceptance of the notion that meanings change with time and are always influenced by the procedure that produced the relevant evidence. "The idea that the extensions of our terms are fixed by collective practices and not by concepts in our individual heads is a sharp departure from the way meaning has been viewed ever since the seventeenth century" (Putnam, 1983, p. 75). I do not suggest that all definitions are functional or that *a priori* axioms are not theoretically useful, but rather that all evaluations of the meaning of an empirically derived proposition are, simultaneously, evaluations of both the proposition and its evidential origins. This conclusion does not limit the creativity of the investigator; it only urges care in making assertions and a tolerance toward new meanings for old ideas.

2

Twentieth-Century Trends in Developmental Psychology

The ways in which conditions in society and practices in the laboratory cohere to create temporary nodes of scientific inquiry are not well understood. It is not clear, for example, why seventeenth-century naturalists chose to study flowering plants more often than mammals, or why early nineteenth-century scholars were more interested in evolution than in locomotion. The wisest scholars in the beginning of the nineteenth century could not have anticipated the questions developmental psychologists would ask a century later.

A post hoc analysis of the growth of the natural sciences suggests that at least three relatively independent factors contribute to the popularity of an empirical question. They are (1) novel methods, (2) new theory, and (3) events in the larger society, some with a long historical prologue, that create a broad concern with a particular phenomenon. The contemporary vitality of genetics and molecular biology provides an example. Inside the academy, Watson and Crick's insight into the double helical structure of DNA motivated the discovery of powerful procedures that cleaved DNA strands at their joints, promising eventually a library of the human genome. Outside the laboratory, citizens in industrialized societies wished to cure and prevent diseases that remained recalcitrant and to create new strains of plants to alleviate hunger in less advantaged areas. The joining of these forces persuaded citizens, legislators, scientists, and students selecting careers that a serious commitment to molecular biology was warranted.

The short history of scholarship in psychological development, a little over 100 years, yields to a comparable analysis. Darwinian theory and parental concern with the child's character and talent guided developmental inquiry during the last two decades of the nineteenth century. Parents wanted to know how to make their children more moral and more intelligent, and evolutionary theory implied a biological contribution to the universal ontogeny of, as well as the wide variation in, both characteristics. But because the only method that enjoyed consensus was to watch children and record what they did, the first information came from the diary entries of educated parents with a scientific interest in human development. Then, as now, gaining pleasure and avoiding pain were assumed to be the primary motivations for action; so diarists like Millicent Shinn unconsciously interpreted their observations in this frame. When she saw her newborn infant turn toward a light, she assumed that the resulting sensations were pleasurable (actually she used the word *agreeable*).

The Rise of Behaviorism

A major change in premise and procedure occurred during the first two decades of the twentieth century, following Pavlov's discovery and Watson's dissemination of the phenomenon of conditioning. Despite the originality and theoretical significance of Pavlov's conclusions, the rapid rise in the use of conditioning explanations in American writings required a secular factor. The necessary social catalyst took the form of a serious political problem.

During the years before World War I, there was a significant increase in racial and ethnic tension between the new European immigrants and the urban black populations, on the one hand, and the established, white middle-class majority, on the other. Cravens (1978) and May (1959), among others, have documented that the increased numbers of European immigrants in the cities raised the level of suspicion and hostility between middle-class whites and the minority groups, culminating in legislation restricting immigration. This strife was especially strong during the middle of the second decade.

Part of the reason for increasing tension was, as in earlier crises, economic. The depression of 1914 revived labor's fears of foreign competition and decreased the employer's interest in a steady flow of immigrant workers. Lawrence and Paterson presented to newspaper readers the picture of the dangerous alien immigrant. And everytime anybody, for any reason, worried about the preservation of old ways, he was likely to glance with alarm, at the annual inflow of half a million newcomers (May, 1959, p. 347).

The highly publicized assumption was that the differences in ability, wealth, status, character, and criminality between established and immigrant groups were essentially biological in origin. Concern with proliferation of a less-advantaged group, which was bound to weaken the capacity of the larger society, led to a national conference on race betterment in 1914. One year later, twelve states had passed sterilization laws. Then, as now, the bias toward blacks centered on intellect. In April 1916 a writer in the *Archives of Psychology* put his conclusions in terms of statistics: "Pure negroes, negroes three-fourths pure, mulattoes, and quadroons have roughly 60, 70, 80 and 90 percent respectively of white intellectual efficiency" (Ferguson, 1916, p. 125, quoted in May, p. 349). And Karl Pearson (1925), who was uneasy over the consequences of immigration into England wrote, "The whole problem of immigration is fundamental for the rational teaching of national eugenics. What purpose would there be in endeavoring to legislate for a superior breed of men, if at any moment it could be swamped by the influx of immigrants of an inferior race, hastening to profit by the higher civilization of an improved humanity" (cited in Pastore, 1949, p. 7).

The belief that differences in ethnic and racial habits, styles of interaction, and especially mental abilities were genetic was strengthened when the mental tests administered to recruits as America entered World War I revealed that blacks and ethnic minorities had the lowest scores. The interpretation imposed by Robert Yerkes (1921) and Lewis Terman (1916)—two of the most influential psychologists of the time—was that these differences in mental ability were biologically based.

Sixty-five years later government officials again were worried about the very low scores on army intelligence tests produced by army recruits from minority groups—this time black and Hispanic rather than European. But six decades of history had altered the social consensus regarding the meaning of these scores. Hence, in 1980 the Secretary of the Army, Mr. Alexander, was able to do what his counterpart in 1915 could never have done. He challenged the test, removed the scores from the recruits' files, and insisted that despite their low scores these recruits were as capable as their civilian peers (*New York Times,* August 10, 1980).

Although Terman softened his views in his later years, the earlier statement was provocative. These objective mental test scores were regarded as an index of a biological quality; hence, a genetic interpretation forced many Americans to confront an idea that was threatening to the national egalitarian ethos. There was good reason to think that the majority of educated Americans wanted to believe in the ideal of a society in which the poor and disadvantaged could, through effort and motivation, lift themselves to the middle class. Many geneticists and social scientists writing during the first two decades of this century—including Cooley, Watson, Boas, and J. B. S. Haldane—explicitly rejected the conclusions of Galton, Pearson, McDougall, and Terman. Hermann Muller (1933), a Nobel Laureate in genetics, wrote: "There is no sufficient basis for the conclusion that the socially lower classes or technically less advanced races, really have a genetically inferior intellectual equipment, since the differences between their averages are, so far as our knowledge goes, to be accounted for fully by the known effects of environment" (p. 43).

Popular writers also insisted that the low IQ scores of immigrant children were amenable to social engineering. "When a high level of economic independence and common education has been achieved then also will our tests register a higher level of common attainment" (Link, 1923, p. 385). Even Arnold Gesell (Gesell and Lord, 1927) was friendly to this idea. He concluded an empirical paper on class differences in the behavior of three-year-olds with a quotation from a speech that the utopian Robert Owen had given over a century earlier to an audience that included the President and the Congress of the United States.

> External circumstances may be formed as to have an overwhelming and irresistible influence over every infant that comes into existence, either for good or evil . . . To surround him through life with the most agreeable or disagreeable object [will] . . . make any portion or the whole of the human race poor, ignorant, vicious and wretched, or affluent, intelligent, virtuous and happy. (p. 356)

Henry May (1959) affirms the suggestion that there was a national commitment to egalitarianism. "The first and central article of faith in the national credo was, as it always had been, the reality, certainty, and eternity of moral values" (p. 9). In this moral scheme, evil was easy to define for "it was incarnate in extreme inequality, political corruption and ruthless power" (p. 22). May suggests that a majority of Americans would have been bothered—as Adam Smith and Helvetius would have been two centuries earlier—by any fact that threatened this idea. "Most of the custodians of culture prophesied that America would prove able to deal with the immigrant flood, the vulgar plutocracy, the rising materialism of the middle-class, the attacks on sound education, and the many incomprehensible vagaries of the youngest generation. With democracy, but under the leadership of its proper guardians, idealism would be strengthened and culture spread through the land" (p. 51). "By hard work, most of the newcomers could probably be led toward the light" (p. 38).

Essays in the *Atlantic Monthly* during the second decade reflected this premise. H. M. Chittenden (1912) asserted his faith in the basic genetic similarity of all humans. "While human nature is ever the same, the growth and influence of civilization produces from this same nature ever changing results" (p. 781). "What marks us off from our ancestors is a changed environment and not a changed human nature" (p. 782). Samuel Smith (1912) attacked those who were too quick to argue that genetic taint was the cause of criminal behavior; and William Jewett Tucker (1913) wrote, "The demand for equality, like the demand for liberty whenever it is serious, takes precedence" (p. 481).

Some scholars even criticized the institution of science for being too elitist:

> Prostitution of talent and character, the development of an intellectual aristocracy in a democratic land, and absurd clamoring for petty honors increasing gaps and misunderstandings between classes and professions . . . dependence on reputation rather than on genuine worth . . . the effort to serve two masters—truth and the man immediately above one in rank . . . all of these are evils attendant upon our present system of academic honors and badges. (Speech by David Starr Jordan, cited in MacArthur and MacArthur, 1916, p. 466)

The objective mental test scores, therefore, posed a potentially serious inconsistency in national philosophy. If poor Italians, Slavs, and Jews were biologically less talented than middle-class, established Caucasians, individual effort and proper education might not work. The resulting dissonance was as serious a source of unease as E. O. Wilson's suggestion that our moral attitude toward sexuality and aggression should be based on evolutionary facts, or Skinner's claim that each of us is not free because our present behavior is a determined product of past conditioning. It is not surprising that many educated liberals would be eager for any rational weapon that would neutralize the racial inferiority hypothesis.

A second basis for the shift in paradigm lay in the fact that authors of psychological texts trained after 1900 were writing at a time when psychology as a discipline was trying to define itself as an experimental natural science, distinct from philosophy and biology, empirical in character, and pruned of metaphysics. The opening sentence of Watson's 1913 essay in the *Psychological Review* declared: "Psychology as the behaviorist views it is a purely objective experimental branch of natural science" (p. 158). Hence, the critique of racial inferiority had to be based on scientific evidence. Pavlov's work, which was made popular by John Watson, was seized on by the new cadre of psychologists. Conditioning was elegant, experimental science, and its subject matter and language of description (stimuli, responses, reinforcements) belonged uniquely to the new scientific profession of psychology. In addition, conditioning emphasized the role of experience, not biology, in promoting both change and stability of psychological attributes. By the late 1920s learning had become a key mechanism in all texts, and with that change came longer discussions of the influence of experience, especially experience in the family.

The first empirical paper on the role of conditioning in development to appear in the *Pedagogical Seminary*, the chief organ for dissemination of technical papers on child development, appeared in 1916 when Feingold suggested that the imbecile might be taught to inhibit impulsive action. Five years later George Humphrey (1921) argued that the nineteenth-century assumption that imitation is an innate disposition should be replaced with an explanation that uses conditioning principles. And in 1931, Dorothy Marquis reported the successful conditioning of behavioral signs of "eating behavior" in the newborn. Marquis's paper marked the beginning of an increasing number of reports that relied on conditioning explanations of behavior in children. Her final conclusions are worth quoting: "Systematic training of human infants along social and hygienic lines can be started at birth. Since habit function may begin so early the sharp lines drawn by some writers in their classifications of some acts as instinctive and some acts as learned must be viewed with some hesitation" (p. 490).

Whether Watson and his colleagues realized it or not, by emphasizing the role of conditioning in development, they supplied the intellectual weapons necessary to defuse the racial inferiority hypothesis. By the 1930s the battle was over, for the hypothesis of innate racial differences was absent from major texts—the change was that rapid and total. Julian Huxley could now write in the *Yale Review* that the eugenicists had been wrong about racial inferiority.

The ideas of behaviorism were accepted so quickly because there was a fire to put out—the social danger implied by the hypothesis of racial inferiority promoted during the years before World War I.

It seemed to many social scientists that the principles of conditioning would explain most of the individual variation in children's character, symptoms, and intelligence as due to different reinforcement experiences. By the early 1940s the developmental journals contained two types of reports. One described classical or instrumental conditioning of a new response in an animal, usually a white rat. The second described age, sex, or social class differences in a human mental ability or behavior. Both classes of reports implied that the behavior of interest could be explained by application of the principles of conditioning derived from investigations with animals. Government pamphlets offering advice to mothers were dogmatic in insisting that a mother should not attend to her baby just because it cried. Such practices would condition the infant to expect that he or she could get what they want by crying. I recall my mother saying that she followed this advice faithfully, and confessing that she felt guilty when she let me scream in the crib if it was not the correct time for my feeding.

The mood of the faculty involved in learning theory when I entered graduate school in 1950 reflected the assured confidence that a satisfying and relatively complete behavioristic explanation of children's behavior, both universal ontogeny and variation, was only years away. John Dollard and Neal Miller wrote in *Personality and Psychotherapy* in 1950, "Human behavior is learned; precisely that behavior which is widely felt to characterize man as a rational being" (p. 25). This popular book, which began with the above declaration, proceeded to explain all human anxiety and conflict as a product of the learning of responses to particular drive conditions, as did the first edition of Mussen and Conger's text *Child Development and Personality* published in 1956. Few developmental psychologists would interpret infant separation and stranger anxiety in this way today.

The Attraction to Freedom

Developmental psychology has always contained two distinct images of the best way to explain human nature. One celebrates the rational, the pragmatic, the material, and experimental analysis of the separate functional components in isolated agents. The explanations of behavior based on conditioning met all four of these standards. The characteristics of the second ideal, which are a bit harder to specify, award primacy to the more internal and holistic processes, especially emotions, social perceptions, intentions, and desires that are built upon and displayed through relationships with others. The scholars whose ideology and temperament favored these processes found Freud's ideas more attractive than those of Watson. Psychoanalytic concepts and principles, which competed with conditioning theory in some universities and complemented them in others, made emotions rather than acquired habits the central constructs, and posited stages of development that contained an implict set of values, the most important being that restriction of the child's natural freedom of expression was inimical to mental health.

A comparison of a conditioning versus a psychoanalytic explanation of a child's phobia conveys the differences between the two perspectives. Conditioning theory attributed a child's behavioral avoidance of dogs to an accidental pairing of the unpleasant state of fear with an encounter with a large dog. The cause of the phobia was a specific event in the environment, the symptom was reversible, and the explanation had no moral or political overtones. The psychoanalytic interpretation assumed repression of dangerous thoughts that originated in emotionally tense relationships with parents. Thus, the cause of the fear was the product of chronically improper parental behavior, not a single chance event, and the symptom was only reversible if the parents permitted the child sufficient freedom to express his desires and ideas. This explanation is not free of moral and political overtones. Perhaps the most fundamental assumption in the theory of psychoanalytic therapy is that repressed motives, confined to the unconscious, lead to symptoms whose cure requires permitting the imprisoned ideas free access to consciousness. By changing just a few words in that description, one has a political declaration about the importance of freedom for human well-being.

Perhaps the most profound and, at the same time, the most disguised premise in most texts on development is that the child naturally enjoys freedom, an affirmation of Locke's declaration that "children love liberty and therefore they should be brought to do the things that are fit for them, without feeling any restraint laid upon them" (Locke, [1693] 1892, p. 83). Even though all children must be socialized, their personal liberty is the most important inherent property to nurture. This idea is hidden in psychological propositions about play, private conscience, independence, and autonomy.

Freedom has at least two major meanings, one political and one psychological. The political definition refers to a society that awards its citizens as much permissiveness in matters of action and belief as it can without infringing on the actions and beliefs of others. There is no guarantee that each citizen will be able to exploit the freedom of belief and action a particular government permits. From a psychological perspective freedom refers to a *belief* that one is able to act in accord with privately generated goals with minimal external coercion. This private belief is abstract, and, I suspect, does not exist in children before early adolescence. Therefore, observers who use the term *freedom* to describe the state of the child are unconsciously confusing the political and psychological definitions.

In discussing the growth of the child's sense of agency, Baldwin (1895) noted that the child "begins to grow capricious himself and to feel that he can be so whenever he likes. Suggestion begins to lose the regularity of its working; or to become negative and contrary in its effects. At this period it is that obedience begins to grow hard, and its meaning begins to dawn upon the child as the great reality. It means the subjection of his own agency, his own liberty to be capricious, to the agency and liberty of someone else" (p. 125).

Sully (1896) suggested that the infant's protest to the removal of the feeding bottle before full satisfaction had been obtained is "the first rude germ of that defiance of control and of authority of which I shall have to say more by and by" (p. 231). But Sully is not bothered by these rebellious tendencies; he celebrates them. "We should not care to see a child give up his inclinations at another's bidding without some little show of resistance. These conflicts are frequent and sharp in proportion to the sanity and vigor of the child. The best children, best from a biological point of view, have, I think, most of the rebel in them" (p. 269). Indeed, the natural child resents restriction of his liberty because, Sully declares, freedom is a natural desire. "So strong and deep reaching is this antagonism to law and its restraints apt to be that the childish longing to be big, is I believe, grounded on the expectation of liberty" (p. 277).

In a text that purports to be more scientific, Rand, Sweeny, and Vincent (1930) assert,

> The whole process of the child's development has as its goal its emancipation from the parents, so that its own life may be free to

develop to the fullest without the hindrances that are inevitable if there continues an attachment to the home . . . free development of the personality is only possible if it is free from crippling dependence of any sort . . . Therefore, parents who are wise will grant freedom gradually and increasingly and will welcome rather than resent signs of a desire for independence on the child's part. (pp. 351–352)

Even John Watson, who prided himself on being scientifically objective, told parents that if they treat their children properly, "the end result is a happy child free as air because he has mastered the stupidly simple demands society makes upon him" (1928, p. 150).

Play as a State of Freedom

Children are most free, it is supposed, when they are at play. The behavioral category *play* appears in almost every textbook, but the fuzzy quality of its definition leads one to suspect that its popularity rests upon a deep presupposition—play is a celebration of freedom. Most definitions of the child's acts (crying, hitting) or states (fear, hostility) are defined in terms that refer to real events. There is little ambiguity regarding the physical actions or phenomena to which the decriptive term applies. But this is less true for the category of play, where there is no clear guide one can use to diagnose a response as an instance of play. Play is defined neither in terms of antecedent conditions nor observable reactions but as a special state. Few major descriptive terms for the child or his properties are treated this way. Since this class of definition is both unusual and ambiguous, one would have thought that it would have a short life. But the category persists, I believe, because it is filling a vital function. The early definitions of play reveal one reason for its persistence.

"It is in play that [the child] gives free scope to all his aptitudes" (Compayré, 1914, p. 143). William Stern (1930) declared that no child can play under the yoke of necessity, "only that being can play whose consciousness is not quite subjugated under the yoke of necessity, under the stress of the struggle for existence . . . play is neither demanded nor imposed, but bubbles up spontaneously from the individual's deepest craving for action and its nature, form, and duration are determined by the player himself" (p. 307). Piaget, too, emphasizes the freedom in play. "Imaginary play is a symbolic transposition which subjects things to the child's activity without rules or limitations" (Piaget, 1951, p. 87).

The least ambiguous statement is in a book on play directed to the general public—*A Philosophy of Play*—written by Luther Gulick (1920), a leader in developing recreational opportunities for youth and a founder of the Playground and Recreation Association of America. "Play is what we do when we are free to do what we will" (p. 267). "Play as free expression of the self, as the pursuit of the ideal, has direct bearing on the ultimate questions of reality and worth. The spirit of play has value as a philosophy of life" (p. 11). Play is necessary for America, Gulick declares, because "the type of freedom found in play is the type of freedom on which democracy rests" (p. 261).

The words *subjugated, yoke of necessity, compulsion, freedom, rules and limitations,* which are used frequently in descriptions of play, have political connotations. The popularity of play as a scientific category for children may originate, in part, in the deep concern that adults feel about restrictions on their individual liberty and in the devotion they show, at least in the West, to freedom as a cherished state that must be worked for and maintained.

There are other terms an observer might apply to the acts that are now classified as play. When a one-year-old is building a tower with five blocks (a sequence always treated as play) it is not unreasonable to call that event an instance of morality. The child generates a standard (the idea of a five-block tower as a goal to be reached) and feels compelled to persist until he meets that standard. One might even argue that while the child is building the tower he is anything but free. The rough-and-tumble bodily encounters of four-year-old boys could be classified as an example of healthy behavior, hostility, anxiety reduction, or even sexuality. There is so little resemblance between a one-year-old building a block tower and four-year-olds wrestling, it is surprising that so many observers have insisted on calling these activities by the same name.

I am not persuaded that individual freedom is one of the hidden purposes in ontogeny. Reproduction, coordination of limbs, and reflective thought may be biologically adaptive teloi, but freedom is a metaphysical ideal. That does not mean it is less significant, only that the statement "Children should be free" has no firm home either in psychological theory or empirical fact but is based on a political philosophy. The fact that political ideology slips into the descriptions of children's psychological attributes indicates that our wisest observers have permitted their views about individual liberty to affect their classification of children's actions.

Attachment Theory

Both conditioning and psychoanalytic theory had made the nurturing acts of the mother the primary foundation for a child's perception of her as a source of pleasure. Learning theory claimed the mother acquired reward value; in psychoanalytic essays, the infant cathected the caretaker. Both mechanisms were supposed to motivate the child to learn the values, motives, and habits that permitted adaptation to the society. The child's attachment to the mother was the mechanism that made these outcomes possible.

It is important to note, however, that nineteenth-century authors rarely used terms that denoted a child's inclination to establish an affective relation with adult caretakers. Mothers had intense, unrestrained affection for their babies, but babies did not necessarily reciprocate. For example, Elizabeth Evans (1875) asserted that "the strongest human tie is, understandably, that which binds a mother to her child" (p. 7), but nowhere in this 129-page essay on maternity does she ever say that the infant naturally binds itself to the mother. Indeed, one author (Fiske, [1883] 1909) suggested that the function of infant helplessness was not to encourage the infant's attachment to the mother but rather to facilitate the emotional bond between the two parents. The cooperativeness necessary to nurture several children through adolescence would inevitably strengthen the emotional tie between the parents and keep them together.

To the nineteenth-century observer, the infant was, first, a collection of reflexes, instincts, and sensory capacities which developed a sense of self and a burgeoning morality by acting in the natural world. These properties were established through individual action, not mutual interaction and dependence upon parents. But by the late 1920s—and with increasing regularity after Freud's writing became popular—attachment, trust, and dependence became major descriptive terms for the infant and young child. And this concern was accompanied by more explicit preaching about the importance of the proper amount of parental love. Frank Richardson (1926), a physician who tried to disseminate the implications of Freudian theory for parents, opened the first chapter of his book with the simple declaration, "Love is the greatest thing in the world" (p. 3), and warned parents of the dangers of too little or too much affection for their infants. Too little could cause "a definite injury, whose results, may, and probably will, last as long as the life of the individual" (p. 18). Too much love might cripple a child and produce "unfortunate individuals [who] present a sorry sight 10 or 12 years later. They are irritable, dissatisfied, wholly incapacitated for happy middle-age or later life" (p. 22).

One of the strongest statements on the significance of the love relation between child and parent is to be found in the final volume of John Bowlby's ambitious trilogy on attachment and loss (Bowlby, 1980). Bowlby begins the monograph on *Loss* with a conclusion that would be difficult to find in a scholarly essay on human experience prior to 1800: "Loss of a loved person is one of the most intensely painful experiences any human being can suffer" (p. 7). Bowlby argues that an attachment to another person is instinctive, endures from infancy to adulthood, and, most important, an insecure attachment during infancy is likely to have a permanent affect on future vulnerability to psychopathology. On the final page Bowlby celebrates the centrality of affectional relationships. "Intimate attachments to other human beings are the hub around which a person's life revolves, not only when he is an infant or a toddler but throughout his adolescence and his years of maturity as well and on into old age" (p. 442).

This bold hypothesis could not have been written by Erasmus or Montaigne because they did not regard infancy as a formative period and because intimate social relationships were not the major source of gratification or virtue. Although many nineteenth-century observers would have understood and probably agreed with Bowlby, few would have written three books on this theme because, like the blue of the sky, the idea was too obviously true. Bowlby's conclusions are newsworthy in the last half of the twentieth century because historical events have led many citizens to question the inevitability of maternal devotion to the child and the child's love for his family.

After World War II, middle-class American and European communities became appreciably uncertain about the quality of the mother–infant bond, in part because of rising divorce rates, adolescent pregnancies, and working mothers who had to leave their babies with surrogates. The satisfying image of a young mother birthing, nursing, and playing with her baby until it skipped off to school became flawed. Many Americans continue to believe today, as they have since the Revolution, that mothers should be with their babies. Surrogate care, it is assumed, cannot be as good for young children as the concerned nurturance of a biological parent. With half of America's mothers working, many scientists and social commentators suggested that American infants were being harmed permanently, and many Americans were bothered by violation of what they believed to be natural law. Historical changes had prepared the average citizen to believe that a secure, emotional attachment to the mother was the most important psychological function to maintain in the young child.

However, a theory of attachment and historical changes in the family were not enough; it was necessary to have an easily implemented measurement procedure. An important reason for the current popularity of the concept of attachment is the ease of implementation of Mary Ainsworth's Strange Situation. Just as Piaget's simple procedure for assessing conservation of mass and liquid recruited many scientists to the study of concrete operations, so, too, did the Strange Situation attract investigators because it promised in less than an hour to provide them with a window into a characteristic the larger community believed had profound consequences for a child's future.

The Strange Situation consists of a series of three minute episodes in a laboratory playroom in which a one-to-two-year-old child is either alone with its mother, with an unfamiliar woman and the mother, with the unfamiliar woman alone, or with no adult present in the room. The last two situations—when the child is either with the unfamiliar woman or alone—are most stressful, and the child's behavior during these periods, together with its reactions when the mother reenters the room, provide the major information used to classify the child's attachment to the parent. Although the classification scheme is currently being revised, until recently a child was classified into one of three groups.

The securely attached child, who makes up two-thirds of American children and is called Type B, typically shows mild distress when the mother leaves the room but rushes to the mother and recovers quickly when she returns. There are two categories of insecurely attached children. The resistant child, who makes up about 15 percent of American children and is called Type C, exhibits extreme distress when the mother is gone and is not easily soothed when she returns. The adjective *resistant* was chosen because these children push against the mother, as if they were resisting her attempt to calm them.

The avoidant child, who makes up about 20 percent of the sample and is called Type A, does not become upset when the mother leaves and typically continues to play when she returns; hence, the descriptive term *avoidant*.

John Bowlby's fruitful set of hypotheses and Mary Ainsworths' promising method to test the implications of these ideas were a perfect combination for scientific progress. The history of research on behavior in the Strange Situation during the past decade represents an elegant tribute to the power of empiricism to clarify theory. These investigations by many psychologists have made it possible to make some initial judgments about both the ideas and the validity of Ainsworth's method.

Meaning of Behavior in the Strange Situation

Support for the assumption that the Strange Situation assesses both the prior and current relation of the one-to-two-year-old to its mother comes from early studies revealing that children who are classified as securely attached in the Strange Situation become more resilient, curious, and socially adroit with peers than do infants classified as less securely attached—both Types A and C (Arend, Gove, and Sroufe, 1979; Waters, Wippman, and Sroufe, 1979). More recent studies also imply that behavior in the Strange Situation does measure qualities in the child that are due, in part, to the history of interaction with the primary caretaker (Bretherton and Waters, 1985).

But there is also evidence that factors other than the child's experience with the caretaker make a significant contribution to behavior in the Strange Situation. The two most important are the young child's temperamental tendency to become fearful or remain spontaneous in unfamiliar situations (see Chapter 4), and parental socialization practices that do or do not teach the infant to control behavioral signs of anxiety (Grossman, Grossman, Huber, and Wartner, 1981). If these two factors prove to be as important as they seem at the present time, psychologists who use the Strange Situation will have to evaluate them before generating conclusions about security of attachment.

Four facts support a skeptical view of the validity of the Strange Situation. First, although some investigators find good stability of the attachment classification over the second year of life, others do not. In some studies, about one-half of the children change their attachment classification during the second year (Thompson, Lamb, and Estes, 1982; Schneider-Rosen, Braunwald, Carlson, and Cicchetti, 1985).

A second, more serious critique is the fact that major differences in the availability and nurture of the caretaker do not always correlate with variations in attachment. One investigator found no differences in the likelihood of a secure attachment between children living with working mothers and those with nonworking mothers. Moreover, the children whose mothers left home to begin work when the infant was between 12 and 20 months did not change their attachment category—they did not change from Type B to type A or C. The assumptions that lie behind the maintenance of a secure attachment would lead one to expect that at least one child whose mother went to work during the second year would have shifted from secure to less secure status (Owen, Easterbrooks, Chase-Landsdale, and Goldberg, 1984).

Additionally, one study did not find that Type A insecurely attached infants receive less affection, less love, or less playful interaction than securely attached infants (Belsky, personal communication). It is also surprising that the proportions of Type A, B, and C infants in a sample of average Swedish families was not significantly different from the proportions found in Swedish families where the mother had serious psychiatric disturbance during the first year of the child's life: "In fact, the proportion of infants who were securely attached to their mothers tended, if anything, to be slightly higher for mothers who were known to have been psychotic and clearly disturbed . . . No evidence was found that serious active maternal mental disturbance during the infant's first year of life relates positively to anxious attachment to the mother at one year of age" (Naslund, Persson-Blennow, McNeil, Kaij, and Malmquist-Larsson, 1984, p. 238).

A third basis for questioning the validity of the Strange Situation is the belief that the child's temperamental vulnerability to uncertainty and distress, in contrast with emotional spontaneity, in unfamiliar contexts makes a contribution to the child's behavior in the Strange Situation (Kagan, 1984; Gunnar et al., 1988). As we shall see in Chapter 4, these two categories of children, who are called inhibited and uninhibited, behave in predictable ways when they are in unfamiliar contexts. Inhibited children become very anxious and are most likely to be classified Type C. Uninhibited children, who do not become very anxious in unfamiliar situations, are more likely to be classified as Type A or Type B. Support for this claim is the fact that

18-month-olds who were classified as securely attached were minimally shy and maximally social when playing with an unfamiliar
child in a play situation (Easterbrooks and Lamb, 1979).

Further, one-year-old infants classified as Type C-insecurely attached are psychologically different from securely attached babies
from the opening weeks of life. As young infants, Type C children are
much more irritable, more prone to sleep problems, and generally
harder to manage than Type A or B infants. For example, Japanese
newborns in the city of Sapporo who would be classified as Type C
when they were one year old were more likely to cry intensely to the
mild frustration of nipple removal than were newborns who would be
classified as securely attached. When observed at one and three
months of age in their homes, the former group cried more often and
more intensely and, at seven months, showed more fear to an adult
stranger. At two years of age, the irritable newborns were more
cautious and shy with an unfamiliar child than were securely attached
or avoidant children (Chen and Miyake, 1983; Miyake, Chen, and
Campos, 1985). Similar results have been reported for American
infants. Newborns who cried to the frustration of nipple removal
were more likely to be classified as Type C-insecurely attached at 14
months of age than infants who did not cry (Fox, personal communication).

In addition, the newborn infants who are highly aroused by the
unexpected change in sensation they experience when the liquid they
are sucking suddenly changes from water to a sweet solution begin to
suck at a much faster rate. These excitable infants are more likely to
become Type C one-to-two-year-olds than are infants whose sucking
rate does not increase very much to the introduction of the sweet
solution. The latter infants are likely to become Type B (LaGasse,
Gruber, and Lipsitt, in press). We can understand this result if we
assume that the Type C children were born with a low threshold of
limbic arousal to unexpected changes in stimulation (see Chapter 4).
This characteristic, which explains why they become aroused by the
sweet taste, also predicts that they will be more easily aroused by
unfamiliar places and people and, therefore, behave in a timid, inhibited manner.

The prediction of a positive relation, based on temperament, between a Type C classification at one year and shy, timid behavior in
later childhood is affirmed in a longitudinal study of 113 children
who were observed in the Strange Situation at one year and evaluated

again at age six. The boys classified as Type C at one year were judged five years later to be less communicative, more withdrawn, and more shy than children who had been Type A or B infants. Type C girls at age six were both less aggressive and less active than A or B children (Lewis, Feiring, and McGuffog, 1984). This finding is in accord with a study of 96 children observed in the Strange Situation at 12 and 18 months and in a preschool setting at four to five years of age. The ten Type C children were more shy and more anxious than the Type A or B children—exactly what one would expect if temperamentally based inhibition had some influence on the child's behavior in the Strange Situation (Erickson, Sroufe, and Egeland, 1985). A similar result has been reported for premature children (Plunkett, Klein, and Meisels, 1988).

The most persuasive support for the influence of temperament is that inhibition was a better predictor of a Type C classification than a prior history of maltreatment at home. Comparison of the Strange Situation behavior of maltreated and nonmaltreated children from the same social class backgrounds at both 19 and 25 months revealed that children who cried a great deal and remained close to their mother during the first three minutes of the Strange Situation before she had left the room, as well as during a free play episode when the mother was present, were most likely to be classified as Type C (Schneider-Rosen, 1984). The child's timidity and inhibition while with the mother in an unfamiliar room was a better predictor of a Type C classification than was the fact of being maltreated at home.

If a low threshold for uncertainty to the unexpected and unfamiliar, based on temperament, influences the child's behavior in an unfamiliar room with strangers, it must also affect the child's attachment classification in the Strange Situation. Because the best predictor of seeking contact with mother when she reenters the room is the degree of upset and distress shown following her departure, infants who have a close, securely attached relation with the mother but who do not become uncertain in unfamiliar contexts may cry very little—or not at all—when the mother leaves. As a result, they are unlikely to approach her when she returns. These children are apt to be classified as Type A (avoidant). Infants who are moderately vulnerable to uncertainty are a little more likely to cry when the mother leaves and so will approach her when she returns. But because they do not become extremely upset, they will be easily placated and classified as Type B, securely attached. The children with a very low threshold for uncertainty will be very upset by the mother's unexpected departure. As a result, they are difficult to soothe and likely to thrash or push their mother away as they continue to sob. Most of these infants should be classified as Type C. And a study of English two-year-olds confirms that the children who are most fearful to unfamiliar people in a laboratory are apt to be evaluated as Type C (Stevenson-Hinde and Shouldice, unpublished).

After finding that distress to unfamiliar events was stable from 9 to 13 months of age and, in addition, predicted the child's behavior in the Strange Situation, Gunnar and her colleagues (1988) concluded, "The stability in proneness to distress is characteristic of the infant in reaction to strangers, strange places, and maternal separation . . . that stability is [not] the result of the infant's attachment history" (p. 35). I suspect that the persistent irritability to discrepancy is the result of temperamental processes.

The complete corpus of data is at least suggestive of the hypothesis that the temperamental characteristics involving ease and quality of arousal to unfamiliar events make at least some contribution to the classification of secure and insecure attachment in the Strange Situation, despite Sroufe's claim to the contrary (Sroufe, 1985). Even investigators who rely on the Strange Situation as an index of attachment acknowledge that "emerging infant personality characteristics, such as tendencies toward fearfulness or the expression of positive affect may be stronger organizers of behavior when infants [in the Strange Situation] interact with individuals with whom they do not share a relationship history" (Bridges, Connell, and Belsky, 1988, p. 198). Of course, these temperamental qualities also influence how parents interact with their children, and so behavior in the Strange Situation also reflects, in part, the history of parent–child encounters.

A fourth and final source of skepticism regarding the validity of the Strange Situation as an index of attachment are data suggesting that the child's behavior in the Strange Situation is influenced by the degree to which the mother has encouraged her child to control his or her anxiety over the course of the first year. A child with an attentive and loving mother who has encouraged self-reliance and control of fear is less likely to cry when the mother leaves and, therefore, less likely to approach her when she returns. This child is likely to be classified as avoidant. By contrast, the child whose mother has been protective and less insistent that her child deal with anxiety is more likely to cry and rush to the mother when she reenters the room and so be classified as securely attached (see Hock and Clinger, 1981). In sharp contrast with the norms for Americans, where three-fourths of one-year-olds are classified as securely attached, only one-third of a group of middle-class West German children behaved in the Strange Situation as though they were securely attached, and almost one-half were avoidant (Grossman et al., 1981). These data do not necessarily imply that more German than American children are insecurely attached; rather, they could mean that these German mothers promote independence and discourage crying and clinging when their child is anxious. Thus, both temperamental qualities and prior socialization influence the child's behavior in the Strange Situation.

No one, including myself, claims that a child's behavior in the Strange Situation is unrelated to any aspect of the infant–parent dyad during the first year. That would be impossible. But the attachment classifications do not reflect only that history. Behaviors in the Strange Situation are complex phenomena that are simultaneously indexes of the child's temperamental disposition to be maximally or minimally distressed to unfamiliarity, socialization for the control of fear, and, of course, the nature of the emotional relationship with the parent. It is not possible to separate the differential contributions of these three factors in a single ahistorical assay, as it is not possible to separate the influence of mutation from that of dramatic ecological change in explaining the current distribution of mammals across the world.

Reluctance to acknowledge this conclusion is leading to questionable practices among a few who are closely identified with this domain of study. These scientists assume, without adequate empirical justification, that the specific type of early attachment, based on the child's behavior in the Strange Situation, is stable over time and that experts know, intuitively, the psychological characteristics of a securely or an insecurely attached six-year-old. It is not surprising that the American experts guess that a securely attached six-year-old reunited with its mother in a laboratory is relaxed, shows pleasure with the parent, and initiates warm, personal conversation (Main and Cassidy, 1988). Because a secure attachment is a desirable quality and the behaviors described above are, for this society in the present historical moment, desirable dispositions to possess, it is inevitable that a psychologist would expect securely attached six-year-olds to be relaxed, warm, and emotionally spontaneous with their parents while insecurely attached six-year-olds should be restrained and timid.

Nineteenth-century Japanese scholars would make a different prediction. In Scandinavia, where a reserved personality and control of expressions of affect are more desirable than they are in the United States, infants classified at one year of age as Type C-insecurely attached were judged at 5 years of age as having better control of their impulses than securely attached children (Van IJzendoorn et al., 1987). However, the main point is that if the temperamental dispositions for inhibited or uninhibited behavior in unfamiliar settings were stable over time, the same predictions made by Main and Cassidy would hold. But the stability of these two temperamental qualities is based on empirical data, not intuition (Kagan, Reznick, and Snidman, 1988).

Regardless of the future of the Strange Situation as a method, the research on the construct of attachment has had important benevolent consequences for study of the effect of family experience on the child. Traditional constructs continue to describe, as they have for a century, either qualities in the child or qualities in the parents' behavior because of the simplifying assumption that particular parental behaviors produce uniform outcomes in children. The research on attachment, which deals with the relationship between child and adult, has produced a dissatisfaction with this traditional frame, and a small number of investigators are searching for constructs that describe relationships between a profile of qualities in the parents and a profile in the child.

Similar constructs exist in other disciplines but we do not recognize them as such. For example, when biologists learn the cause of a disease, the resulting diagnostic label is, in fact, descriptive of a relation between the pathogen and the symptoms. The construct poliomyelitis refers to motor paralysis due to viral infection of the motor neurons—a relation between a specific virus and a specific metabolic process in the spinal cord.

It will be useful to search for analogous constructs in human development. Children vary in their temperamental vulnerability to uncertainty; parents vary in the degree to which they control the child. Suppose that the combination of a controlling parent and a temperamentally uncertain child produces a specific profile different from a controlling mother interacting with an uninhibited child. Another pair of outcomes is generated when a minimally controlling mother interacts with either an inhibited or uninhibited child. The four combinations require four different constructs to capture the relation between the category of child and the category of experience. Currently, we do not have such concepts in our vocabulary. The invention of such constructs will advance developmental theory; the motivation to search for these concepts is attributable directly to the work on attachment. Thus, in a relatively short time, the work of Bowlby, Ainsworth, and their students has been responsible for major progress in our understanding of psychological development.

The Emergence of Cognitive Development

The simultaneous decline of interest in both behavioristic and psychodynamic views during the 1960s is ascribable to the conditions that produced their initial growth—changed social facts, alternative theory, and the invention of new procedures. Envy of the unexpected surge of Russian technology, which was attributed by Americans to better educational strategies in the Soviet Union, combined with heightened awareness of the variation in educational attainment of children from different social class backgrounds, supplied psychologists with the social incentive to treat cognitive development not as a by-product of conditioning or conflict but as an autochthonous domain with its special origins, profile of growth, and sources of evidence.

Establishment of the discipline of cognitive development was also helped by the growth of developmental psycholinguistics and the popularity of Piagetian theory. Both conditioning and psychoanalysis provided weak explanations of language and reasoning. The first denied their importance, and the second made these talents derivative of emotional conflict. But the new generation of social scientists was not satisfied with an explanation of the acquisition of reading skill that treated it either as a conditioned response or a derivative of fear or pleasure. I blush to admit that I repeated to my first class in child psychology what I had been taught as a graduate student. I said with certainty that some children found it difficult to learn to read because they interpreted the act of reading as aggressive behavior toward their parents, and their socialization had made them anxious or guilty over hostile motives. Younger readers are probably smiling, but that explanation was treated as a serious hypothesis in the 1950s.

Piaget's Contribution

It was apparent by the late 1960s that the universal milestones of development—reaching for a cup at four months, symbolic play at one year, and speaking sentences at 24 months—could not be easily explained by either conditioning or the structures of the oral stage. The progress of every science is marked by historical moments in which a compromise position is needed to accommodate two powerful views which have become inconsistent, or to correct a position which has begun to violate educated intuitions. The scholar who has the talent and persistence to fill the compromise role is rightfully celebrated, as Jean Piaget is today.

Nineteenth-century psychology conceived of the child in a Darwinian paradigm. The infant inherited dispositions to imitate, to exert will, to symbolize, to reason, and to sympathize with others. These properties would be actualized as long as the child grew in a world of objects and people. Children needed sensory experience and models to imitate, but their instincts were fundamental forces for growth. When American psychology became behavioristic after World War I, it rejected concepts implying the force of instincts. Every disposition and competence had to be acquired through contingent reinforcements. Although persistent application of this principle was supported by many, by the late 1960s it failed to explain a great deal of the data that had been gathered by child psychologists. Hence, many were ready for Piaget's corrections to this view.

Additionally, the doctrine of logical positivism, which was growing in influence during the opening decades of this century, had insisted on constructs that referred to overt behavior and rejected purely mentalistic notions. Piaget's suggestion that the interiorization of experience was the source of new cognitive structures appeared to meet the new philosophic requirements. Finally, Piaget's emphasis on adaptation as the criterion for evaluating new competences was in accord with the increasing reliance on pragmatic criteria for action and decision which became ascendant early in this century, partly as a result of the implications of Darwinian thought and partly as a function of the secularism that was necessary to accommodate to the diversity of values that mass European immigration made necessary.

Thus, developmental psychologists became receptive to a theoretical view which balanced experience with maturation, was potentially verifiable, and made adaptation to the world a criterion of growth. Piaget's theory met these stiff requirements. Even though his books had been available for several decades, it was only when the intimidating power of behaviorism had begun to wane in American psychology that an eager, enthusiastic audience turned to Piaget. His theory relieved the child from the chains of reward and punishment, made him active rather than passive in dealing with experience, and assumed that intellectual growth consisted of a connected series of structures from birth to adolescence. When a theory serves that many needs, it deserves to be awarded the highest praise.

There are several basic presuppositions in Piagetian theory. The first is that the child's activity is the fundamental source of new knowledge. This view is to be contrasted with the assumption of Enlightenment scholars that knowledge originates in the more passive process of perception. Second, the primary function of knowledge is adaptation. Although private states of understanding occur, they are secondary in importance to the pragmatic press of more successful adjustment to the world of objects and people. The child looks at a strange animal in order to act—not merely to create a perceptual representation. This assumption was in accord with evolutionary theory and the writings of Peirce, James, and Dewey. Third, the structures created through action form a continuous and invariant sequence of stages. Hence, the actions of a one-year-old become participants in the logical deductions of the adolescent.

Although these suppositions were attractive to the younger cohort of developmental psychologists, what perhaps was most critical for the adoption of Piaget's theory were his amazing empirical discoveries. Piaget uncovered a host of fascinating, hardy phenomena which were under everyone's nose but which few were talented enough to see. Those discoveries—the eight-month-old who suddenly becomes able to retrieve a hidden toy, the egocentric answer of a five-year-old on the mountains test, and the shift at age seven from a nonconserving to a conserving reply to the beakers of water—were so consistent across cultures that they resembled demonstrations in a chemistry lecture hall. Child psychology had never possessed such a covey of sturdy facts. Additionally, Piaget made cognitive constructs, rather than affect or motivation, bear the burden of explanation. The scheme, operation, and group seemed to provide satisfactory explanations of the empirical phenomena, and assimilation and accommodation, although loosely defined, made it possible to imagine how changes in cognitive structures might have occurred. Few would question the conclusion that Piaget's writings have been a primary basis for the centrality of the cognitive sciences in contemporary psychology.

My own view is that Piaget will be celebrated most for his descriptions of formal operational thought. Piaget claimed that the adolescent can manipulate propositions logically, detect inconsistency in those propositions, and realize when all solution possibilities are exhausted. Piaget's theoretical descriptions of the infant and school-age child are less satisfying. First, it is unlikely that all the infant's knowledge is contained in sensorimotor schemes. The powers of discrimination and recognition memory shown by very young infants seem resistant to an explanation that relies on manipulation of the environment. Second, others have suggested, although far less formally, that important psychological changes occur at around seven years of age. Parents in the third-world villages around the globe give responsibility to their children at this time, and the Catholic Church declared centuries ago that the child of seven was responsible for his actions. But Piaget's suggestion that a major cognitive restructuring occurs at adolescence is, in my opinion, original and of immense importance for understanding this period of development. If, as Piaget claims, the 14-year-old is disposed to examine the logical consistency of his existing beliefs, we should expect a special tension that is not solely the product of emerging sexuality. The adolescent must deal with the temptations of sex, new evaluations of his parents, and, in America, incessant demands for independence. These perceptions and associated experiences rub up against old beliefs, and the resulting incompatibility is usually resolved by delegitimizing the earlier assumptions. As a result of the cognitive competences that accompany formal operational thought, the adolescent begins to question old ideas and search for new premises. Piagetian ideas lead us to expect that the adolescent will be in a state of uncertainty and provoked to resolve that state. As a result of the mental work, older premises will be changed. The ideational rebellion that is definitional of adolescence in the modern West does not primarily serve hostility to the parents but rather the more pressing need to persuade the self that its mosaic of wishes, values, and behaviors derives from a personally constructed ideology. This conception of the psychological state of the adolescent flows directly from Piagetian theory.

When a scholarly corpus has the vitality and scope that characterizes Piaget's writings, one can expect it to be informed by a basic *Aufgabe*—or frame—which crystallizes early and becomes polished with time and reflection. The young Piaget, motivated to explain the moral nature of human beings, sided with those who felt that moral propositions were to be based on biological fact. The next major transition was his decision to make the development of cognitive functions the form that the biological facts assumed.

The decision to let morality be led by thought, rather than by affect, motivation, or interpersonal experiences, provided a corrective to the moral relativism that swelled during the first quarter of this century. Nineteenth-century theorists insisted that all children knew what was moral, but they provided no intellectually satisfying rationale for that declaration. Piaget also insisted that there were universal aspects to the establishment of standards, but he explained why. Contemporary essays on the cognitive bases for the human affects, not just guilt and shame, owe some of their originality to Piaget's fresh conception of the contribution cognitive function makes to human feelings. Although it is too early to judge the ultimate consequences of Piaget's ideas for educational practice, the new science curricula and the replacement of rote memorization with discovery are traceable to Geneva.

It is impossible for a scholar as ambitious as Piaget to create a totally invulnerable theoretical edifice. First, as many have noted, the constructs of assimilation and accommodation are not sturdy enough to bear the burden of accounting for the transition from one stage to the next. Second, it is still difficult for Piagetian ideas to explain important aspects of cognitive functioning. Language provides the best example. Some two-year-olds use and understand words like *you, is, like,* and *why,* which have little relation to overt action and cannot easily be explained as a function of the growth of sensori-motor schemes. Third, psychologists, Margaret Donaldson being one, are discovering that preschool children possess some of the competences that Piaget claimed were not possible, including a nonegocentric attitude and the concrete operations of conservation and class inclusion, if standard Piagetian procedures are altered. Donaldson suggests that one reason for the less mature answers young children often give to Piagetian probes is that they are answering questions other than the ones the experimenter poses because their interpretations are not in accord with those of the examiner. Donaldson notes, "When a child interprets what we say to him his interpretation is influenced by at least three things (and the ways in which these interact with each others)—his knowledge of the language, his assessment of what we intend (as indicated by our non-linguistic behavior), and the manner in which he would represent the physical situation to himself if we were not there after all" (p. 68).

Piaget may have been too quick to assume that a cognitive competence generalizes across varied problem contexts. Investigators in all areas of psychology are now beginning to appreciate that generalizations about competences, motivations, and dispositions must be accompanied by a detailed statement describing context.

Perhaps the most basic criticism is that Piaget assumed that Western logic is universal and that the fundamental principles of Western logic and mathematics are demanded by each child's experiences in the world. These bold declarations are subject to question. In Western logic, the affirmative statement "The sky is blue" is logically equivalent to a double negative—"It is not true that the sky is not blue." But in a logical system used in one form of Indian philosophy, these two statements do not have identical meaning. Second, Piaget claims that the experiences of all seven-year-olds should lead them to conclude, in the conservation of quantity procedure, that the transformed and untransformed pieces of clay have the same amount of material. But experience suggests that most people should not give a conservation answer when the examiner changes the shape of one piece of clay, since a little bit of material is always left on the examiner's hand when he or she changes its shape. Indeed, a few children insist that this is the correct answer.

One reason for Piaget's insistence on the role of experience was his conviction that the function of knowledge is action. This is a choice other scholars have not always shared. In John Locke's famous seventeenth-century essay, he made understanding and a sense of knowing the primary purpose of knowledge. Correspondingly, Locke made perception and reasoning, rather than action, the mode by which knowledge was gained and a criterion for growth. Indeed, the intuitions from sensory experience that Locke viewed as the most certain knowledge are the same sources that Piaget regarded as immature.

Nonetheless, Piaget has been a central figure in the renascence of cognitive psychology and has contributed to the important link between this discipline and biology. Although he specifically avoided discussion of biological preparedness, fortunately his followers have interpreted his writings as indicating the importance of biological maturation and in that way helped to make the psychological community receptive to the new data on early development. With Freud, Piaget has been a seminal figure in the sciences of human development.

The Current Era

The last decade of developmental inquiry affirms the simultaneous influences of history, theory, and method. Four of the most prominent nodes in contemporary research are (1) perception and attachment processes in the infant and, in the older child, (2) cognitive functions, (3) peer-group relations, and (4) morality.

The Infant

The enthusiasm for the infant is due, in part, to Piaget and Bowlby, who treated infancy as a critical stage in ontogeny. But American child psychologists are empiricists first, and the infant became an attractive research subject because of the appearance of new methods, like the object permanence procedure, the Strange Situation, and especially Fantz's discovery that differential attention to visual events could be used as an index of discrimination. This discovery is now being used to measure the infant's ability to perceive a feature that might be shared by events from two sensory modalities. The possibility that a nine-month-old can recognize that a segmented line and an intermittent tone share a quality one might call discontinuity is one of the most exciting ideas in this century.

But history also made a contribution. Contemporary Americans continue to worry about the dramatic differences in academic accomplishment between advantaged and disadvantaged children, assume that these differences were formed during the first few years of life, and want to intervene early to prevent the later academic failures. The most expensive research projects in child psychology in the last twenty years have involved tests of possible interventions, reflecting the strength of the twin beliefs that the best time for prophylaxis is the first few years of life and that proper experiences can produce changes that will be stable indefinitely.

The belief that early experience has a profound and permanent effect on human infants has been held firmly by Western scholars for a very long time. It is reasonable to ask, therefore, what experiences support that belief. The human mind has a natural tendency, when faced with an event that is not well understood, to find a familiar, better understood phenomenon that shares primary features with the novelty. If successful in this search, the mind then slips easily into the assumption that the accepted explanation of the familiar event applies also to the new one. When the shared qualities are not intended to be literal, we called the shared relation a *metaphor*. When we believe the shared features imply a common mechanism, we treat it as an *explanation*. Galen, along with other ancient Greek naturalists, believed the warmth of the human breath indicated that the body contained heat. Since fire was one of the most familiar and best understood sources of heat, Galen assumed that the body contained a fire-like heat generated by the heart. Because fires can become too hot and have to be cooled, he assumed that the function of respiration was to regulate internal heat. Although that was a scientific explanation for Galen, to modern minds the relation between the heart and a fire is a popular metaphor in love songs.

It is likely that several common phenomena have supported the belief that early experience is formative, including the fact that seeds planted in poor soil grow less well, unusually sickly infants become adults with less endurance than most, and that children from poor families often turn out to be less well adjusted to the society than children from advantaged homes. If one were friendly to the doctrine of infant determinism, it would be easy, and likely, that one would recognize the similarity between the familiar events of plants and sickly children and a nonnuturant home and assume that just as poor soil has a permanent influence on the growth of the plant, a psychologically inadequate family is potentially dangerous to the child's psychological growth.

This folk explanation was supported by Harlow's dramatic demonstration with monkeys that several months of isolation after birth had a profound, and what appeared at the time to be permanent, effect on the animal. The discovery that rehabilitation was possible and that some species of monkey were less affected by isolation than others were published much later and did not do much damage to the original assumption, even though neuroscientists were reporting on the plasticity of the young central nervous system and the longitudinal studies initiated in the 1930s were not verifying in a commanding way the belief that the experiences of the first few years set the course of the child's development.

Historical nodes of worry. Each historical era has its special sources of angst. During most of the nineteenth-century a materialist science continued to erode confidence in the premises of Christian philosophy, generating tension over the soundness of the golden rule. Members of the community wanted to know whether kindness and love or their opposites were the true moral imperatives. Evolutionary theory seemed to resolve some of the ambiguity by legitimizing the competitive self-interest that was impossible to suppress as Europe and America industrialized at a more rapid rate. The facts of science had become a source to which educated citizens turned in times of ethical ambiguity, and Darwinian theory helped parents accept, and in some cases encourage, more narcissism, defiance, and self-expression in their children.

By the turn of the century the tension had become focused on a particular moral act, namely, sexual behavior. Dissemination of the apparently valid idea that humans are close relatives of sexually active, furry animals permitted erotic thoughts to mingle more often with daily plans. The comingling was disturbing to European and American adults, and, again, citizens turned to science for help. This time the oracle was Freud, who reassured troubled parents that sexual excitement, even occasional masturbation, was natural and no cause for alarm. As we noted earlier, when Americans were troubled by rumors that the European immigrants were genetically flawed, the society relied on Pavlov and Watson and the results of laboratory experiments with animals for proof of the falsity of such propaganda.

For contemporary Americans the sources of worry include apprehension over polluted air and water, terrorist bombs, vandals on city streets, drug addiction, and, always in the background, the terrible possibility of nuclear war. These anxieties have replaced the traditional preoccupations with hunger, ghosts, sorcery, and state tyranny. They remain salient because the majority of Americans live miles away from childhood friends and family, with neighbors they do not know. Hence, a mood of uncertainty about each day, as well as the future, is not quieted by a fabric of trusting interactions with friends and intimates. This mood of anxiety has been projected onto the infant and young child and contributes to the scientific curiosity about the child's anxiety, trust, and attachment.

Jung, but not Freud, recognized that history exerted an influence on the preoccupations of the community as well as the concepts of the theorist. Jung sensed that historical conditions had increased the salience of sexual motivation and suggested to Freud that both the real and psychic products of industrialization had a profound effect on human consciousness. In one of his last letters to Freud, in the summer of 1913, Jung tried to explain that sexual conflict was not the primary cause of sexual dreams or a symptom, but reflected a specific adaptation for those living in a particular historical moment. He pointed out that the easy availability of contraceptives, rather than child-rearing, had contributed to the prominent position of sexuality in human consciousness at the turn of the last century. Jung was implying that historical circumstances had so altered European and American consciousness that some citizens were prepared to regard psychoanalytic theory as a profound statement about humanity. A more contemporary example was the reception of *The Greening of America* by the youth of the 1960s.

Perhaps Jung's deepest insight, which Freud may not have understood, was that Freud's choice of libido as a primary explanatory construct was determined, in part, by the fact that the human mind finds this idea attractive. Today, Jung would have said that the human mind is prepared to describe psychological qualities with an energy metaphor. Like many post-World War I philosophers of science, Jung recognized that a scholar's choice of concepts was influenced by his or her personal conflicts and cultural location. Freud, however, regarded the idea of libido as a discovery of one of nature's great secrets.

Contemporary research supports Jung's intuition. Glen Elder has described the effect of the depression on Americans who were adolescents in the decade between 1930 and 1940. And analyses of the consequences of the Vietnam protests on youths' academic motivation are beginning to appear. The historical description of Vienna at the turn of the century by Toulmin and Janik argued that social attitudes and class structure existing at the time of the collapse of the Hapsburg empire exposed Wittgenstein to ideas that were far less salient to young adults in Scandinavia or England.

Jung appreciated that the ethical concerns of a society are generated from nodes of uncertainty. The virtues easiest to promote in others and to defend to oneself are those that can mute or prevent the uncertainty that accompanies temptations to violate a standard or the discomfort that follows such violations. The varied uncertainties are provoked by conditions that occur with different probabilities across communities. Five potential candidates are the anticipation of the different varieties of anxiety that occur in response to possible physical harm, social rejection, or task failure; feelings of empathy toward those who are in need; feelings of responsibility that follow causing harm to another; feelings of fatigue following repeated gratifications of desire; and the feeling of uncertainty that accompanies encounters with discrepant events that are not easily understood or the recognition of inconsistency among beliefs or between beliefs and actions. Because people do not like to feel uncertain, sorry for someone less privileged, guilty, bored, fatigued, or confused, these states will be classified as bad and people will want to replace, suppress, or avoid them. The acts, thoughts, and beliefs that accomplish these goals will be good and, therefore, virtuous. Each culture in each of its historical enactments presents a unique profile of provocative conditions for these unpleasant feeling states and opportunities for behaviors that prevent or alleviate them. As a result, different definitions of the concrete, morally praiseworthy characteristics will be encouraged and new sources of guilt will be created.

An example Jung might have liked is found in what appears to be a secular change over the last half-century in the degree of guilt, anxiety, and depression experienced by mothers who have given birth to a handicapped infant. There are at least two reasons for the presumed change in the intensity of their emotional reaction.

The first rests on the principle that violated expectations generate emotion. During the first decades of this century, prior to the rise of modern medicine and the more regular institutionalization of handicapped children, it was a common experience to see children with physical handicaps on the streets of every American city. Most American mothers, like mothers in all settings, realized that a handicapped newborn was always a possibility. However, when early prenatal diagnoses of anomalous development became a reality, there was something a mother could do to prevent the birth of a handicapped infant.

Simultaneously, magazines, newspapers, and television began to remind the mother that her diet and life pattern could affect her unborn child. Excessive smoking and drinking were clearly teratogenic, and perhaps too many colds, too much stress, frequent airplane travel, excessive exercise, and a host of other activities might influence the fetus adversely. The message was clear: In light of new scientific knowledge, each mother was responsible for guaranteeing the birth of a healthy newborn. As history shifted the blame from chance to the mother's will, it is not surprising that the average mother began to feel guilty if she birthed a flawed infant, for she could have avoided this catastrophe if she had been sufficiently conscientious during her pregnancy.

There is, in addition, a mood of perfectability among Americans. Advertisements for jogging, vitamins, low-fat diets, organic foods, sodium-free antacid pills, and high-fiber breakfasts generate a sense of obligation—for some a moral imperative—to strive continually for bodily perfection. The media imply, moreover, that such perfection is attainable. It follows that if mothers did everything correctly every day of their pregnancy, they could prevent accidents of fate and expect a perfect newborn.

Thus, a handicapped child is a more serious violation of modal expectation today than it was a century ago. Although modern mothers could have blamed these events over which they have no control on leaching toxins in the soil, freeways perfused with leaded gasoline, and disguised food preservatives, they did not. They usually blamed themselves, because the culture expected them to be vigilant and to cope with these dangers. I believe Jung would have argued that the more intense dysphoria created by giving birth to a handicapped infant among modern parents is due more to historical events that changed parental expectations than to the childhood experiences of the mothers.

Cognitive Development

A second major feature of contemporary research in cognitive development is recognition of the particularity of a child's cognitive competence. J. P. Guilford's suggestion that cognitive performances vary across different classes of information and types of cognitive processes is being confirmed. For example, the correlation between recall memory for verbal versus pictorial materials is often low, and the difference between recognition and recall memory for a small number of independent items of information (less than seven) is much larger for children than it is for adults, perhaps because of the validity of John Flavell's suggestion that the child's lack of knowledge about the processes of memory influence performance in the laboratory.

Refinements of Piaget's interviewing techniques have, oddly enough, provided data that challenge his statements about age norms. It appears that preschool children know much more about the concept of number than we suspected and even have some appreciation of the relations between categories. Piaget had assumed that both of these talents were victories belonging to the school-age child.

Peer Relations and Morality

Investigations of cognitive functions remain in a constructive tension with studies of emotion, peer relationships, and morality. The latter three themes have also been aided by new methods. Videocassette recorders have made it possible to apply Izard's and Ekman's protocols to study the facial expressions that are supposed to accompany certain emotions. Data produced by these techniques reveal that fear and anger appear later in the first year, a conclusion which implies that maturation of the brain may be a necessary prior preparation for certain human emotions. Investigations of the relation of momentary changes in facial muscles to external incentives have also revealed that the facial profiles are not always correlated with theoretically expected changes in voice, biochemistry, or self-report. Thus, the next wave of investigators may begin to invent new terms for the popular affects. For example, they may replace the generic concept of anger with a family of emotions, just as taxonomists have replaced classifications based on fossil evidence alone with classifications that combine biochemical, behavioral, and fossil information.

The videocassette recorder has also made study of social relationships easier, whether the context is a group of children on a playground or a parent and child at home. The permanent record relieves the investigator from uneasy reliance on one or two numbers to summarize a half-hour of interaction and replaces the observer's rating with fine-graded, quantitative analyses of a large number of interactions. This strategy will force new constructs and eventually generate better theory.

Finally, the study of morality, which has idled since Piaget's early, influential book, is experiencing a renaissance, in part because of Kohlberg's inventive use of responses to hypothetical moral dilemmas and in part from the recognition that children appreciate moral standards several years before they enter the Oedipal period. New cross-cultural information using moral dilemmas has forced recognition of the difference between the Western conception of the individual as an independent, personally responsible agent and the Eastern view that each person is an interdependent part of a larger group which can require special loyalty. Thus, methods invented to test an earlier theoretical idea have yielded facts that have required alteration in the original conception.

Certainty or Relevance?

Many developmental scientists selecting a problem for study experience a tension over the decision to examine a domain that is knowable because a minimally uncertain fact can be discovered or to probe an area that is of interest to many and, therefore, discover a fact that is presumably important to know. A preference for the knowable leads psychologists to perform experimental manipulations on animals that are not possible with human infants. A preference for the relevant leads psychologists to the study of human infants in natural contexts where the behaviors appear to be more applicable to the conditions of everyday life.

Most investigators desire both recognition from their peers as well as the satisfaction of communicating with and assisting the larger society. However, the prizes symbolizing peer recognition by the scientific community are most often given to those who produce knowledge that seems minimally uncertain. The public, in contrast, awards its acclaim to those who produce knowledge that, on the surface, appears to be helpful to society. Those for whom the motive to be helpful is felt more urgently are likely to choose problems that appear to be socially relevant. In making that choice they must often sacrifice certainty in their conclusions. Bohr noted that there is a complementary relation between clarity and truth. As one moves toward clarity in describing a phenomenon, one moves away from truth; if one offers a description that corresponds more accurately with nature, one will ordinarily be less clear. In a similar vein, there is a complementary relation between research that yields facts which seem minimally ambiguous and research that produces facts which seem relevant to the concerns of citizens.

This tension has important implications for the future of developmental psychology. The idea of the prototype, a fruitful concept in cognitive science, implies that children and adults favor those representations of a domain that are close to the prototype. I believe that the disposition to feel positively toward the prototype and less positively toward serious deviations affects the direction and growth of scientific domains. The features that define the prototype of a psychological investigation differ for the two classes of behavioral scientists

I have just described. For those who try to maximize certainty, the primary features involve experimental manipulations, objective data, and interpretations that emphasize a process as a cause of a phenomenon. For those attempting to produce relevant knowledge, the primary features of the prototype are naturalistic observations, judgments of human states, and interpretative statements that emphasize a process as a part of a larger coherence. Because each of these classes of investigation strays far from the prototype of the other, and unconscious attitudes always influence the awarding of resources, there is a danger, which institutions supporting social science are beginning to display, that future support for developmental psychology will come from two different sources.

Part Two

Temperament

3

The Idea of
Temperamental Types

The mind, always attracted to differences, follows Mill's canon of inference if it has any way to link qualities that covary and will assume that they are linked causally. People assumed the causal relation between the shortening of the day and the changing colors of trees long before they knew the reasons for this odd correlation. Distinctive and characteristic styles of human behavior and mood are among the most obvious facts of our experience, and the presumed bases for this variation have oscillated between external conditions, like climate and early experience, and internal ones, like brain structure and, currently, balance among neurotransmitters.

Although contemporary psychological research remains part of a cycle, now almost 75 years old, that has preferred an external environmental interpretation of behavioral variation, a majority of scholars from the immediately prior cycle believed that inherited temperamental factors exerted considerably more influence. Freud's suggestion that the psychological products of early experience were the most important basis for adult moods and symptoms was an original and not a consensual view at the turn of the century.

The meaning of the term *temperament* has changed over time. Hippocrates and Galen were thinking of the small number of emotional profiles that seemed to differentiate adults. The qualities were affective rather than intellectual because their presumed origins were bodily substances that permeated the soma. Intellectual faculties, by contrast, were located in the brain. Most important, Hippocrates and Galen believed that these temperamental qualities could be created by stable environmental conditions, especially climate and diet. The assumption that temperamental characteristics are influenced by inherited biological processes is a relatively modern idea.

The nineteenth-century essays on temperamental types were remarkably similar in premise and substance. The shared assumption was that children began life with biologically based biases favoring certain emotional states. The environment, acting on those states, led to a variety of stable profiles of emotion, behavior, and motivation. Most theorists affirmed three of the four Galenic types—sanguine, choleric, and phlegmatic. Apparently, it is easy to discern the small number of adults who, most of the time, are cheerful-sociable, irritable-hostile, or listless-unexcitable. However, nineteenth-century European observers made Galen's melancholic type a derived category, and added a neurotic, sensitive type, which became Jung's introvert.[1]

Contemporary investigations of temperament have focused most often on the contrast between the sanguine and the nervous—the extravert versus the introvert—and ignored the angry and the listless types, perhaps because the latter two are not as obvious in childhood as the contrast between sociability and shyness. Although a belief in the reality of the sanguine-extravert and melancholic-introvert has survived for over 2,500 years, that fact should be neither treated as proof of its validity nor ignored.

The terms for most of the temperamental categories—ancient and modern—refer to profiles of action and mood that are easily assimilated by the average citizen and used in everyday conversations about friends. But the growth of physics, chemistry, and biology during the last 200 years teaches us that the constructs that account for important phenomena had to be invented because they were not part of public discourse. Consider seventeenth-century explanations of visual perception as compared with the modern view. The earlier descriptions relied on words like light rays, eye-ball, and brain. Modern writers, exploiting new knowledge, talk about rods, cones, bipolar cells, and center-on- and center-off-neurons, structures that are neither available to the unaided eye nor understood by the untutored reader. It is likely that the current terms for temperament, which are

1. It is not clear why Galen did not treat the tall, thin, nervous adult, so obvious to nineteenth-century northern European observers, as a basic type. One possibility is that ectomorphic body builds were less common in Mediterranean countries.

small in number and part of the vocabulary of the educated citizen, are inexact and new concepts will have to be generated. The fact that few constructs in modern biology were employed by seventeenth-century naturalists implies that we will need to invent new temperamental concepts, some of which will be difficult to assimilate initially. Alfred North Whitehead (1925) wrote, "We forget how strained and paradoxical is the view of nature which modern science imposes on our thoughts" (p. 122).

Constitution and Temperament

Belief in an association between external physical characteristics and personality was popular in seventeenth- and eighteenth-century Europe, so popular it guided the selection of wet nurses. Mothers were advised to choose women who had brown hair, darker complexions, and a muscular build because they were easy going and strong and to avoid blonde, fair-skinned, blue-eyed ectomorphs and, especially, women with red hair and freckles because they were likely to be impatient, easily fatigued, and a source of less nutritious milk (Fildes, 1986).

It is not inaccurate to mark the modern history of temperamental types with Franz Gall (1835), who incurred the enmity of his community by suggesting that variation in human intentions and emotions was due directly to differences in brain tissue detectable though measurements of the skull. The dominant view in the late eighteenth century was that the anatomy of the brain was a legitimate focus of inquiry, but it had no implications for human behavior, which lay outside the domain of natural science. Gall and his student Joseph Spurzheim (1834) accepted prevailing dictionary terms as references for primary human characteristics (for example, hunger, sex, and greed) and, acting as psychological geographers, assigned each quality a location in the brain. They hoped that psychological function revealed structure and that the basic human qualities would provide a clue to the basic organization of the brain. That is, they reversed the modern strategy of using knowledge of the brain to explain behavior; they wanted to use knowledge about behavior to infer brain structure.

Gall's argument, which paralleled the form Darwin used in *Origin of Species,* was to first state a thesis, follow it with his understanding of the community's objections, and then marshall evidence refuting the popular critique. Like Helmholtz and Watson who followed, Gall wanted to eliminate the idea of soul from explanations of behavior, but his materialism was so crass he angered both colleagues and the citizenry by insisting that a person's character was determined by brain tissue alone and not subject to an agent's will. "The degree of moral liberty, of merit and of demerit, is as different in individuals as their cerebral organization is different; and, consequently, that education, morals, religion, legislation, rewards and punishments, are essentially allied to the nature of man" (p. 46).

Spurzheim consolidated Gall's ideas, retaining the essential premise of a location for each primary human quality and, reflecting nineteenth-century biases, assigned more space in the cranial cavity to emotional than to intellectual processes. Love was in the cerebellum, aggression in the temporal lobe, and timidity in the upper lateral and posterior part of the head, near the middle of the parietal bones. The vigor of Spurzheim's arguments derived, in part, from the same force that motivated Francis Bacon's *Novum Organum*. It was necessary to expunge metaphysical, religious ideas from scientific explanations of human nature. It was time, as the Scottish philosopher George Combe (1829) noted, to place human behavior in its proper place as part of natural law.

The rash of essays on constitutional causes of human behavior that followed Gall was due, first, to the fact that many in the European community were ready to believe that the physical differences between the lean build, narrow face, and light skin and hair of the Scandinavian and the short, broad, darker Neapolitan were predictive of popular stereotypes of regional differences in mood and behavior. Natural science came of age during the 200 years between Locke and the first studies of sensorimotor physiology by Magendie and Müller, furnishing theorists with preliminary possibilities of how the central nervous system might be linked to perception, attention, and behavior. The mind must be given some possible mechanisms if a novel idea is to be treated as rational. As scholars began to learn about the relation of brain to behavior, they became less resistant to the possibility that the nervous system had a recognized place in the science of mind. Thus, only 60 years after the rejection of Gall's views, Bain (1861) speculated on the cerebral localizations of motor and sensory functions.

Darwin provided the capstone only 70 years after Gall by uniting three separate ideas into a coherent and dynamic argument. The three ideas were: (1) living things vary in their biology, (2) the variation is differentially supported by the environments in which organisms live and reproduce, and, (3) because of continuous change in environments, there will be continuous changes in the predominant morphology and behavior of animal groups. The only element missing, which was supplied before the century ended, was the idea of mutations contributing to the variation the environment acted upon.

After Darwin it was more reasonable to assume that groups of people living in different places for an extended period would eventually differ in their biology because each group would have been forced to adapt to unique environmental challenges. Since few Neapolitans moved to Stockholm to marry Swedish women, the physical differences among Europeans, Africans, and Asians were likened to the morphological variation among tortoises on the islands of the Galapagos or the variation in quality of song between small, dark birds in German forests and large, white ones on the shores of the Aegean. The fact that differences in morphology were associated with differences in behavior among animal species made it reasonable to generalize this principle to humans.

The first important transformation of Gall's phrenological ideas was an expansion of the set of relevant biological features and, more important, recognition that the features were only signs of the real, invisible causes, and were not directly influential. Many writers proposed that the shape of the body and face and the color of eyes, hair, and skin were reliably linked to particular behaviors; but both characteristics were the product of common biological, but as yet unknown, factors. Until these mysterious factors were discovered it was reasonable practice to use the visible marks as diagnostic of temperament and predictive of a person's future actions. Skin, hair, bones, eyes, skull, and eyebrows contained the most sensitive clues to an individual's personality.

In a book that enjoyed eight editions, Joseph Simms (1887) awarded the face more diagnostic power than the contemporary psychologists Paul Ekman or Carroll Izard would have dared. Simms acknowledged, however, that both heredity and postnatal experience produced the characteristic facial and bodily forms. This is not a minor addition to the discourse, for Gall ignored the effects of diet, disease, and style of living on morphological shape. Simms described five ideal types: two variations of the contemporary mesomorph, two of the ectomorph, and one endomorphic type and assigned the expected psychological traits to each. The *osseous* type is cautious, the *thoracic* is cheerful, and the *muscular* is energetic and amoral. Simms listed over twenty psychological qualities, most of which had a familiar meaning to the average citizen—ambitious, watchful, playful, monoerotic—and unself-consciously presented as fact the unique profile of face and body that was most closely associated with each trait. Even American school teachers were indoctrinated with these ideas. Jessica Fowler (1897) prepared a manual to help teachers diagnose in their pupils qualities like "veneration for elders" from the presence of excessively drooping eyes.

Although both Gall and Simms were on the intellectual periphery of their respective professional communities, these ideas were occasionally proposed by scientists who enjoyed considerable legitimacy. An example is Paolo Mantegazzo, a nineteenth-century Italian anthropologist who awarded special significance to the shape of the face and the color of the iris. He also imitated his colleagues by including an illustration of a tree of intellectual ability in which the branches closest to the ground represented the less competent, darkly pigmented racial groups, while those at the top were the highly competent Caucasians.

Constitutional hypotheses were also applied to illness. George Draper (1924), a physician at Columbia University, was motivated by the observation that some body types were more vulnerable to contracting polio during the 1916 epidemic. He presented table after table of numbers indicating associations between selected bodily features and susceptibility to a small number of diseases. Draper suggested that brown-eyed individuals were more likely to have ulcers and gall bladder problems, while blue-eyed adults were especially susceptible to pernicious anemia and tuberculosis.[2]

Two classic treatises by the physicians Caesaro Lombroso and Ernst Kretschmer postulated an association between body type, on the one hand, and crime or mental disease, on the other. Lombroso's book (1911) acknowledged that crime had social and climatic correlates but claimed that adults who fell at one of the extremes on a normal body type were more often represented among criminals. Dark-haired men, for example, were more likely to be criminals than those with light hair.

2. It is of interest that a recent study reporting that ectomorphs were vulnerable to tuberculosis (Catsch, 1941) verified Hippocrates' belief that tall, thin adults (*habitus Phthisicus*) were vulnerable to lung disease.

Kretschmer (1926) invented new names—*asthenic, pyknic,* and *athletic*—for the three classic physiques and awarded differential vulnerability to major mental illnesses to the first two body types. Schizophrenics were more often found among the asthenics; manic depressives among the pyknics. Kretschmer was able to take advantage of new biological evidence suggesting that physiological factors, like hormones, might be causes of both body shape and mental symptoms. Kretschmer and Lombroso enjoyed greater acceptance than Gall because they offered explanatory statements referring to body humors which made their arguments more palatable. Explaining the relation between manic depressive illness and a pyknic build, Kretschmer wrote, "One must look out particularly for a connection with certain diseases of metabolism . . . connection between exophthalmic goitre and manic depressive insanity . . . circulars suffer from local dystrophy in the formation of the body, which points to severe endocrine disturbances" (Kretschmer, 1926, p. 84).

Kretschmer's conceptualization formed the basis for Sheldon's (1940) famous book on personality and physique. Sheldon measured a large number of morphological dimensions from the photographs of 4,000 college men and collapsed the resulting 76 categories into three basic body types, each type rated on a seven point scale. The pure *ectomorph* was tall and thin; the *endomorph* was round and fat; the *mesomorph,* broad and athletic. A fourth type, called *dysplastic,* was less coherent. Sheldon suggested that there was a relation between each of the ideal types and three families of psychological qualities which he called *cerebrotonia* (characteristic of the ectomorph), *viscerotonia* (characteristic of the endomorph), and *somatotonia* (for the mesomorph). The ectomorph was the classic introvert, the endomorph, the relaxed extravert, and the mesomorph was described as active, energetic, and assertive. In a prescient section in the closing chapter, Sheldon suggested that "behind the whole pattern of these observable phenomena a deeper constitutional factor may be at work" (p. 232). Sheldon argued, as Simms did 40 years earlier, that the personality type was not a direct result of biology but the product of environmental pressures acting upon a person with a particular physique. "It seems almost fatuous to attempt to draw a line between what is organic and what is functional in the human personality" (p. 235).

The year of publication of Sheldon's work was also the time when the Nazis were threatening Europe. The idea that physical qualities

were associated with characteristic human behaviors was too close to
Hitler's vision of Aryan types, and this research suddenly stopped.
The abruptness is not surprising, for tucked away in Sheldon's book
is the dangerous suggestion that Negroes are more often aggressive
mesomorphs while Jews are more often intellectual ectomorphs.
When the Harvard anthropologist Earnest Hooton (1939) wrote that
some bodily constitutions were naturally inferior and linked to criminality, there was a defensive tone to his essay because in 1939 Hooton
was aware of how unpopular this view had become to most Americans.

   Nevitt Sanford (1943) and R. N. Walker (1962) were two strag-
glers who affirmed the significant relation between an ectomorphic
body build in children and shy, timid behavior. But their monographs
came after the successful revolt against constitutional typologies. The
failures to replicate the claims of Kretschmer and Sheldon, as well as
the promotion of psychological variables with continuous variation,
created a hostile attitude toward temperamental categories. (I received no reprint requests for a paper published in 1966 describing a
relation in children between an ectomorphic body build and a reflective, cognitive style.) For an instructive review of much of the work
on constitution and behavior, see Myrtek, 1984.

Consciousness as the Mediator

A second perspective on temperamental types ignored features of
morphology and emphasized variations in psychological states
derivative from processes of the central nervous system. One of these
states was dependent upon the amount of energy available to consciousness. Freud acknowledged, in the monograph on hysteria, that
adults with a tall, thin body build and narrow thorax were prone to
hysteria, but he ignored that observation, presumably because he did
not believe these somatic features were relevant (Breuer and Freud,
1956). Although Freud agreed with colleagues that children were
born with different brain states, he broke with them by awarding to
early experience the power to influence these states and, therefore,
future symptoms.

   There are at least three reasons why Freud suggested that hysteria
was due to a special mental state influenced by childhood experience.
The most popular and reasonable account is that he realized he could
not explain the symptom patterns with the physiological knowledge
available to him; thus, he entertained psychological factors. But there

has always been, as there is now, a tension in Western views toward the origin of psychological differences and a desire, supported by a commitment to egalitarianism, to minimize biology and maximize experience. During this century, at least, scholars from minority groups have more often promoted the politically liberal emphasis on the formative role of experience. Thus, Freud, who felt the anti-Semitic prejudice of the Austrian community, might be friendly to this view. Jung was not.

A third, less obvious, reason is the referent population studied. Kretschmer and Lombroso regarded world-wide variation as their proper domain. Lombroso, for example, compared both past and present crime rates across Europe and Africa and could not help but attend to the obvious differences in body build. By contrast, Freud's primary evidence came from his Caucasian, central European patients, most of whom shared a more homogeneous constitution. Otto Klineberg, Solomon Asch, and Helen Block (1940) were on the faculty of New York's City College when they published a collaborative study refuting the constitutional theorists. But they, too, sampled minimal variation in constitution because most of their subjects were Jewish students. There is an old joke about a fisherman who had a net with four-inch holes who claimed the sea had no fish smaller than four inches around.

One can study the growth of flora in a forest from two perspectives. The observer who bends down to note the different heights of a group of six ferns will look for local variation in shade and weeds to explain the variation. But the observer on a plateau overlooking the entire forest who notes that the ferns grow only in the southeast corner will hypothesize different influences on the growth of these plants. Kretschmer wondered why more schizophrenics came from northern than from southern Europe. Freud wanted to explain why Schreber became a paranoid schizophrenic while his neighbor did not. The two questions are different and so are the explanations. The reasons for the differences in industriousness between two sisters are not the same as those that explain why modern Japanese are more industrious than the Indians Darwin saw at Tierra del Fuego.

The Metaphor of Energy in Conscious Processes

Janet and Freud, among others, found a generative metaphor for psychic events in the first law of thermodynamics and its principle of energy conservation. Many nineteenth-century scholars were certain that this physical law could provide a bridge between physiological and psychological phenomena because it implied convertibility of the physical energy in the body to the energy required for psychic processes (see Cleland, 1882). The power of this metaphor rests, in part, on its match to intuition. Every person has experienced the feeling of being drained of energy at the end of the day and an impaired ability to concentrate after several hours of strenuous physical exertion. These, and so many other related experiences, rendered reasonable the belief that each person, like a closed container of gas, had a fixed amount of available energy, and expending a proportion of that total in one activity meant that another would have less.

Middle-class European scholars wrote, in obvious self-interest, that mental work, not felling trees, lifting sacks, or washing clothes, was the one human activity requiring the greatest expenditure of energy. One defense of this view was the folk belief that poets and writers were sickly and, on average, died at a younger age than most other men. Lombroso exploited this idea to explain why geniuses were precociously gray, bald, and without the normal amount of sexual and muscular vitality.

Nineteenth-century writers often compared the energy necessary for thought with that necessary for sexuality, as if this particular contrast had an obviously special salience (Russett, unpublished). Balfor Stewart (1881) wrote, "Every throb of pleasure costs something to the physical system and two throbs cost twice as much as one" (Stewart, 1881, p. 228–229).[3] The decision to pit thought against sexuality was influenced, in part, by a preoccupation with sex differences. The contrasting stereotypes of male intellectual inventiveness versus female emotionality were presumably explained by the law of conservation of energy. Since women required more energy for reproductive functions—maturing ova, pregnancy, lactation, and care of the young—it followed that they have less energy for thought. This simple idea was used as a rationalization for not sending young women to college. It was not possible for young women to invest a

3. These ideas were popular in Europe before Freud wrote his seminal papers. Freud's original contribution was to suggest, first, that early experiences in the home influenced the distribution of the energy and, second, that the primary source of energy for psychological functions was libidinal. This choice implied that sexual pleasure had a special force, while permitting other sources of pleasure to contribute to the total reserves. But the idea of libido would appeal only to those communities in which many were experiencing consciously the frustration and guilt of sexual restraint.

great deal of concentration in academic work because their energy was being invested in the growth of primary and secondary sex characteristics and preparation for marriage and maternity.[4]

Edward Clarke (1873) wrote of a female patient who had attended the New York State Seminary for Girls and graduated, at 19 years of age, a scholar and an invalid. Clarke describes this young woman.

> She was well and would have been called robust, up to her first critical period. She then had two tasks imposed upon her at once, both of which required for their perfect accomplishment a few years of time and a large share of vital force: one was the education of a brain, the other of the reproductive system . . . the school, with Puritanic inflexibility, demanded every day of the month; nature, kinder than the school, demanded less than a fourth of the time . . . She put her will into the education of her brain and withdrew it from elsewhere . . . Presently . . . the strength of the loins, that even Solomon put in as part of his ideal woman, changed to weakness . . . Doubtless the evil of her education will infect her whole life. (p. 69–72)

The idea that men and women, as well as individuals within each gender, differ in the amount of energy available for the psychological work performed by consciousness was a central basis for Janet's explanation of hysteria. Janet (1901) assumed, as an axiom, that a weakened consciousness was the immediate cause of hysterical symptoms, but let the reader infer that the weakness had a specific physiological foundation. Breuer and Freud tried to explain the reasons for the weakness by claiming that the repression of sexual ideas removed energy from consciousness and left it in a weakened state. Because women were more likely than men to repress sexual ideas, they were more vulnerable to a weakened consciousness and hence to hysteria. That argument is reasonable, given their six premises.

(1) The brain operates on physical energy.
(2) The cells of the brain attempt to achieve a quiescent state of energy equilibrium.

---

4. Modern theorists approach human behavior with the equally abstract idea that self-interest is the major guide to all decisions. Sociobiologists suggest that some animals help their kin at the expense of their own fecundity in order to enhance the actualization of their own gametes in a future generation. Western theorists are attracted to abstract, unifying Platonic principles that seem to be part of a natural plan which is, at root, an accountant's table amenable to arithmetical judgments of correct or incorrect for each action.

(3) Any increase in the energy of the brain must be discharged.
(4) Sexual ideas are a primary cause of an increase in the brain's energy.
(5) Early childhood experiences make adults vulnerable to the repression of sexual ideas.
(6) When a sexual idea is repressed, the energy attached to it is not discharged, as it should be, and, as a result, consciousness is weaker and hysterical symptoms may appear.

Freud acknowledged, as did Janet, that individual differences in vulnerability to hysterical symptoms were due, in part, to hereditary differences in the excitability of the brain. Freud and Breuer wrote, "The fundamental pathological change (in hysteria), which is present in every case and enables ideas as well as non-psychological stimuli to produce pathological affects, lies in an abnormal excitability of the nervous system" (p. 191). "These differences, which make up a man's natural temperament are certainly based on profound differences in his nervous system—on the degree to which the functionally quiescent cerebral elements liberate energy" (p. 198). Thus, Freud and Breuer held what we call today a diathesis-stress theory in which temperamental differences in states of excitability were a major factor in symptomatology.

The Contrast between Freud and Jung on Consciousness

Jung (1924) accepted the theoretical centrality of consciousness but rejected Janet's notion of a division in this state. The differences between introverts and extraverts, which he also believed were temperamental in origin, included the attitude consciousness assumed toward an object and the degree to which libidinal energy could be withdrawn from an object. By replacing Janet's concept of the "contraction of consciousness" with the "target of consciousness," Jung attained a more value-free description, while challenging the popular view that all persons possessed the same unitary consciousness.

Even though Freud acknowledged that people differed in amount of libido, he assumed that all humans possessed essentially the same consciousness during the early years of life. Childhood conflict could change the quality of conscious feeling tone. But if these conflicts were resolved, the original functions, presumed to be identical for all, would return.

Jung denied the Platonic idea of a universal consciousness, believing that introverts and extraverts inherited qualitatively different brain structures which could not be changed. Hence, the same external events might not have the same significance for the two temperamental groups. This fact of nature could not be altered by social legislation. "It may well serve a useful purpose, therefore, to speak of the heterogeneity of men. These differences involve such different claims to happiness that even the most consummate legislation could never give them approximate satisfaction" (Jung, 1924, p. 619).

In attempting to understand why Freud and Jung held such different views on the variation in conscious feeling tone of the two temperamental groups, it may be relevant to note that their young adult years were separated by an important 20-year interval. In 1875, the year of Jung's birth, Freud was 19 years old, Europe was relatively stable, and Darwin's ideas and the principle of the conservation of energy supplied over-arching metaphors for development and behavior. It would have been difficult for any scholar concerned with human nature to be indifferent to two of Darwin's basic ideas: humans are closely related to animals, and the key to species survival is reproduction. When these premises were combined with the conception of a nervous system that runs on a fixed source of energy that is conserved, a creative mind searching for universals might well have generated the idea of libido, assumed sexual drives to be primary, and posited a stage-like ontogeny paralleling the phylogenetic stages in animal evolution. Darwin believed he was writing about universal processes and not inventing generalizations that accommodated to local history and culture. Freud shared that ambition.

But the Hapsburg empire was collapsing when Jung was 19 years old, permitting him to experience a community changing its basic assumptions and adults expressing ideas and actions that seemed to be independent of the particular events of their early childhoods.

It is likely, also, that Jung was an introvert and Freud an extravert.

> The introverted, thinking type is characterized by a priority of the thinking I have just described. Like his extraverted parallel, he is decisively influenced by ideas; these, however, have their origin, not in the objective data but in the subjective foundation. Like the extravert, he too will follow his ideas, but in the reverse direction: inwardly not outwardly. (p. 485)

> Continually emancipating itself from the relation to the object this feeling [of the introvert] creates a freedom, both of action and of

conscience, that is only answerable to the subject, and that may even renounce all traditional values. (p. 491)

His [the extravert's] entire consciousness looks outward to the world, because the important and decisive determination always comes to him from without. (p. 417)

The egoism which so often characterizes the extravert's unconscious attitude goes far beyond mere childish selfishness; and even verges upon the wicked and brutal. It is here we find in fullest bloom that incest wish described by Freud. (p. 424)

If Jung's characterizations are correct, and he was an introvert and Freud an extravert, we might expect Jung to award priority to feelings, which are transient and yoked to contexts, but Freud to award salience to stable objects, like parents and libidinal energy, neither of which changes its essential qualities. Freud, like Russell, saw the world as objective, materialistic, and following universal causal laws. Jung, siding with Whitehead, conceptualized reality as composed of families of events whose components changed with conditions. Because both men used introspective analysis of their feelings, thoughts, and history as a central source of evidence for their theoretical views, we might expect them to arrive at different premises. Again, knowing the source of evidence aids understanding.

The class and ethnic differences between the two men may also clarify their different views on temperamental types. Although Jung's father was not wealthy, he was a respected pastor in a small community that awarded the family social status. After Jung married the daughter of a wealthy and prominent Zurich family, he became a member of the elite class in Swiss society. Freud, by contrast, grew up in a middle-class Jewish family in an anti-Semitic society and throughout his childhood perceived himself as an outsider. Children who confront the fact that the other—the legitimized majority—regards the self as less pure develop special beliefs to explain the chronically uncomfortable feeling of being outside of or unwanted by their community. It is more comfortable to conclude that the mood of illegitimacy was produced by one's experiences, in Freud's case the attitudes of the majority, than to attribute the dysphoric mood to an endogenous quality. By contrast, Jung would be motivated to regard his more secure status and accompanying feelings as inevitable and not the product of chance experiences. Hence, he might be tempted to emphasize the role of heredity in the formation of his personality.

The different attitudes toward myth held by the two men are concordant with this argument. Freud, oppressed by an outside world he believed held a false idea about Jews, treated myth and religion as childish and regressive. Only facts should persuade, and if the facts showed that Jews were not evil, the Gentile world would have to change its mind. Jung, an elite member of a Christian majority, treated myth and religion as adaptive human qualities. Truth was gained by intuition and listening carefully to one's anima.

Jung's ideas were rejected by most American psychologists during most of this century, in part, because he wrote at the wrong time. Egalitarianism has dominated American essays on human nature. Nurture, not nature, was the sculptor, and few Americans wanted to listen to a European nativist who questioned equality. Jung ended *Psychological Types* (1924) with an undemocratic reference to the French Revolution:

> Although every man should stand equal before the law and no man, through inherited social position should unjustly over-reach his brother, nevertheless it [the idea of egalitarianism] is less beautiful when the notion of equality is extended to other provinces of life. A man must have a clouded vision to cherish the view that a uniform distribution of happiness can be won through a uniform regulation of life. (p. 618)

Freud could not have written those sentences. Thus, the resistance to Jung's ideas was due, as he would have predicted, to historical conditions.

Relations between Body and Mind

Biology, chemistry, and physics have no difficulty dealing with the notion of emergent phenomena derived from the interaction of processes that are described in different languages. The gravitational attraction between earth and moon, described in a metric that combines force and distance, is the basis for the emergent phenomenon of the tides described in hours and heights. The rate of movement of sodium and potassium ions in and out of the membrane of the axon leads to the emergent phenomenon of an action potential described in millivolts. But scholars have had difficulty describing psychological phenomena as emerging from central nervous system states.

One basis for the tension is traceable, I believe, to our phenomenology. Because each of us is an actor with a consciousness, there is a sense, as compelling as the conviction of medieval citizens that the sun moves around the earth, that our actions begin in the intentions generated in our minds. Christian philosophy insisted that God made all souls identical; only bodies were different. Intuition and reason belonged to the soul. This position made psychological phenomena more basic than bodily processes. It would have been impossible for a medieval philosopher to treat the soul as derivative of, or emergent from, physiological events. When the fourteenth-century skeptics documented the flaws in human perception, the integrity of the soul was threatened. In an attempt to rescue the soul from this attack on its purity, Descartes cut all connections between soul and body and placed reasoning in the soul. After acknowledging that our senses deceive us, Descartes (1641/1980) concluded in the sixth meditation that "my essence consists in this alone: that I am only a thing that thinks . . . it is therefore certain that I am truly distinct from my body and that I can exist without it" (p. 93). A mind so isolated from bodily processes cannot be derivative of them. The doctrine of a sovereign mind made it easier for John Locke to ignore the body and assert that sensory impressions changed the mind directly and, as a consequence, actions and moods were altered. Mind was primary; body, secondary. But the advances in natural science in the late eighteenth century encouraged a small number of theorists to place the psychology of human nature in a Newtonian and, therefore, mechanical frame. Even though Gall's crass materialism was satirized by his colleagues, he was arguing that variation in human behavior could be emergent from brain states. The fact that his specific ideas were incorrect is independent of the soundness of his ambition. Darwin was wrong in claiming human morality was a product of a Lamarckian mechanism, but correct in claiming that all children inherit a moral sense.

The manipulation of mood and action by drugs and lesions is one source of evidence favoring an emergent view, although that conclusion does not mean that mental phenomena do not influence physiological ones. Sperry (1977) has argued, convincingly, I believe, that there is mutuality between psychological and physiological phenomena. Psychological events should be seen neither as isolated from brain states nor as independent origins of action. Even though the action potential is a significant basis for a motor reflex, it is not independent of the ion exchange at the axon hillock. Leonard Carmichael understood the error of conceiving of biological and psychological processes as separable. During the third decade of this century, less than twenty years after Pavlov's discoveries, a large number of American psychologists were replacing the nineteenth-century conception of instinct with an environmentalism so extreme it came close to claiming that no response was possible without some form of external stimulation. Kuo (1924), who led the attack on endogenous hereditary mechanisms, argued that the appearance of behaviors formerly regarded as hereditary instincts was, most of the time, the product of postnatal conditioning. This radical suggestion provided the incentive for Carmichael's (1926; 1927) elegant experiments on the frog and salamander larvae he gathered from small ponds near Princeton, New Jersey.

The experimental larvae, which had been placed in the anesthetic chloretone to block motor responses, swam less than a half-hour after being freed of the anesthetic and close to the time noted for the control larvae who grew under natural conditions. Because the anesthetized larvae could not execute small muscle movements, the later display of coordinated swimming could not be attributed to prior conditioning or external stimulation. However, Carmichael recognized that invoking the concept of maturation would not explain the swimming movements and, in a rejection of both the preformationists and environmentalists, suggested that the swimming required prior periods of nerve–muscle stimulation during the time the larvae were anesthetized. Although swimming was dependent upon structures determined by heredity, that action required functional neural activity for its actualization. Carmichael appreciated that although scientific prose can describe heredity and environment as separate factors, in nature the two forces are inherently a unity.

Why did Carmichael have to perform these experiments, and why did Richard Solomon, years later, have to demonstrate that instrumental learning can occur without the organism having to make the unconditioned response? Part of the answer is that many American psychologists resisted then, as a few continue to do now, the idea that some forms of behavioral change require neither prior action nor interaction. The traditional environmental perspective remains attractive, despite persuasive counter-evidence, because of a wish to have most of the control of behavior rest with external events acting on the organism. If that premise were generally true, adults would have greater power to change young children and, by affirming

Locke's image of the growing mind, maintain the hope that the actions of parents and peers might be so perfectly orchestrated that we could approach a politically and socially egalitarian society.

Some contemporary writers invented the concept of internalization to summarize the psychological consequences of experience. After presenting persuasive data indicating that signs of self-recognition appear during the second half of the second year, Lewis and Brooks-Gunn (1979) suggested that this competence "has as its source the interaction of the young organism with others—both people and objects. The implication of this is that action within the interaction of the organism and its environment precedes knowledge. Indeed, it is from action that knowledge develops" (p. 241).

Piaget made internalization the central mechanism in early cognitive growth, while recognizing that environmental experience alone is insufficient to create cognitive structures. In the section of *Play, Dreams and Imitation in Childhood* (1951) in which he is describing the stages of imitation during the sensorimotor period, Piaget states that the child's behavioral "experimentation is interiorized and coordination takes place before there is external adjustment" (p. 62). A few pages later, in a section on the function of mental images in imitation, Piaget asks, "Why should it, therefore, not be the product of the interiorization of imitation once this has reached its full development, just as interior language is both the draft of words to come and the interiorization of acquired exterior language" (p. 70).

Piaget did not want psychological functions like imagery to be biologically prepared talents that would occur eventually in all children just because they lived in the world. Piaget assumed that the only obvious alternatives to this view were a pan-behaviorism or autochthonous, but unspecifiable, processes in the brain leading to new responses. The problem with the latter position is that if scientists can only know as real what they can sense, and all else is nonsense, then to suggest, as Preyer (1888-1889) did, that the child will become aware of himself, imitate his parents, speak a language, and have images because these competences are part of the hominid genome is to yield to occultism. Twentieth-century empiricists who wish to be part of the scientific enterprise must avoid such explanations. This popular materialistic view of ontogeny was bolstered both by Pavlov's experiments and John Watson's later dogmatism, "There are no instincts, we build in at a early age everything that is later to appear" (Watson, 1928, p. 38).

Carmichael's belief that natural events, like swimming salamanders, were unities derived from a structural entity functioning in a specific surround is a premise of contemporary biology, chemistry, and physics. No biologist would try to quantify the separate influences of nuclear DNA and the cytoplasm with respect to the production of a protein. And Lorenz did not think of evaluating the separate contributions of the young gosling's ability to locomote and the experience of seeing an adult walk to the phenomenon of imprinting. Nor would a physicist be concerned with the differential influence of the temperature of the air and the qualities of water molecules on the formation of ice when the temperature falls below freezing. Yet, some psychologists continue to argue about how much variance in intelligent behavior is attributable to genes and how much to pre- and postnatal environmental events.

I suspect that whatever reluctance there is to accept Carmichael's conclusion is due partly to the fact that the human mind has difficulty uniting ideas from two different lexicons and so conceptualizes them as separate forces. When the psychological phenomena involve physiological processes, the natural entity in theoretical descriptions is often named with a biological word—gene, hormone, neuron, synapse—while the facilitating experiences are described in psychological language. The mind–body dichotomy is a linguistic problem, not a natural one. When a particular female wrasse becomes dominant over the other females in the harem in which they live, she begins to make sperm. As long as that phenomenon is described only with biological concepts (place in the dominance hierarchy; production of gametes), we do not feel the need to know the differential contribution of (1) the events that led one female to become dominant and (2) the characteristics of that particular female. But should someone suggest that the dominant female wrasse experiences a special psychological state, I suspect that the introduction of a psychological term would lead some scientists to wonder whether they might measure the psychological state of the fish separate from the exogenous and endogenous events that transformed her sexuality.

Finally, there is a political motivation for keeping environmental factors separate from biological ones. A good number of American psychologists, many of them developmental scholars, would like to believe that, regardless of children's genotypes, it should be possible to discover environmental manipulations that will produce equally competent children and adults. The possibility that some genotypes are more and some less malleable to a given class of experience implies an unfair constraint on benevolent intervention, even though no one believes it is possible to make a wolf as relaxed as a beagle. Even home-reared chimps treated with gentling affection become dangerous after a few years. The idea that a class of behavior is influenced by biological events is often misinterpreted as implying limitations on the potency of experience when, in fact, experience is absolutely necessary for every psychological outcome. It is just that we cannot specify with exactitude its influence independent of the organism that accommodates to it.

Had Carmichael had the advantage of reading W. V. Quine, he might have altered a pair of sentences Quine used to describe his view of the relation between fact and convention and written something like the following: "The behavior of every organism can be likened to a pale gray fabric. Although some fibers are black with biology and others white with experience, I have found no substantial reason for concluding that there are any quite black threads in it or any white ones."

These philosophical issues are relevant to contemporary views on temperament. My colleagues and I have found that about 10 to 15 percent of young children typically stop what they are doing when they encounter an unfamiliar event. This form of reaction emerges from central nervous system states created by detection of discrepant experience. Infants who will become behaviorally inhibited in their second year probably establish a relation with their caretakers that differs from the relation established by uninhibited infants. But the early and later behaviors should be viewed as part of a sequence that has some basis in the child's biology. We do not have to decide whether psychology or biology is more basic; each has the opportunity to be both origin and consequent.

The Return to Temperamental Categories

The reasons for the return of temperamental concepts during the past decade, following over a half-century of exile, are multiple. First, research on the role of the family has produced too few robust generalizations to mute a growing skepticism over the power that had been awarded to this class of experience. Second, the most central idea in psychoanalytic theory—namely, that acquired sexual conflict is the basis of neurosis—has been tested by history. Despite an obvious reduction in the repression of sexual ideas, the profiles of agoraphobia, paranoia, depression, crime, and schizophrenia are still with us, and some symptoms—for example, suicide—are increasing in frequency. Third, laboratory research has undermined the traditional tenets of learning theory. Adult monkeys learn new responses without any obvious reinforcement; infant monkeys spend more time on a cloth surrogate that is not a source of food than on a wire one that is; and ethologists have found a host of species-specific responses that do not yield easily to a behavioristic analysis.

Further, pharmacological treatment of depression and anxiety has been more effective than most psychiatrists had expected. One conclusion, although not logically impeccable, has become popular. If extreme anxiety in a 28-year-old woman is reduced by a drug that alters the biochemistry of her brain, it is reasonable to assume that the anxiety might have been due to brain biochemistry in the first place. And it seemed easier in the 1980s to speculate on how genes might produce a biochemical profile that, in turn, influences psychological profiles than to speculate on how treatment by parents and friends might have done so.

Finally, the modern synthesis in evolutionary biology has articulated a conceptual strategy to combine biology and experience. Biology provides a varied set of agents, each of whom confronts different experiences. Knowledge only of the biological state of an agent permits no prediction. Knowing the genomes of the mammals who lived 50 million years ago would not have allowed any biologist to predict the rise of apes and baboons. The evolutionary biologist also needs to know the specific ecological changes that selected some species rather than others. Had different droughts and temperature changes occurred, *homo sapiens* would not exist.

The idea that environments act on varied phenotypes differentially may seem simple, but it took over 2,000 years to invent. Everyone knows that large red roses require both special seeds and much sunshine. Change the seeds or the weather and we get either white roses or tiny red ones. But this common knowledge did not generalize to human behavior until recently because prior to 1900 we did not have a conceptual frame to describe environmental variation and after 1910 we did not want to acknowledge biological influences. Thus, many forces came together to lead Thomas and Chess (1977) to suggest what mothers had known intuitively, namely, that infants differed in reactivity from the first days of life. But their message would not have been promoted if scientists had not been transformed by these profound changes in the Zeitgeist.

Modern Temperamental Categories

Hans Eysenck (1953; 1957), one of the influential contemporary theorists, posits four types formed from the conjunction of two orthogonal dimensions: extraversion–introversion and emotional lability–stability. The *dysthymic* type is introverted and labile; the *hysteric* and the *criminal* are extraverted and labile; the *introvert* is introverted and stable; and the *extravert* is extraverted and stable. The modern feature in Eysenck's writing is the attempt to relate the four types to profiles of cerebral excitability and inhibition. Extraverts and hysterics generate excitatory potential slowly and to a lower average level; thus, the energy dissipates quickly. Introverts and dysthymics generate stronger excitatory potential more quickly; hence, the energy dissipates more slowly.

Thus, Eysenck retains, in subtle form, Janet's notions of potency and energy. Janet thought that panic attacks resulted from a weakened consciousness; Eysenck suggests that the cause lies with a central nervous system that cannot dissipate high levels of excitatory potential generated in a brief period. Both descriptions conjure up the image of an impotent brain unable to deal with the energy it has created. The most recent research on panic patients by biologically oriented psychiatrists has expunged language implying a weak brain and speaks, in a more neutral tone, of excited limbic areas that respond readily to challenge or novelty. Variation in the excitability of cells and circuits does not have the evaluative connotations of variation in strength.

Although the current temperamental categories of children are free of both evaluative language and an energy metaphor, they are conceptually conservative for at least three reasons. First, a majority of the most active investigators are empiricists, not theorists, and the judicial hand of Vienna Circle positivism is still felt on their shoulders. Second, these scientists are aware of the resistance, among many developmental scholars, to the idea of temperamental types, as well as overly abstract ideas unsupported by evidence. Thus, these investigators avoid categories that cannot be easily assimilated to everyday experience and extant knowledge. Finally, a fair proportion of these investigators are interested in either clinical problems or the characteristics of infants that might interfere with the mother–child relationship. Indeed, the source of the Chess–Thomas temperamental categories was parental descriptions of their infants. A mother can only speak about the qualities she has articulated in consciousness and for which she has a vocabulary. Mothers are likely to talk about behavior that either worries or pleases them. It is not a surprise, therefore, that activity level, crying, sleeping, feeding, soothability, adaptation to new contexts, and a happy or a fearful mood dominate the current set of temperamental categories.

Buss and Plomin (1975; 1984) posit three basic temperamental types for both children and adults, each believed to be under genetic influence. *Emotionality,* which refers to the ease with which infants and children become distressed, shares major features with Eysenck's concept of lability. *Sociability* is an obvious analogue of extraversion. The third category, *activity,* refers to variation in vigor and tempo of behavior and is one of the Chess–Thomas dimensions.

Rothbart and Derryberry (1981) also award salience to the ability to control emotional arousal, for they posit *reactivity* and *self-regulation* as the two basic temperamental functions. The former shares features with Buss–Plomin emotionality; the latter with Eysenck's notion of the brain's ability to dissipate excitation. Goldsmith and Campos (1982) are unique among modern theorists in restricting application of temperamental constructs to infants and awarding the term a special meaning. *Temperament* refers to processes that organize the expression of emotion, especially in interpersonal contexts. They award importance to the display of affect because of a concern with how the child's behavior influences the parent–child relationship.

Types versus Dimensions

The return of the concept of temperamental types to developmental dialogues requires consideration of the theoretical utility of qualitative categories of persons compared with a set of continuous psychological dimensions. Stated differently, are the psychological variations among people a matter of degree or of kind?

The twin missions of science are to determine the form of the functional relations between events and to describe the structure of the entities that participate in those relations. In the initial parsing of each of these missions the investigator often asks whether a functional relation is linear or nonlinear and whether the differences between the participating entities should be conceptualized as quantitative or qualitative. To illustrate, an inquiry into the relation between local food supply and the fecundity of baboons and hyenas sharing a savannah should be sensitive to the exact form of the function and the possibility of treating the two classes of animals as members of qualitatively different categories or as variations on one of a small number of continuous dimensions.

The answers to scientific questions are always idealizations, for empirical data rarely, perhaps never, reveal their unambiguous membership in one and only one invented conceptual space. Bohr's complementarity principle suggests that the choices are influenced by theory, procedure, and the analytic methods imposed on the evidence. Depending upon the preferred concepts, apparatus, and the data-reduction techniques applied to a problem, it will be more or less fruitful to regard functional relations as linear or nonlinear and the participating entities as varying continuously or as qualitatively discrete.

The empirical and mathematical discoveries that led to quantum mechanics substituted the discrete photon for the assumption of continuous light waves, while replacing the promise of determinacy and perfect prediction with the absolute impossibility of both. The reverse change in perspective occurred when Darwin substituted a dynamic evolutionary continuum between humans and apes for the traditional assumption of a qualitative discontinuity between these biological categories.

During this century the disciplines that study behavior, thought, and affect have favored continua over categories and linear over nonlinear relations. These presuppositions, fundamental to Newtonian physics and the philosophical writings of Kant and Leibniz, dominate the modern psychological laboratory, partly as a consequence of the dissemination of statistical procedures in the interval between the two World Wars. By the Second World War, the use of inferential statistics became the mark of the sophisticated social scientist. Investigators who ignored statistical analyses were regarded as less competent. The correlation coefficient, t test, and analyses of variance are computed on continuous variables. Experimental psychologists assumed there were no types; all humans could be treated as substantially alike in studies of sensation, perception, and memory. Analyses of variance were performed upon sets of continuous scores produced by classes of experimental conditions, not initially different classes of people. The only popular exceptions were gender and age.

Many psychologists, whether in the role of scientist or journal referee, have a condescending attitude toward statistics applied to categorical data, like chi square, because they believe such methods are wasteful of information. This opinion remains strong despite important empirical examples to the contrary, including the categorical perception of qualities of tastes and smells, dramatic changes in performance that occur as new maturational stages are attained, and the psychological differences among groups with distinct genotypes. Thus, some social scientists are pulled in opposite directions when they design investigations and later when they analyze their evidence, for they suspect that some basic constructs should be treated as qualitative categories.

Categories and Continua

A majority of scientists in every discipline assume that natural phenomena are best described as products of classes of entities and the specific functions or processes in which the entities participate. Electrons spin, molecules adhere, neurons discharge, muscles contract, and bats echolocate. A second, less frequently articulated, assumption is that the entities—whether electrons, neurons, or bats—and the processes are concepts defined by a family of correlated values on *n* dimensions or features. That is, they are prototypes. I know of very few useful theoretical entities in the life sciences that are defined by a value on a single dimension. Psychological concepts are frequent exceptions to this claim, for concepts like *introvert* and *genius* are often defined by a narrow range of values generated by one procedure.

Further, in the biological sciences each class of process is linked to specific kinds of entities, even though some features of a process might be shared with related ones. For example, both nerve cells in the hypothalamus and Sertoli cells in the testes, but not receptor cells on the basilar membrane, secrete chemical substances. But the specific features of the production and dispersal of the chemical substances differ for the two secretory cells. A major difference between psychological and biological research is that the latter discipline is more sensitive to the need to link particular entities with particular processes. With the exception of neuroscientists, most psychologists focus almost exclusively on processes and push against limitations on the generality of a process, hoping that it will be applicable to a very broad set of phenotypically different entities.

When traditional learning theory guided laboratory work before and right after World War II, experimental psychologists believed that learning ability was a continuous process from rats to humans. Technical reports compared the number of trials a monkey and a child required to learn a perceptual discrimination, expecting a linear relation between phylogenetic status and rapidity of learning. Such an approach is more controversial today, when both biologists and psychologists emphasize qualitative differences among varied species as often as they note similarities. The premise that the process of learning is similar across different classes and ages of individuals is obvious in Pavlov's writings, but one would have thought that the work of ethologists would have countered that optimism.

Reflect upon natural entities, both sensed events like rocks and flowers, as well as invisible ones like molecules and viruses. Each class of entity is a patterned structure qualitatively different from members of other classes, even though one can invent a quantitative relation among related classes for the qualities that, considered together, define each type of entity. The molecules of epinephrine and norepinephrine are composed of similar atoms and are very similar in size and weight. However, some of the functions and sites of production of the two molecules are qualitatively different. Although molecules can be placed on a continuum of weight and size, the form and function of the chemical reactions in which they participate involve the entire molecule, not just its weight. The unique spatial pattern of atoms located at the end of the Y-shaped arm of an antibody molecule, not the continuous characteristics of length or weight, determines the molecule's immune reactions in the body. Similar arguments for qualitative distinctions apply to animal families, genera, and species. Closely related strains of mice are similar in size, anatomy, and number of chromosomes. But their behavioral and biochemical reactions to stress are often qualitatively distinct.

The usual reply to this brief for qualitative distinctions is to point to the fruitfulness of the physical concept of energy. Fire, friction, water, and light are very different qualitatively, yet each of these phenomena can be placed on a single continuous metric that refers to the potential or kinetic energy of each source. But physicists mute the fact that it makes a difference whether the source of energy is sunlight or friction when they study the relation between amount of energy and a particular phenomenon. A growing plant requires the energy contained in photons; a spring rose will not blossom if it is warmed by rubbing. Although the theoretical concept of energy refers to a continuous quantity, the functional relations in which energy is a mediating process depend upon qualitative features of the energy, in this case its source.

Although the continuous dimensions scientists measure are often used as signs, or clues, to help them detect the presence of an entity, these dimensions are not always the functionally most important ones. For example, an early step in a new procedure that analyses the location of a gene involves placing tiny pieces of DNA, created by restriction enzymes, on special paper and observing how far each piece migrates. The smaller, lighter pieces migrate further than the larger ones, and the distance migrated is an important continuous dimension geneticists use to infer the presence of a specific gene. But no geneticist claims that the size of a segment of DNA, which is correlated with distance migrated, is important with respect to the specific proteins the gene directs or the disease it may eventually influence. Once the locus of the gene for Huntington's disease was found, the technical prose describing the discovery referred to a qualitative property of the gene—its chromosomal location—not to its size. One day we may learn its qualitatively distinct molecular structure.

The EEG spectra from the human brain can be described with terms referring to the continua of frequency and amplitude. Scientists use these two continua to detect the probable origin of a cortical discharge. But no physiologist claims that the state of sleep, with its unique EEG signature, differs only quantitatively from the state of alertness in a performing cellist. The two states are considered to be qualitatively different. Similarly, the vocal greeting of a friend is composed of a set of quantitative dimensions, but the difference between the voices of a friend and stranger seems qualitative. The concept that is the referent for, or sign of, an event can have a meaning different from the one that summarizes the event's primary functions or structure.

Consider the phenomena of short- and long-term memory which are detected by evaluating the relation between the probability of recall of information and the delay between exposure and the subsequent recall performance. If the recall is exceptionally good after a 10-second delay but poor after a 30-second delay, the phenomenon is classified as belonging to short-term memory. If the performance is good at both delays, the phenomenon is classified as belonging to long-term memory. Because temporal delay and amount of information recalled can be arranged to form continua, some investigators have been tempted to treat the concept of memory trace as varying continuously in strength. However, neurological evidence implies a qualitative distinction between the ability to retrieve a fact learned 10 years ago and one learned 10 seconds earlier, despite the fact that the procedures used to detect the two qualities rely on a continuum.

The probability of occurrence of a conditioned response (for example, the classically conditioned nictitating membrane reflex in the rabbit) is a linear function of the number of conditioning trials. This fact leads psychologists to describe the response with a continuous metric, often called *response strength*. But the neurons and brain circuits that participate in the acquisition and display of this reflex are very different for the unconditioned and conditioned forms, and lesions in different parts of the circuit have different effects on the response. Conditioned and unconditioned eye blinks in rabbits are qualitative categories because they involve special brain circuits, and each is actualized differently when conditions of arousal, incentive, or setting are varied.

Although the frequency, loudness, and rise time of an auditory tone are continuous dimensions, tones with particular values on the three dimensions have qualitatively different effects on infants. Tones of high frequency (100 Hz) that are loud (80 db) and have fast rise times (50 msec) startle infants and make them cry. By contrast, tones of low frequency (50 Hz) and low intensity (40 db) with slow rise times (3 sec) lead the infant to open its eyes and appear alert. An investigator who treated frequency, loudness, and rise time as three independent continua and implemented an analysis of variance to test the consequences of each would find no main effect for frequency, intensity, or rise time nor any significant interaction term. However, it would be incorrect to conclude that these continuous dimensions do not influence newborn behavior, for qualitative categories of sounds, each of which is a unique combination of frequency, loudness, and rise time, are extremely effective in changing behavior.

More important for this discussion is the fact that the modern concept of species, which is so fundamental in evolutionary biology, is a qualitative category defined primarily by reproductive isolation. Each of the separate, graded dimensions that characterize a species—

weight, length, lifespan, pigmentation—is of secondary importance. An example of the qualitative nature of species is found in a comparison of the behavior and physiology of three closely related macaque species—rhesus, bonnets, and crabeaters. Within rhesus and bonnets, but not among crabeaters, there is no correlation between changes in corticosteroid secretion and motor activity following encounter with the stresses of novelty or restraint. Crabeaters show the largest increase in corticosteroids and behavioral signs of fear when placed in a novel environment; but, in the wild, rhesus, not crabeaters, are the least tolerant of unfamiliar animals. It is not possible, therefore, to arrange the three species on a continuum of either fear of, or arousal to, unfamiliarity. We must view them as three qualitatively different types of animals (Clarke, Mason, and Moberg, 1988).

A temperamental type is analogous to a biological strain. Each type refers to a class of people who share a biological constitution and a history of changing, but correlated, characteristics. The temperamental category my colleagues and I call the *inhibited child* is characterized by a reactive limbic and sympathetic nervous system (which is often reflected in extreme irritability or sleeplessness during the first year), fearfulness during the second year, and consistently shy, timid behavior in unfamiliar settings in the third year. A three-year-old child who possesses only one of these features is not a member of this temperamental category.

The usual research sample of volunteers may contain only a small number of children who belong to a distinct temperamental category. We have been studying a group of Caucasian children who were not preselected on any psychological quality and have evaluated them at 14, 20, 32, and 48 months of age. Of the original group of 100 children seen at 14 months, 77 were studied when they were four years old. We have also studied two other longitudinal groups of children who were preselected originally to be inhibited or uninhibited—each group representing about 10 to 15 percent of a volunteer sample (see Chapter 4). At every age, significantly more of the extremely inhibited children showed an acceleration of heart rate from the beginning of a testing session to the end one hour later. Further, at 7½ years of age, more of these inhibited children showed a large increase in heart rate when their posture changed from sitting to standing.

However, when we correlated these two cardiac variables with a continuous index of inhibited behavior for the unselected group of children seen at age four, we found no relation between degree of inhibited behavior and any of the heart-rate variables. We then selected two smaller groups of children who were either consistently inhibited or uninhibited over time. A comparison of the two groups revealed that more of the children in the inhibited category showed an acceleration of heart rate from the beginning to the end of the episode and a large increase in heart rate when their posture changed from sitting to standing. We interpret these results as supporting the claim that a lack of correlation among single dimensions in a sample of volunteers may obscure the existence of a distinct psychological category containing a small number of children.

A second illustration of this point is found in an extensive study using a battery of self-report and psychophysiological variables on large groups of normal subjects and patients (Myrtek, 1984). The correlational matrices and the resulting factor analyses revealed minimal relation among the many continuous variables. However, interesting findings emerged when Myrtek examined a combination of variables involving body type and pattern of reaction of heart rate and blood pressure to a change from supine to standing. Myrtek concluded that "classification procedures seem to have more potential and are superior to the global correlative concept," that is, to factor analyses of many continuous variables on a sample of normal subjects (p. 216).

Single dimensions are, of course, legitimate targets of empirical study when we wish to understand the factors that control a dimension like body weight. However, when the primary question is, "Why does one group of animals survive in a particular ecological niche and others do not?" the species is the more useful unit of analysis. I believe this principle applies to psychology.

The social environment usually acts on a type of person, not on a single psychological characteristic. Teachers, for example, chastise a restless child whose history contains no stigmata but will be supportive of restless children who have other qualities characteristic of the category called *attention deficit disorder*. Further, recent research makes clear that mothers react differently to a particular action, depending upon whether that child belongs to the category *son* or *daughter, infant* or *child*. Thus, in studies of personality, a category of person should be the preferred unit of analysis, or, at least, a possible unit of analysis. That suggestion does not imply that we should ignore the study of single dimensions. Knowledge of the conditions that lead to chronically restless behavior would be useful. But investigations restricted to the correlates of single personological dimension (aggression, anxiety, conformity) do not permit robust understanding or prediction of patterns of behavior with others. That victory will require constructs that refer to types or categories of persons (Hinde and Dennis, 1986). David Magnusson (1988) came to the same conclusion after following a large group of Swedish children from 10 to 26 years of age. Single continuous dimensions like aggressivity or restlessness in children were not related in any simple way to adult outcomes. However, a small group of boys who were restless, aggressive, and had lower levels of urinary epinephrine were at greater risk for adolescent problems, especially delinquent behavior. Magnusson concluded that "there is continuity and stability in the patterns of individual functioning. It is individuals who are stable across time, not variables" (p. 186).

Freud was a central figure in accelerating the change from categories of people to continuous psychological processes. During the last half of the nineteenth century, when a strong form of biological determinism was ascendant, patients with specific psychological profiles like aphasia, hysteria, and somnambulism were regarded as members of a qualitative class because they were presumed to have specific lesions or particular dysfunctional brain processes. One popular explanation of hysteria at the turn of the century emphasized a lack of harmonious balance between the two hemispheres (Harrington, 1987). A woman who fainted regularly, or had a sensory anesthesia, was presumed to have a discrete abnormality of brain function. However, when Freud reluctantly came to the conclusion that available knowledge about the brain was not deep enough to permit him to explain neuroses in physiological terms, he abandoned physiological categories, claiming that his theory of neurosis was purely psychological and should not be regarded as referring to anatomical locations. However, that shift entailed a replacement of constructs referring to categories of patients with psychological concepts such as repression, anxiety and libido, which refer to continua. And since that time personality constructs have been similarly conceived.

This error was due, in part, to a failure to differentiate between the aim of an action and its form. Both bonnet and rhesus mothers nurse and protect their infants. However, the inherited behavioral styles of these two species of monkeys are very different. Rhesus mothers hover over their infant and reject intrusions from other animals. Bonnets are more relaxed and are willing to share their infant with other females. During most of this century psychologists assumed that because childhood experiences were the major influence on an individual's hierarchy of motives, such experiences were also the major cause of the variation in the form or style of the motivated acts. But it appears that temperament influences the form of behavior in a major way, and, as a result, we may require typological descriptors.

Describing Types

The preference for quantifying concepts that are amenable to a continuous metric, in contrast with concepts referring to categories of individuals, affects our interpretation of the prose used to describe behavioral phenomena. Imagine a histogram in which the ordinate is the number of children behaving in a particular way (for example, failure to initiate conversation with a stranger) and the abscissa is a set of two dozen different situations in which this class of behavior might occur. Investigators can focus on the differential power of each situation to induce this form of shy behavior or on the children who fall at the extremes of the distribution—those who are extremely shy or are extremely sociable in 90 percent of the situations evaluated. Scientists interested in the variance ascribable to situations are likely to invent constructs that refer to contextual features that are easily changed (for example, number of people, unfamiliarity of the people or objects in the setting). By contrast, those interested in the children who fall at the extremes will invent constructs that refer to the less changeable features of these subjects; for example, inherent physiological states or well-practiced habits established over a long period of time.

Most developmental psychologists remain more interested in the variance attributable to contexts than to persons because such a strategy is in accord with the premise that behavior is malleable to the features of settings. This tension is present in the construction of our sentences. Consider the following two propositions which seem to have the same sense meaning but begin with different ideas.

1. Eating frequently is a characteristic of obese people.
2. Obese people eat frequently.

The topic of sentence 1 is an act that does not occur continuously; hence, the mind focuses on the situations that promote the act of eating. In sentence 2, however, the focus is on the stable characteristics of obese people.

Similarly, sentence 1 below, which begins with an action in a setting, implies a feature of a context that can be changed easily, while sentence 2 implies a set of permanent characteristics belonging to some children.

1. Becoming quiet with unfamiliar adults is a characteristic of inhibited children.
2. Inhibited children become quiet with unfamiliar adults.

Sentence 1 tempts the reader to compare "becoming quiet" with "talking" and to minimize the type of child. Sentence 2 tempts the reader to compare inhibited with uninhibited children and to minimize the influence of the social situation.

The placement in the initial noun position of terms that refer to actions, or processes, in contexts subtly biases the reader or listener to treat the topic as a transient event that is vulnerable to control. Similar initial placement of terms referring to people biases the reader to treat the person's qualities as relatively permanent.[5] One reason for this effect on our inferences is that propositions that begin with a type of person as the noun (for example, *introverted adults*) imply a contrast with other classes of people. Propositions that begin with an action or process in the noun position imply a contrast with another act or process. All descriptions require a choice of terms, and the choice is often guided by an assumed conceptual complementarity or contrasting idea. Four fundamental complementary dimensions that guide description in the sciences include inner-outer, continuous-discontinuous, material-nonmaterial, and, permanent-transient.

Sentences attributing the causes of action to the permanent qualities of individuals, rather than characteristics of contexts, tempt readers to assume that biological processes, rather than contextual events, are causal. The mind–body duality reflects, in part, a complementarity between the more transient and the more permanent qualities of organisms.

5. Roger Brown has presented a different example of the subtle effect of language on inference. In interpreting the sentence "Ted likes Paul" most readers assume that Paul is likeable rather than Ted being an especially friendly person because the predicate *like* evokes the adjective *likeable* which is more appropriate to the object *Paul* than the agent *Ted*. But in "Ted bores Paul" the reader assumes that it is Ted who is boring, not Paul, for similar reasons.

However, concepts that refer to types of organisms, whether animals or humans, must also specify the settings in which the behavior of interest occurs, for no defining behavior occurs in every setting. When we write about inhibited children, we specify that the shy, quiet behavior occurs only in unfamiliar contexts, not at the dinner table. When behavioral biologists write "Wolves are predatory," they recognize that the sentence refers to a specific class of action in a specific species of animal in selected settings. A phagocyte engulfing a bacterium is not regarded as an instance of predation.

It will be theoretically useful, therefore, if social scientists begin to invent constructs that simultaneously provide information on (1) the type of agent, (2) the class of context, and, if possible, (3) the nature of the mediating process. The meaning of the construct should combine all three sources of information. The biological process called *bleaching* refers to a specific chemical change in the pigment of retinal cells following exposure to light. It is never used to describe the lightening of a lizard's skin following an aggressive attack by a larger animal.

When members of our laboratory use the term *inhibition* they intend to refer to an increase in quiet, avoidant, timid behavior to unfamiliar incentives in children who were born with a certain physiological bias. They do not mean the display of timidity in any child on any occasion—for example, confronting a snarling dog. As a domain of inquiry matures, robust phenomena become linked to specific contexts and entities so that the name for the phenomenon automatically implies a set of contexts, objects, and mediating processes. However, the delineation of these more fully articulated constructs will require both more, and different, sources of evidence. New data delineate the boundaries of the phenomenon, sometimes expanding their sphere, sometimes restricting them, and frequently changing the meaning of the concept chosen to describe the events.

The New Metaphors

The recent research on temperamental types awards considerable influence to brain biochemistry and, in so doing, is changing the metaphors chosen to describe the determinants of human behavior. Modern neuroscience implies that the central nervous system operates in accord with a set of rules dictated by the structure of the brain and the actions of neurotransmitters. Some humans are anxious or shy in part because that is how their central nervous system is constructed; the person's conscious will is limited in its power to alter these reactions.

A similar implication can be detected in the research of the last half-century by psychologists who assumed that variation in the generic qualities of self-esteem and anxiety, produced by variation in social rejection and task failure, would account for differences in shyness among children and adults. But for both social rejection/ acceptance and task failure/success the actions of others and local circumstances outside the complete control of the person were significant causes of variation in self-esteem and anxiety. Thus, whether the primary influence rests with biochemically mediated neural circuits, or the whims of others, the individual is portrayed as a partial victim of circumstances over which he or she has incomplete control.

By contrast, the two dominating nineteenth-century metaphors for human nature—conservation of energy and natural selection—treated the individual as a primary unit. The person could act to alter his or her profile of energy expenditure or to seek a more adaptive niche. Thus, the new metaphor in which invisible events on chromosomes and between neurons hold the share of power generates a special view of our relation to nature.

The paradox, however, is that one of the defining premises of Western civilization is the belief that each person is an active, not a passive, agent in his or her life itinerary. A partial resolution of this paradox is possible if we assume that the active component refers to each person's response to fate. Although each of us has no control over our heredity and only limited control over how others treat us, we can insist that each individual has the will to cope with the consequences of chance's whims. Odysseus could do little to subvert Athena's decision to beach him high on a rock in the middle of a storm. Dylan Thomas exhorts us to rage, rage against the dying of the light.

Contemporary understanding of human temperamental types is more penetrating than the views held by Kretschmer or Sheldon. This progress required more careful measurement of both behavioral and biological variables, a respect for the power of context, and a developmental orientation that acknowledged dynamic changes in phenotypic displays as a consequence of maturation and experience. We must now invent a new set of constructs for temperamental categories in which biological, psychological, and contextual features are combined. Put plainly, it is time for a more powerful vocabulary.

It makes me furious not to be a poet—to be so ponderously tethered to prose. I'd like to be able to create those sparkling, absurd objects: poems, resembling a ship in a bottle, which are like an instant's eternity. But there's something throttled in me—my feelings haven't found their language . . . I don't know what the solution is . . . I prefer these two [lines] which apparently come from a song:

"Oh you'll find boulders on every roadway,
On every roadway you'll find some woe . . ."
(J. P. Sartre, *The War Diaries,* p. 314)

4

Inhibited and
Uninhibited Children

One of the few obvious behavioral differences among humans that is not correlated with social class is the initial reaction to unfamiliar or challenging situations for which the person does not have an immediate coping reaction. Some children and adults become quiet and restrained while they assess the situation and their resources before acting. Others act spontaneously, as though the distinctions between familiar and novel were of minimal psychological consequence. The situation that reveals this quality most often in children and adults is an encounter with unfamiliar people, especially if the context is evaluative. Of course, it is rare to find many people who are consistently shy and affectively restrained or outgoing and spontaneous in every social context. There is, however, a small group of children—estimated to be about 10 to 15 percent—who consistently bring one or the other of these behavioral styles to such situations.

Almost every commentator on human nature, from Hippocrates to modern personologists, has noted these two contrasting characteristics, and empirical indices of these constructs are among the most stable and heritable in contemporary psychology (Conley, 1985; Floderus-Myrhed, Pedersen, and Rasmuson 1980; Loehlin, 1982; Plomin, 1986). Further, many theorists have assumed that physiological processes make a partial contribution to the two styles (Thomas and Chess, 1977). Jung's (1924) complementary categories of introversion–extraversion, which represent the most complete elaboration of this idea, must have appealed to European and American minds; these terms continue to be the most popular names for these classes of behavior, even though most American scholars ignored Jung's more extensive theoretical analyses of personality.

Jung's Conception

Jung regarded introversion and extraversion as complementary processes, similar to the Chinese conceptualization of Yin and Yang. Every adult's animus (or anima) possesses one of these biases as its primary quality, but each person also tries to achieve a psychological balance by adopting, in surface behavior, qualities that define the complementary type, which Jung called the *persona*. Gellhorn (1967) invented the terms *ergotrophic* and *trophotrophic,* which came close to being physiological parallels to introversion and extraversion, to describe the complementary relation between the activity of the sympathetic and parasympathetic nervous sytems.

Jung chose the targets of a person's interests as a distinctive feature differentiating the two types. The extravert is concerned with people and objects; the introvert chooses to concentrate on thoughts, fantasy, and feelings. Jung wrote,

> The names and forms in which the mechanism of introversion and extraversion has been conceived are extremely diverse, and are, as a rule, adapted only to the standpoint of the individual observer. Notwithstanding the diversity of the formulations, the common basis or fundamental idea shines constantly through; namely, in the one case an outward movement of interest toward the object, and in the other a movement of interest away from the object, towards subject and his own psychological processes. (Jung, 1924, p. 11)

Intrapsychic processes take precedence over motivation and action in Jung's list of the four psychological features that distinguish introverts from extraverts: thinking, feeling, sensation, and intuition. The major difference between introverts and extraverts is in the quality of their consciousness, not in their everyday behaviors. Perhaps that is one reason why American psychologists have ignored Jung, for Watson and the behaviorists that followed him took exactly the opposite position by making subjective processes secondary to action.

Jung believed that inheritance of a strong or a weak nervous system would explain the two types. Although it is unclear whether Jung borrowed this idea from Pavlov, he obviously appropriated Freud's concept of libidinal energy, while changing its primary function. Introverts, Jung suggested, have more intense primary forces and so appear more tense than extraverts. Because introverts have more libido available to be aroused by challenge or novelty, the secondary, or assimilative, function requires a longer time to recover. Thus, the brain of the extravert possesses a "higher restitutive capacity than that of the introvert" (p. 355; see Strelau, 1985, for a modern version of this view). Modern investigators might rephrase this idea and say that both central nervous system arousal following an encounter with an unfamiliar event and the time required to assimilate such experiences are greater in introverts. As we shall see, Jung's speculation was prescient, for the children my colleagues and I call *inhibited* show greater arousal of the sympathetic and hypothalamic-pituitary-adrenal axis following challenge and unfamiliarity and require more time to adapt to unfamiliar situations than uninhibited children. Although Jung did not wish to underestimate the importance of parental behavior in sculpting a child's future profile, he believed "that the decisive factor must be looked for in the disposition of the child" (p. 415), a hypothesis that is being verified in many laboratories.

Animal Work

Comparative psychologists and zoologists have noticed two contrasting clusters of behaviors, similar to Jung's concepts, that differentiate among species or even within strains of closely related animals. Schneirla (1965), who named the contrast approach-withdrawal, implied that the balance between the two processes might distinguish among animals from the same or similar strains. Like Jung, Schneirla also tied withdrawal to sympathetic arousal, but he believed prenatal experiences (rather than genetics) produced the bias favoring one or the other of these dispositions. The facts supporting this class of differences are persuasive. Dogs, mice, rats, wolves, cats, cows, monkeys, and even paradise fish differ intraspecifically in the tendency to approach or to avoid novelty (Royce, 1955; Murphey, Duarte and Penendo, 1980; Blanchard, Flannelly and Blanchard, 1986; McDonald, 1983; Csanyi and Gervai, 1986; Dantzer and Mormede, 1985; Adamec and Stark-Adamec, 1986; Cooper, Schmidt and Barrett, 1983). Both Suomi (1987) and Stevenson-Hinde, Stillwell-Barnes, and Zunz (1980) have reported that laboratory-reared rhesus monkeys differ in degree of fearfulness and maintain these differences from infancy through puberty. In addition, the physiological differences between the fearful and less fearful monkeys in Suomi's studies are similar to those we shall describe for inhibited and uninhibited children.

The most extensive study of the genetic origins of these behavioral qualities was published by Scott and Fuller over twenty years ago. Scott and Fuller (1974) studied five breeds of dogs—basenji, beagle, cocker spaniel, Shetland sheep, and fox terriers in the Jackson Laboratories in Bar Harbor, Maine. Over 250 puppies from the five breeds were studied longitudinally from birth, with some puppies cross-fostered to mothers from a different breed. An additional group of about 200 dogs was the product of matings between breeds, including back-crosses. In one of the more sensitive assessment procedures, a handler took the puppy from a holding cage and returned it to the common room. The handler then placed the puppy one or two feet away, stood still, and noted the animal's behavior. The handler then slowly turned and walked toward the puppy, squatted down, held out his hand, stroked the puppy, and finally picked it up. The puppies classed as timid ran to the corner of the room, crouched down, and gave a high-pitched yelp early in this sequence. The five breeds differed dramatically in the degree of timidity shown in this situation; basenjis, terriers, and shelties were much more timid than beagles and cocker spaniels. However, the rearing environment made a significant contribution to this behavior, for if the puppies of the various breeds were raised in a home rather than in the laboratory, they showed less extreme signs of timidity.

Differences among the five breeds in resting heart rate revealed a correlation between timidity and a high heart rate. Basenjis had the highest heart rates, cocker spaniels the lowest, and beagles, shelties, and terriers were in the middle. Further, the rank order of the five breeds on a measure of "disposition to escape" was very similar to the rank order for the heart rate scores, with basenjis highest on both variables and cocker spaniels lowest. A factor analysis of the data from a large sample of dogs from all the breeds revealed a factor characterized by a high heart rate and behavioral timidity. An earlier analysis of similar data from the Jackson Laboratories revealed a major factor defined by early motor freezing, withdrawal to novelty, and high blood pressure (Royce, 1955). Years later Goddard and Beilharz (1985), who studied puppies from four different breeds (laboradors, Australian kelpies, boxers, and German shepherds), found that avoidance of unfamiliar objects on a noisy street differentiated the four breeds, with the German shepherds most, and the labradors least, fearful of novelty. Among three closely related species of macaque monkeys, crabeaters are most likely to display signs of fear while rhesus react with anger or protest (Clarke and Mason, in press).

A series of studies of defensive versus aggressive cats, summarized by Adamec and Stark-Adamec (1986), provides some clues to the possible neural bases for these differences. Ordinary house cats (*Felis catus*) vary in their disposition to retreat from or approach unfamiliar rooms and humans, as well as to avoid or attack rats. A small group, about 15 percent, show prolonged inhibition of approach to novel events and people and also fail to attack rats, while a larger complementary group—about 40 percent—show no tendency to retreat from novel objects and typically attack rats. The avoidant-defensive cats show both greater neural activity in the basomedial amygdala when a rat is introduced, as well as larger evoked potentials in the ventromedial hypothalamus following stimulation of the basomedial amygdala, implying greater synaptic transmission from the amygdala to the hypothalamus. By contrast, electrical stimulation of the basomedial amygdala of aggressive cats produces larger potentials in the ventral hippocampus. These facts imply, although they do not prove, that the connections between the amygdala and the hypothalamus and sympathetic chain are more excitable in defensive cats, while the connections between the amygdala and the motor actions serving attack are more excitable in the nondefensive cats.

Similarly, strains of rats bred to differ in fearful behavior also vary in the profile of neural discharge of a selected group of neurons in the central nucleus of the amygdala, suggesting that the behavioral differences between the strains are associated with the differential responsiveness of these cells (Henke, 1988). (See Cubiccioti et al., 1986, for differences in physiological responsiveness between squirrel monkeys and titi monkeys, and Kling et al., 1987, for the response of the amygdala to novelty.)

Longitudinal Studies of Inhibited and Uninhibited Children

No one disputes that some two-year-olds are consistently shy, timid, and wary with strangers or in unfamiliar contexts, while others are immediately sociable and exploratory. These contrasting qualities were the only ones preserved from the first three years of life through childhood and adolescence in the Fels Research Institute's longitudinal population (Kagan and Moss, 1962). A subsequent longitudinal study with infants and children from Caucasian and Chinese families living in and near Boston found that behavioral timidity in unfamiliar situations and a stable heart rate, which were correlated, were the best preserved characteristics from 3 through 29 months of age (Kagan, Kearsley, and Zelazo, 1978; see also Plomin and Rowe, 1979). It is important to emphasize that the defining feature of this classification is initial behavior to unfamiliarity and challenge, not habitual behavior in familiar contexts, a fact also emphasized by Suomi (1987) in his study of comparable differences in rhesus monkeys.

Our laboratory has been studying two independent groups of Caucasian children from intact, middle- and working-class families who were selected from larger samples when they were either 21 or 31 months of age because the child was either consistently shy, timid, and fearful (we call such children *behaviorally inhibited*) or sociable, bold, and fearless (*uninhibited*) when exposed to unfamiliar rooms, people, and objects. We had to screen over 400 children, using both telephone interviews and laboratory observations, in order to find 54 consistently inhibited and 53 consistently uninhibited children, with equal numbers of boys and girls in each group (see Garcia-Coll, Kagan, and Reznick, 1984; Snidman, 1984, for details). (It is of interest that when German kindergarten teachers in Munich were asked to select only those children who were extremely shy, only 15 percent of the total school population of 1,100 was chosen; Cranach et al., 1978; only 8 percent of 101 Parisian children, studied from birth, were regarded as extremely shy and timid at 18 months; Dargassies, 1986).

The original index of inhibition on cohort 1 at 21 months of age was based on behavior with an unfamiliar woman, unfamiliar toys, a woman displaying some acts that were somewhat difficult to recall and to imitate, a metal robot, and temporary separation from the mother. The behaviors that were regarded as operational definitions of inhibition were long latencies to interact with or retreat from the unfamiliar people or objects, staying near the mother, and cessation of play or vocalization. The index of inhibited behavior in the second cohort at 31 months of age was based primarily on behavior with an unfamiliar child of the same sex and age and behavior with an unfamiliar woman. However, the definitions of inhibition were similar to those used with the first cohort, namely, long latencies to interact with the child, adult, or toys and long periods of time remaining near the mother. Each of these groups has been seen several times since the original selection. Cohort 1 was seen again at 4 years, 5½ years, and 7½ years of age. Cohort 2 was seen at 43 months, 5½ years, and 7½ years of age (see Kagan et al., 1984; Kagan, Reznick, and Snidman 1987; Reznick et al., 1986; Snidman, 1984, for additional details).

At the last assessment at 7½ years there were 41 children in each cohort—a loss of about 20 percent of the original sample. The phenotypic display of the two temperamental tendencies changed with age because of learning and maturation. A two-year-old will become uncertain in an unfamiliar room with unfamiliar objects, but older children require more potent incentives, especially unfamiliar children and adults. Thus, the specific laboratory procedures we used changed across the four evaluations.

The index of inhibition on the second assessment (3½ or 4 years) was based on behavior in two separate 40-minute laboratory play sessions with an unfamiliar child of the same sex and age with both mothers present. At 5½ years the children in both cohorts were observed in four different unfamiliar situations. The indexes of inhibition, for each situation, were based on: (1) long latencies to initiate play or interact with an unfamiliar child as well as time spent near the mother in a laboratory playroom, (2) spatial isolation and infrequent interaction with classmates in the child's school setting, (3) long latencies to talk and infrequent spontaneous comments with a female examiner who administered a 90-minute cognitive battery (including recall and recognition memory, match to sample, and discrimination of pictures), and (4) reluctance to play with novel toys suggestive of risk in an unfamiliar laboratory room (a large black box with a hole, a beam set at an angle to the floor). The theoretically relevant variables from each situation were aggregated to form a composite index of behavioral inhibition.

The index of behavioral inhibition at 7½ years was based on two situations separated by several months. The first was a laboratory play situation involving 7 to 10 unfamiliar children of the same age and sex; a single unfamiliar child does not generate sufficient uncertainty in a child this old. Approximately 50 minutes was devoted to structured, competitive games and a total of 30 minutes to unstructured free play intervals interposed between each of the games. The two variables indexing behavioral inhibition were: infrequent spontaneous comments to the other children and long periods of playing or standing apart from any other child in the room. The second assessment context was an individual testing session with an unfamiliar female examiner. The two variables were: latency to the sixth spontaneous comment to the examiner and the total number of spontaneous comments over the testing session. The results are similar if latency to any of the first six comments is used as the component of the index. The inter-coder reliabilities (correlation coefficients) for the variables quantified from video tapes were generally above 0.90 at each age.

Preservation of Social Behavior

There was moderate preservation of inhibited and uninhibited behavioral styles from 21 months through 7½ years with interage correlations averaging 0.5. About three-fourths of the children classified as either inhibited or uninhibited at 21 or 31 months retained their expected behavioral classification at 7½ years, and one-third of the original group of the inhibited two-year-olds were still unusually shy. Although about half of the children changed their extremely inhibited profile over the five-to-six-year interval, very few were as spontaneous and sociable as the typical uninhibited child. A smaller number— about 10 percent—of the original group of uninhibited children had become shy and timid at 7 years of age.

The qualities of inhibition and lack of inhibition generalized to an ecologically natural context. Children originally classified as inhibited were more isolated, withdrawn, and quiet than uninhibited children when they were observed in their kindergarten classrooms at 5½ years of age (Gersten, 1986). An extremely sensitive index of inhibition is seen at age 4 when a child meets an unfamiliar peer of the same sex and age in a play situation with both mothers present. The inhibited child stays close to the mother, remains quiet, and does not initiate play with the other child. However, by 5 to 6 years of age, such a situation is less sensitive because most children have learned how to interact with a single, unfamiliar peer. At this age, the child's behavior with an unfamiliar adult in a testing situation better discriminates the two groups. At 7½ years most of the formerly inhibited children waited more than 10 minutes before making their sixth spontaneous comment to a friendly female examiner and, additionally, made less than 40 spontaneous comments to her across the

90-minute testing session. By contrast, the majority of the uninhibited children issued their sixth spontaneous comment before five minutes had elapsed and made more than 70 spontaneous comments to the examiner.

Inhibited children were also shy and quiet at 7½ years when they were with a large group of unfamiliar children. The two variables that best discriminated inhibited from uninhibited children were the total number of spontaneous utterances across all the episodes and, second, the amount of time the child stood apart from other children during the free-play intervals between the structured games—defined as the proportion of time each child was greater than an arm's length from any other child. The formerly inhibited children were more often standing or playing distant from any other child and much less likely to talk either to another child or to the two women monitoring the session. A frequent scene during the play sessions was a cluster of three or four children playing close to one another, often talking, and one or two children standing or playing alone 3 to 12 feet from the center of social activity. These isolated, quiet children were typically those who had been classified as inhibited five or six years earlier.

When the index of inhibition from the testing situation (long latency to talk and few spontaneous comments) was combined with the peer-play index (playing apart from peers and not talking) to create a single aggregate index of inhibition, 77 percent of the children classified as inhibited but only 26 percent of those originally classified as uninhibited at 21 months were above the median on this aggregate index.

The 7½-year-old inhibited children had more unusual fears than the uninhibited children, including fear of talking in the classroom, attending summer camp, remaining alone in the house, taking out the rubbish at night, or going to their bedroom alone at bedtime. Almost three-fourths of the 7½-year-old inhibited children in cohort 2 had one or more unusual fears, compared with only 20 percent of the uninhibited children. Further, 35 percent of the siblings of the inhibited children had one or more of these unusual fears, while not one sibling of an uninhibited child had an unusual fear. Finally, two-thirds of the mothers of inhibited children, compared with only one-fourth of the uninhibited, reported either chronic fears, social anxiety, or panic disorder during their adult lives.

The two groups also differed in their motoric style. During the testing situations more inhibited children sat with a tense posture, often displaying small finger movements and speaking in a soft voice. The uninhibited children were more likely to make large trunk movements and to speak with normal loudness. The faces of the inhibited children maintained a serious expression and they smiled or laughed infrequently. On the second or third assessment, when asked to fall backward onto a mattress, more inhibited children either refused or fell back to a sitting position. The uninhibited children let their bodies fall freely so that their head struck the mattress. The descriptors that capture the total quality of the inhibited child are quiet, tense, and affectively subdued. The best adjectives for the uninhibited child are talkative, relaxed, and spontaneous.

Cognitive Performance and Inhibition

Some cognitive functions are more easily disrupted by task-related stress in inhibited than uninhibited children. Deterioration in recognition and recall memory performance is a sensitive psychological index of the uncertainty created in a child by an evaluating adult and the possibility of task failure (Messer, 1968). At 5½ years of age significantly more inhibited than uninhibited children showed a loss in accuracy of recognition memory following a series of difficult cognitive tests. At 7½ years of age we replaced the recognition memory test with a test of recall memory. After the child had received electrodes for the recording of heart rate and had remained quiet for a 1-minute baseline heart rate recording, a pre-stress memory recall task was administered. The child listened to a male voice narrate a 3-minute story about a boy and a girl. When the story was over the child was given a set of 18 colored pictures—each about 3 × 3 inches—and asked to arrange the pictures so that they matched the chronology of the story just heard. (Each child was given an initial practice story to acquaint him or her with the requirements of the task.) Subsequently, the child was administered four different, difficult cognitive tasks that involved some failures, followed by a parallel version of the recall memory test. The child then heard a narration that was a continuation of the initial pre-stress story and at its completion was given another set of 18 pictures and asked to arrange them to match the chronology of the story. A significantly larger proportion of inhibited than uninhibited children in cohort 1 showed poorer performance on the second than on the initial recall memory test (59 percent versus 31 percent, chi square = 3.1 $p < .05$), suggesting that the intervening cognitive tests generated more uncertainty/arousal in the inhibited children (see Doerr and Hokanson, 1965, for a parallel phenomenon). However, the inhibited children took much longer to arrange the pictures, implying a caution that was motivated by a desire to avoid making errors.

A second procedure administered at 7½ years suggests that task-generated uncertainty also impairs the inhibited child's ability to make fine perceptual discriminations. Following a set of appropriate practice items, each child was shown a series of 32 pairs of chromatic pictures of people or objects. The child was told that some of the pairs were identical and some differed in a very subtle way (a button missing on a shirt; a different angle of a person's foot). The child had to decide if the pair of pictures projected on the screen were identical or different and, if different, to indicate the exact nature of the difference. Half of the pictures were similar and half different; half were neutral in content and half had an affective content that involved fear or anxiety (a person bleeding, a person tied with rope). If inhibited children have a lower threshold of arousal to uncertainty, they should show impaired discrimination on the affective scenes but not necessarily on the neutral scenes; the uninhibited children should perform equally well on both sets. This expectation was affirmed, for more inhibited than uninhibited children in cohort 1 made more errors on the affective than on the neutral scenes (73 versus 36 percent; chi square $= 5.4$, $p < .05$). Moreover, 40 percent of the inhibited, but only 10 percent of the uninhibited, children showed both indexes of reaction to stress (that is, more errors on the recall of the second story and more errors on the affective pictures).

These procedures also may help to discriminate between those temperamentally inhibited children who have become more sociable by 7½ years and the temperamentally uninhibited children. Although a small number of formerly inhibited children showed sociable behavior with the examiner and peers, all made more errors on the affect than on the neutral scenes. By contrast, neither of the two formerly uninhibited girls whose external demeanor had become timid and shy showed an increase in errors on the second recall story or an excess of affect over neutral errors on the discrimination task.

However, the easy generation of uncertainty characteristic of inhibited children might lead them to be more accurate in recognition memory when the events are moderately threatening or arousing, rather than neutral, as they were in the laboratory procedure described above. To determine whether inhibited children might show this asymmetry in recognition memory—that is, better recognition memory for emotionally arousing events than for neutral ones—Cybele Raver retested children from both cohorts when they were between 8 and 9 years of age. The test materials were color photographs of adult male and female faces displaying facial expressions that were emotionally neutral or smiling, on the one hand, or fearful, sad, angry, or disgusted, on the other.

Of the children retested, 28 children had been classified at either 21 or 31 months as inhibited and 26 children had been classified as uninhibited. We also tested 18 children who had been observed in the laboratory at 21 or 31 months because their parents' answers on a telephone interview had suggested they might be inhibited or uninhibited, but their laboratory behavior was not consistent enough across episodes for them to be included in the longitudinal study. Thus, these 18 children are neither representative of a random sample of volunteers nor as extreme in their behavior as the groups called inhibited and uninhibited. All children were tested at home, usually in the afternoon after they had returned from school.

Each child first inspected a series of 48 color photographs, half male and half female, devoting five seconds to each photograph. Each facial photograph, taken against a homogeneously white background, showed only the face and upper trunk of the person. Each person who posed for a photo produced two facial expressions, one neutral and one emotional, either happy, sad, angry, fearful, or disgusted. Twenty-four of the familiarization photos had either neutral or happy expressions, and 24 had a negative affect (seven fear faces, five sad, eight angry, and four disgusted). After a 10-minute delay during which the examiner, an adult female, talked with the child about neutral matters, the child was administered a test set of 48 photographs containing 24 old and 24 new pictures and asked to say which of the 48 photos had been seen 10 minutes earlier and which were new. The test set contained half neutral-happy photos and half with a negative emotional expression.

The average percent of photographs correctly recognized by all children was 81 percent, but over 95 percent of the recognition errors were to the familiar pictures; that is, most errors occurred because the children said that they did not recognize a photo they had actually inspected earlier. Neither the gender of the face in the photograph nor that of the child was related to errors. All children were more accurate in remembering the negative affect than the neutral pictures; the difference between total errors on neutral-happy faces minus the total number of errors to the negative affect faces was +3. This result is reasonable, because the faces with negative affects were more discrepant from every-day experience and should have generated a brief change in emotional state. But inhibited children had a larger difference score (4.0) than did either the uninhibited (1.9), or control children (3.0).

The inhibited, compared with the uninhibited, children were most accurate on the anger or fear photographs which, we suggest, were more arousing than the faces displaying sadness. It appears that inhibited children were provoked to a more vigilant state by these emotionally arousing faces.

The fact that inhibited children made more recall and recognition memory errors than uninhibited children with neutral information, following cognitive stress, but fewer recognition errors to more arousing information implies that emotion influences memory in different ways for inhibited children. On the one hand, the affect generated by the stress of a series of difficult tests, which we might call *task-related anxiety*, interferes with recognition and recall memory for neutral information. But the affect generated by threatening stimuli, which we might call *stimulus-related arousal*, seems to facilitate recognition memory.

An Unselected Cohort

Our laboratory has recently completed a third longitudinal study of Caucasian middle-class children of both sexes who were not selected to be extreme on the two behavioral profiles. The children in cohort 3 were observed initially at 14 months ($n = 100$) and again at 20 ($n = 91$), 32 ($n = 76$), and 48 months of age ($n = 77$). The indexes of inhibition at 14 and 20 months were based on behavior with an unfamiliar examiner and with unfamiliar toys in laboratory rooms. The index of inhibition at 32 months was based on behavior in a 30-minute free-play situation with two other unfamiliar children of the same sex and age with all three mothers present. The index of inhibition at 48 months was based on behavior with an unfamiliar child of the same sex and age, with an unfamiliar examiner in a testing situation, and in an unfamiliar room containing objects suggestive of risk. The original variation in inhibited behavior for the entire group at 14 months was correlated with the variation at 20 and 32 months (r = .52, .44, $p < .01$), but the indexes at 14 and 20 months did not predict differences in behavioral inhibition at 4 years of age. However, when we restricted the analysis to those children who fell at the top and bottom 20 percent of the distribution of behavioral inhibition at both 14 and 20 months (13 children in each group), the two groups were significantly different at 4 years of age (t = 2.69, $p < .01$). Almost half of the inhibited, but only 8 percent of the uninhibited, group had a positive standard score on the index of inhibition at 4 years of age. This finding, together with the data from cohorts 1 and 2, implies that the constructs *inhibited* and *uninhibited* refer to qualitative categories of children. These terms do not refer to a behavioral continuum ranging from timidity to sociability in a volunteer sample of children, even though such a continuum exists. Psychiatrists also differentiate between bipolar depressive patients and a random sample of adults, even though reports of sadness from both patients and nonpatients form a continuum.

Physiology and Inhibition

As noted earlier, intraspecific variation in behavioral withdrawal to novelty in rats, cats, and monkeys is often correlated with physiological reactions that imply greater arousal in selected limbic sites, especially the amygdala and its projections to the hypothalamus. If this relation were present in humans, inhibited children should show more activity in biological systems that originate in these sites. Three such systems are the sympathetic chain, reticular formation with its projections to skeletal muscles, and the hypothalamic-pituitary-adrenal axis.

Sympathetic Reactivity

Five potential indexes of sympathetic reactivity include a high and minimally variable heart rate, as well as heart-rate acceleration, pupillary dilation, and norepinephrine level to psychological stress and challenge. We measured each child's heart period and heart-period variability both under minimally stressful baseline conditions and during moderately stressful cognitive tasks on every one of the four assessments. Heart-period variability was the average standard deviation of the interbeat intervals during the trials of the test episodes.

Mean heart rate and variability were always inversely correlated—a higher heart rate was associated with lower variability—both under relaxed conditions and during cognitive activity (product moment correlations were between -0.6 and -0.7). Individual differences in heart rate and variability were preserved from 21 months to 7.5 years in cohort 1 ($r = .62, p < .001$ for heart rate; $r = .54, p < .001$ for variability), and from 31 months to 5½ years for cohort 2 ($r = .59$, $p < .001$ for heart rate and $r = .61, p < .001$ for variability). Further, the index of inhibited behavior was typically associated with a higher and more stable heart rate on the early evaluations (average $r = 0.4$), but on the last assessment at 7½ years this relation was less robust ($r = 0.3$). However, the inhibited children with the highest heart rates on the earlier assessments were most likely to have remained very inhibited through 7½ years, compared with the inhibited children who had lower heart rates earlier. The heart rate at 5½ years for cohort 2 children was an exceptionally good predictor of preservation of inhibited behavior. Sixty-percent of the inhibited children with high heart rates remained unusually inhibited through 7½ years, while only one inhibited child with a low heart rate maintained an extreme inhibited style. For cohort 1, 84 percent of inhibited children with a high heart rate (above the median value) remained very inhibited, and only one inhibited child with a low heart rate continued to be very shy and timid. Although most of the inhibited children with a lower heart rate had lost their extreme shyness, many were still less spontaneous than the average uninhibited child. It is relevant to note that heart rate in young children is heritable, and shy children with a high and minimally variable heart rate are the most inhibited at 14 months of age (Fox, personal communication). Further, unusual fears at both 5½ and 7½ years (of violence on television or in movies, of kidnappers, or of going to the bedroom alone in the evening) were most frequent in inhibited children with the highest heart rates (60 percent of the group) and rare in uninhibited children with very low heart rates.

In addition, at every age inhibited children were more likely than uninhibited ones to show an increase in heart rate, (about 10 beats per minute) across the trials of a test or across the entire battery of cognitive tests. This increase in heart rate was also found among the cohort 3 children who had extreme scores on the index of inhibition at 4 years of age. Further, the inhibited children were more likely to attain their maximal heart rate early in the testing session, usually during the first cognitive procedure following the initial baseline. We also evaluated, for the first time at 7½ years in cohort 2 and at 4 years in cohort 3, the change in heart rate when the child was asked to change his or her posture from sitting to standing. Inhibited children showed a significantly larger increase in mean heart rate (10 bpm) over a 60-second period than uninhibited children, despite a slightly higher heart rate during the preceding sitting baseline. This result suggests that the inhibited children maintained a brisker sympathetic response to the drop in blood pressure that accompanies the rise to a standing position. In addition, the inhibited children in cohort 2 showed a significantly higher diastolic, but not a higher systolic, blood pressure during the testing session at 7½ years, implying greater sympathetic tone in the vessels of the arterial tree. Almost twice as many inhibited compared with uninhibited children had high values on both acceleration to the posture change and diastolic blood pressure (66 versus 37 percent).

Several months after the laboratory session with cohort 1 at 7½ years we recorded the child's heart rate during one night of sleep. We eliminated the first and last hours of sleep on the assumption that sleep would be lighter during these times, and examination of the continuous respiration record allowed us to eliminate epochs of active sleep. The mean sleeping heart rate was correlated with mean heart rate obtained in the laboratory at each of the four ages ($r = .37$, .40, .61, and .49, $p < .05$) and was related to two of the four components of the composite index of inhibition at 5½ years: reluctance to play with novel toys suggestive of risk in an unfamiliar room, and shy, restrained behavior with an unfamiliar peer.

Pupillary dilation, which is another potential index of sympathetic activity, was assessed only at 5½ years. Although both cohorts showed a reliable increase in pupil size of about 0.3 mm to cognitive test items (an increase of about 5 percent), the inhibited children in both cohorts had significantly larger pupil diameters during test questions as well as during the intertrial intervals between test items.

Muscle Tension

Projections from limbic structures to the skeletal muscles of the larynx and vocal cords also appear to be at higher levels of excitability in inhibited children. Increased tension in these muscles is usually accompanied by a decrease in the variability of the pitch periods of vocal utterances, called *perturbation*. The increased muscle tension can be due to discharge of the nucleus ambiguus as well as sympathetic activity that constricts arterioles serving the muscles of the larynx and vocal folds. Because the vocal cords do not maintain a steady rate as they open and close, the perturbations in the rate at which they open and close is a consequence of many factors, one of which is the degree of tension in the laryngeal muscles. We measured the vocal perturbation of single-word utterances at 5½ years in cohort 1 and 3½ years in cohort 2. The inhibited, compared with the uninhibited, children showed a significantly greater decrease in vocal perturbation when the single words were spoken under moderate versus low stress. The inhibited children also showed less variability in the fundamental frequency of all the single-word utterances spoken during the episode (Coster, 1986).

Urinary Norepinephrine

Norephinephrine is the primary neurotransmitter in the postganglionic synapses of the peripheral sympathetic nervous system. A urine sample collected from each child in cohort 1 at the end of the test battery at 5½ years was assayed for norepinephrine and its derivatives (normetanephrine, MHPG, and VMA) using mass fragmentography. Concentrations of each compound were transformed to micrograms per gram of creatinine, and a composite index of total norepinephrine activity was computed. There was a very modest correlation between this index and inhibited behavior at both 4 and 5½ years ($r = .34, p < .05$ with the index at age 4; $r = .31, p < .05$ with the index at age 5½ years).

Salivary Cortisol

To assess activity in the hypothalamic-pituitary-adrenal axis, we gathered samples of saliva at both 5½ and 7½ years from the children in cohorts 1 and 2. The children in cohort 1 with early morning cortisol values above the median value for their age group on both occasions were likely to have been classified as inhibited at 21 months (11 of 12). By contrast, only 4 of 12 children with low cortisol values at both ages were originally classified as inhibited. Similarly, cohort 2 children with high cortisol values at both 5½ and 7½ years were more likely to be inhibited than those with low values. When we pooled the data from cohorts 1 and 2, 88 percent of the children who had high cortisol values at both ages had been classified originally as inhibited, in contrast to 30 percent with low cortisol values. Finally, 8 of the 12 children from the unselected cohort who remained extremely inhibited at both 32 and 48 months of age had high cortisol values at both ages, in contrast to only 3 of 13 who had low cortisol values. Combining the data from all three samples revealed that the inhibited children were more likely to have consistently higher cortisol values than the uninhibited children ($p < 5 \times 10^{-5}$).

Aggregate of Physiological Variables

With the exception of heart rate and heart-rate variability, correlations among the remaining physiological variables were low, ranging from $-.22$ to $+.33$ with a median coefficient of $+.10$. This phenomenon has been noted by others (Nesse et al., 1985). However, it is likely that an aggregate index of physiological activity might be more highly correlated with inhibited behavior because any single variable could be the result of a factor unrelated to the hypothetical processes mediating inhibited and uninhibited behavior. Pooling several indexes would dilute the contribution of any of these other factors. For example, a child who did not belong to the inhibited category but who was highly motivated to solve the cognitive problems might show a high and minimally variable heart rate and a large pupil, but this child should show average cortisol levels and variability in the vocal perturbation index.

Consider the following analogy. High body temperature, fatigue, thoracic discomfort, and pneumococci in the sputum are not highly correlated in a random sample of the population. But persons with high values on all four variables meet the criteria for a special disease category. We averaged the standard scores for eight peripheral psychophysiological variables gathered at 5½ years on cohort 1 to create a composite index of physiological arousal (mean heart period, heart period variability, and pupillary dilation during cognitive tests, total norepinephrine activity, mean cortisol level at home and in the laboratory, variability of the pitch periods of vocal utterances under cognitive stress, and the standard deviation of the fundamental frequency values of the vocal utterances). There was a substantial positive relation between this composite physiological index and the index of inhibition at every age ($r = .70$ with the index at 21 months, $r = .64$ with the index at 7½ years of age).

Theoretical Meanings

A majority of the 1½ or 2½-year-old children who had been selected because they were extremely shy, quiet, and restrained in unfamiliar contexts became 7-year-olds who were quiet, cautious, and socially avoidant with peers and adults. A majority of children selected because they were extremely sociable and affectively spontaneous became talkative and socially interactive at 7 years of age. However, the preservation of these two behavioral styles, albeit modest and different in form at the two ages, holds only for children selected originally to be extreme in their behavior. There is no predictive relation between indexes of inhibited behavior assessed during the second and fourth years in an unselected group of children. Only when we restricted the analysis to the behavioral extremes in cohort 3 did we find preservation of the two behavioral categories as well as an association between inhibition and both heart-rate acceleration to mild stress and high early-morning levels of salivary cortisol.

The behavioral differences between the two groups were most consistently associated with peripheral physiological variables implying greater sympathetic reactivity among the inhibited children, especially larger cardiac accelerations to cognitive activity and to a postural change from sitting to standing. We suggest, albeit speculatively, that most of the children we call inhibited belong to a qualitatively distinct category of infants who were born with a lower threshold for limbic-hypothalamic arousal to unexpected changes in the environment or novel events that cannot be assimilated easily. This hypothesis is consonant with the views of a number of physiologists, with comparable data gathered on rhesus monkeys, and especially with animal data implying that the amygdala is an important mediator of states which would be regarded as resembling anxiety or fear in humans. Although the reasons for the lower thresholds in limbic-hypothalamic sites are unclear and likely to be complex, tonically higher levels of central norepinephrine and/or greater density of receptors for norepinephrine in these areas are possible contributing factors. This suggestion is supported by evidence indicating a close covariation in free-moving cats between activity of the locus ceruleus, the main source of central norepinephrine, and acceleration of heart rate to the stresses of white noise and restraint. Further, the conditioned cardiac acceleration appears to require the amygdala (Cohen, 1987).

However, we believe that the actualization of shy, quiet, timid behavior at two years of age requires some form of chronic environmental stress acting upon the original temperamental disposition present at birth. Some possible stressors include prolonged hospitalization, death of a parent, marital quarreling, or mental illness in a family member. These stressors were not frequent in our samples. However, in both longitudinal cohorts, two-thirds of the inhibited children were later born while two-thirds of the uninhibited children were first born. An older sibling who unexpectedly seizes a toy, teases, or yells at an infant who has a low threshold for limbic arousal might provide the chronic stress necessary to transform the temperamental quality into the profile we call behavioral inhibition. Thus, it is important to differentiate between those children and adolescents who are quiet and restrained in unfamiliar social situations because of the influence of temperamental factors and those who behave this way because of environmental experiences alone. Physiological measures might be helpful in distinguishing between these two groups. We suspect that the contemporary concept of introversion, which is usually applied to adults, contains both types. These data support Jung's claim, which Freud rejected, that temperamental factors contribute to the development of social anxiety and avoidance and to the symptoms of panic and agoraphobia which had been classified earlier in the century as components of hysteria.

My colleagues and I do not conceive of the psychological or physiological states mediating inhibited or uninhibited behavior as essences, even though our language contains that implication. Unfortunately, use of phrases like *inhibited to the unfamiliar* tempts readers to conceive of the referent as a unitary, stable characteristic—like the shape of the moon—rather than as a family of related states that are malleable to change and actualized in different forms depending upon the procedural probe (see Armario et al., 1986, for an example of habituation of the pituitary-adrenal response to stress in rats). Although we believe some infants are born with a low threshold for limbic-hypothalamic arousal to stimulus novelty, a minimally stressful environment over the first two years can reduce the likelihood that such children will develop the profile of inhibited behavior, and a proportion of inhibited children lose their extreme timidity by age five. Further, the power of a specific situation to generate limbic-hypothalamic arousal and inhibited behavior varies with development.

The complementarity in evolutionary theory between the genetically based variation of phenotypes and the environmental niches to which the diverse forms adapt provides a fruitful analogy for the relation between temperamental variation and experience. The different temperamental qualities of infants, many of which are to be discovered, provide caretakers, siblings, and peers with a diverse set of behavioral surfaces. The specific form each child's development assumes is a result of the meeting of its behavioral surface with the specific environments it encounters.

Imagine two boys born with high limbic arousal who are irritable and sleepless in the opening months of life and fearful at one year. One boy is born to parents who have been planning their first child for several years, are not easily frustrated, enjoy financial security, and live in a small, middle-class town of 30,000 people with good schools and minimal adolescent gang activity. The second boy is born in Chicago to a family that is under more stress. The parents lose their tempers easily because of frustration, both in their jobs and in their marital relationship. Further, they have a three-year-old boy and had hoped that the second child would be a daughter.

The infant born to the first family will experience fewer occasions of stress and, I believe, is unlikely to become an extremely timid, shy child, despite the fact that he was born with the appropriate temperament. The boy in the stressed family is much more likely to become a fearful, inhibited child.

The contrasting pair of infants born with a low level of limbic arousal will also develop differently in the two homes. The boy in the small-town setting is unlikely to become associated with a peer group having an asocial agenda. However, the boy born with the same temperament growing up in the urban environment may enter school with hostility toward his irritable parents which might lead, in turn, to lower motivation for academic success. Should this boy perform poorly in elementary school he would become vulnerable to adopting the values of his peer-group, and if the group were asocial, there is a reasonably high probability that, as an adolescent, he will engage in delinquent activity. Should psychologists discover at least several dozen temperamental types and as many classes of rearing environments one can imagine a large number of different life itineraries that could be actualized.

Preparedness and Inhibition

The concept of preparedness, a dividend of the recent influence of biology and ethology on the social sciences, offers an explanation of inhibited behavior that contrasts with the traditional emphasis on conditioning. The sense meaning of preparedness is that biological structures and processes, whether present at birth or products of maturation, bias the organism to react to events in particular ways. Newborn human infants orient to those visual arrays that have a great deal of contour; newborn goslings follow moving objects. Although the idea of preparedness was proposed to explain behavioral differences between species, not intraspecific variation, this concept can enhance our understanding of the emergence and maintenance of temperamental inhibition.

Encounters with unexpected or novel events, such as the entrance of a stranger or a visit to an unfamiliar home, are frequent experiences in the lives of most children. All observers of young children have noted that the usual, prepared reaction to such events is a brief period of quiet staring at the source of unfamiliarity and seeking proximity to a familiar person. However, about 10 to 15 percent of children are biased to become extremely quiet and, sometimes, distressed to a much larger proportion of such events than the average child. For these children, the prepared reaction to novelty that is characteristic of all children is exaggerated. We believe this exaggerated bias is a result of lower thresholds of excitability in selected limbic-hypothalamic structures. But even if this particular explanation proves to be incorrect, it is useful to contrast it with the traditional account that relies on learning.

Psychologists used to explain consistent withdrawal and shyness in a 5-year-old by suggesting that these behaviors began as conditioned responses. Interactions with certain people or encounter with events led to an unpleasant state of fear or pain, and the child avoided such events in order to reduce the unpleasant state. The act of withdrawal was reinforced by reduction or removal of the unpleasant state. Consider a 2-year-old who, upon entering an unfamiliar room with his mother, stays close to her for 20 minutes, rather than explore the room full of attractive toys, as a majority of children would have done. The traditional psychological explanation interprets the act of remaining near the mother as an instrumentally conditioned response. In the past, the child happened to remain close to the mother in an unfamiliar place and that act led to a state that was reinforcing. Presumably the reinforcing state was a reduction in the degree of uncertainty or fear, although that extra statement is not always present in modern behavioral essays.

A second possibility is that the child's behavior is a classically conditioned response. The novelty of the room is the unconditioned stimulus that creates a brain state that elicits inhibition of exploration and the seeking of a target of attachment. The problem with this explanation is that novelty is not a specific external stimulus but a relation between an external array and the child's schemata. Further, it is not clear what the conditioned stimulus might be in such a paradigm, for there is no stable object or feature in the room that could become a signal for future inhibition in other unfamiliar places.

The explanation that relies on individual differences in preparedness for inhibition holds that an unfamiliar room, which is not a threatening stimulus for most children, produces simultaneously both limbic-hypothalamic arousal and inhibition of action in a small proportion of children. Hence, these children stay close to the mother and become quiet. It is possible, of course, that although the initial tendency to become quiet and to remain proximal to the mother is a prepared response, repetition of these behaviors over a period of years might be maintained by the principles of instrumental conditioning. Further, instrumental learning might be involved in the attempts of older inhibited children to control their state of fear and inhibit their usual inclination to withdraw. As the child successfully inhibits uncertainty and avoidance and, instead, initiates interaction with others, the uncertainty is extinguished and, as we have shown, some of the peripheral physiological signs can disappear. It is important to distinguish between a state of uncertainty produced by an unfamiliar setting and a specific fear or avoidance reaction that was acquired through experience. This distinction can be observed, in rats, in a comparison of the spontaneous avoidance of novel foods in an unfamiliar environment with a conditioned taste aversion to saccharin. The central and basolateral amygdala are necessary for display of avoidance of a novel food but are not necessary for the acquisition of a conditioned aversion to saccharin (Dunn and Everitt, 1988). This interesting fact suggests that the amygdala, at least in the rat, may mediate a state that is analogous to the state generated in children when they encounter an unfamiliar event.

Gray (1982; 1988), however, awards less influence to the amygdala in his theory of anxiety. Gray distinguishes between the biologically prepared responses of fight or flight to painful or directly threatening events, on the one hand, and an initial inhibition of action to discrepant events or stimuli that have become conditioned signals for pain or fear, on the other. Gray suggests that the amygdala is critical to the former but that a circuit involving the hippocampus and septum mediates the latter phenomena and is a unified system forming the basis of human anxiety. Although Gray's hypothesis is in accord with the data on the effects of tranquilizing drugs on human patients, it is much less persuasive in explaining the differences in fearfulness among related animal strains or the spontaneous avoidance of novel foods described above. Once again, we have a nice example of the principle that the source of evidence affects the meaning of propositions. In this case, the propositions involve the idea of anxiety.

The reason why shyness with strangers seems to be such a sensitive index of the temperamental quality of inhibition is that, for humans, people are probably the most frequent basis for categorizing a setting as unfamiliar. The initial avoidance of strangers need not be the result of a conditioned habit based on prior unpleasant experiences with people, but, like the rats' avoidance of a novel food in an unfamiliar environment, the product of a temporary state of uncertainty in an unfamiliar setting. Perhaps that is why intensity of social anxiety in adults is not highly related to phobias of specific objects or places.

Recent work on the neurophysiological circuits involved in classically conditioned responses forms a link between traditional conditioning theory and the idea of biological preparedness. Rather than manipulate the parameters of the unconditioned and conditioned stimuli (as investigators did thirty years earlier), scientists now use lesions and electrical recordings to study the circuits and structures of the nervous system that mediate the classically conditioned response. For example, Thompson and his colleagues (1987) suggest that two different parallel circuits are involved in the conditioning of the nictitating membrane reflex (NMR) to a tone. The conditioned stimulus acquires the power to elicit both the state of fear and the skeletal motor response. These two links are regarded as separate, although the first facilitates the second. This conception differs from earlier accounts that assumed a linear process in which the conditioned stimulus first acquired the capacity to elicit a central state, something like fear, which, subsequently, elicited the reflex.

The more important change wrought by the modern work is the omission of any reference to reinforcement or reward. The deepest philosophical assumption in conditioning theory is that there is a purpose for a response and a goal to be obtained for its display. It is assumed, implicitly, that organisms will not issue a response if there is no advantage to be gained from the action. Traditional theorists wrote that a reflex (for example, leg withdrawal to shock) reduced the unpleasant state of fear or pain produced by the unconditioned stimulus. The new theorists see no need for such language. They postulate that both the physiological and behavioral phenomena occur because of the way in which the nervous system is constructed. A more satisfying explanation will probably involve propositions with more biological language, rather than concepts such as effort, reinforcement, pleasure, or pain.

This profound change in philosophical presuppositions is analogous to the change in the sixteenth and seventeenth centuries that followed the use of mathematical descriptions of physical phenomena, such as the velocity of falling bodies. These mathematical descriptions replaced explanations that relied on concepts referring to obscure forces imposed from without or residing within the object. As the neurosciences gradually move into areas that have been primarily psychological, the substitution of descriptions with biological language for sentences containing terms like motive, pleasure, pain, and reinforcement will become more frequent. I do not claim this development is to be celebrated. I suggest only that use of physiological descriptions will alter the philosophical assumptions and everyday conceptions of these psychological phenomena, just as the language of artificial intelligence is changing the community's view of human thought by bleaching it of emotion and exaggerating its propositional and logical qualities.

A Possible Role for Norepinephrine

A second speculation involves the potential role of norepinephrine. Inhibited children who also had a consistently high and stable heart rate had the greatest number of specific fears at every age (for example, large animals, the dark, violent shows on television). Even though this fact may seem intuitively reasonable, its explanation is not immediately obvious. I have suggested that inhibited children may possess higher tonic levels of limbic-hypothalamic arousal that facilitate the conditioning of a fear reaction toward specific objects or events. One potential basis for the arousal is higher levels of central norepinephrine, most of which is produced by the locus ceruleus located near the pons in the brain stem (Redmond, 1986). It is important to note that levels of dopamine-beta hydroxylase, an enzyme that mediates the final metabolic step in the production of norepinephrine, is controlled by a single gene locus (Dunnette and Weinshilboum, 1982), and the enzyme's activity is highly heritable (Weinshilboum, 1979). Further, panic disorder and agoraphobia are more frequent in adults who were inhibited children and appear to be heritable. Some investigators have suggested that high levels of norepinephrine characterize the panic patient (Torgersen, 1988).

One indirect index of central norepinephrine is detection thresholds for sensory events because studies with animals indicate that stimulation of the locus ceruleus is followed by suppression of background activity of neurons in sensory areas; as a consequence, there is enhancement of the signal-to-noise ratio (Aston-Jones, 1985; Segal, 1985). Because Eysenck's theory of introversion–extraversion was based on the premise of greater cortical arousal in introverts, investigators following that tradition have compared the performance of introverts and extraverts on perceptual vigilance tasks. In some of these studies introverts performed better when they had to detect an infrequent, and often subtle, signal embedded in a background. For example, introverts detected low-frequency auditory signals (500 Hz) better than extraverts, although there was no difference between the groups in detection of 8,000 Hz sounds (Stelmack and Campbell, 1974). In a later study, Stelmack, Achorn, and Michaud (1977) reported that introverts showed a larger amplitude of the N1-P2 component of the auditory evoked response to 500 Hz, but not to 8,000 Hz tones. Additionally, Hockey (1986) reported better performance for introverts than extraverts when subjects had to detect the infrequent occurrence of a slight increase in the brightness of a circle on a black background.

Before presenting our study of sensory thresholds, it is necessary to note first a surprising discovery that would have made nineteenth-century constitutional theorists smile. In each of five independent samples of Caucasian children between two and eight years of age, including our three longitudinal cohorts, more inhibited children are blue-eyed while more uninhibited children are brown-eyed. The probability that these five results could have occurred by chance is less than 6.2×10^{-8}. In one of these studies two-year-olds were selected only on eye color, not behavior, and observed in the laboratory. The blue-eyed children were much more inhibited than those with brown eyes. One blue-eyed boy who had been stung by a bee became terrified whenever he saw a bee (Rosenberg, 1987).

Other investigators have also been surprised by finding an association between an inhibited profile and blue eyes. The small group of Canadian school children in kindergarten and grade two who were extremely shy and socially isolated were more likely to be blue-eyed than their classmates (70 versus 48 percent; Rubin, personal communication). A survey of over 200 students in a small New England college revealed that more blue- than brown-eyed students reported being shy and experiencing physiological symptoms when they were in unfamiliar social situations (Cheek, personal communication).

However, recent advances in physiology and neurochemistry permit an interpretation that renders this unexpected association at least credible. Higher levels of central norepinephrine during prenatal, and perhaps early postnatal, life could be partially responsible for blue eyes because norepinephrine can inhibit the production of melanin in the melanocytes of the stromal layer of the iris (Rosenberg and Kagan, 1987). The higher levels of norepinephrine could be due to direct genetic influences on the production of this neurotransmitter or, indirectly, to biological factors that lead to increased cortisol levels, for cortisol stimulates the production of norepinephrine. In either case, the enhanced norepinephrine levels should be associated with shyness, lower sensory thresholds, and blue eyes.

Thus, it is of interest that blue-eyed Caucasian adults have lower tactile thresholds on the cornea than do brown-eyed Caucasian subjects (Millidot, 1975). Further, we have found that blue-eyed male adults who report being extremely shy and experiencing physiological reactions, such as a rapid heart rate, sweating, or dizziness, in unfamiliar social situations have a significantly lower olfactory threshold to butanol than brown-eyed males who report being very sociable. We chose olfaction as the modality to test because it is known that norepinephrine disinhibits the mitral cells of the olfactory bulb and, therefore, enhances the signal from the bulb to the cortex and amygdala (Jahr and Nicoll, 1982).

Among many vertebrate species, including fish, amphibia, and reptiles, the animals lose their external coloration when stressed (Bagnara and Hadley, 1973). For example, male pumpkinseed sunfish lose the bright color in the eyes and opercular fold when they become subordinate to another male (Stacey and Chiszar, 1978) because the melanophores are affected by the hormones and catecholamines produced by the stress of subordination. Because both melanocytes and the ganglia of the sympathetic nervous system originate in the neural crest, it is not unreasonable to expect that the melanin-producing cells would be responsive to norepinephrine. Thus, at least one of the morphological features that eighteenth-century mothers used to select wet nurses—recall they were advised to pick dark-haired, brown-eyed wet nurses—may turn out to be valid for reasons they could not have imagined.

If inhibited children do indeed secrete more central norepinephrine, we could explain, in a parsimonious way, a number of superficially diverse findings. First, this idea would explain the vigilance of inhibited children to discrepancy because norepinephrine affects the responsivity of the hippocampus to unfamiliar events. Second, it would explain the greater sympathetic reactivity and timidity of inhibited children because norepinephrine lowers the threshold of reactivity of the amygdala whose projections to the hypothalamus and sympathetic chain are central to a fear state and the display of avoidance reactions to novelty. This hypothesis would also explain the preponderance of blue eyes among inhibited children because, as noted, norepinephrine can inhibit the production of melanin in the melanocytes of the developing eye. Norepinephrine is present very early in the mammalian embryo, and any genotype that produced higher levels of this transmitter at this early phase of development would have pleiotropic effects on the physiological reactivity and morphology of the infant.

Nonetheless, the suggestion that inhibited children are born with lower thresholds of excitability in limbic areas remains speculative. One source of support is the retrospective recall of the mothers of inhibited two-year-olds claiming that their children had been irritable and wakeful during the first year. However, we are gathering information on a large group of infants seen at 2, 4, 9, and 14 months of age whose families volunteered to participate in a longitudinal study. A majority of these infants differ on two behavioral qualities which appear to be independent but may predict inhibition and lack of inhibition in the second year.

When the two- and four-month-old infants are shown interesting visual stimuli—for example, mobiles with varying numbers of objects hanging from them—or hear tape recordings of human voices varying in intensity and content, they display different amounts of motor activity, despite equivalent interest in the stimuli. Some infants lie quietly, eyes and posture alert, occasionally moving an arm or leg or protruding their tongue. At the other extreme are infants who show a dramatic increase in motoricity when the stimuli are presented. These infants protrude their tongues and move their arms and legs repeatedly during the stimulation. Occasionally these infants become so excited their arms, hands, and legs become almost spastic for a few seconds. The striking difference between these two extremes is stable from 2 to 9 months of age. Because the events that produce these behavioral differences are simply a mobile and recorded human voices, it appears that the excited infants have a very low threshold for arousal of motor activity to changing, unfamiliar stimulation. Recent advances in neurobiology provide an initial basis for understanding the difference between the two extreme groups.

An important neural circuit involving the basal ganglia that leads to motor activity originates in sensory association areas which project to the hippocampus and basolateral nucleus of the amygdala. The amygdala, in turn, projects to the ventral striatum and ventral pallidum and, via the thalamus, to the supplementary motor cortex and, finally, to the skeletal muscles. If, as is likely, this circuit mediates the tongue protrusion and arm waving display to our unfamiliar stimuli, low thresholds of reactivity in this part of the amygdala should be associated with more frequent motor movements to the mobiles and voices.

A second quality, which is relatively independent of degree of motoric arousal, might be called irritability. Some infants smile and babble to our stimuli, a smaller group frets or cries a great deal. These extremely fretful infants can be either high or low in motor arousal. There are at least two different ways to interpret the differences between the infants who cry minimally and those who cry often. One possibility is that the distress is simply a result of very high limbic arousal. I do not favor that interpretation because, as I noted, many infants with high levels of motor arousal will smile but never cry, while some infants with low motor arousal will fret and cry frequently. For that reason, I favor an explanation that relies on the recent work of Richard Davidson and Nathan Fox, who have suggested that infants differ in the relative dominance of the left or right frontal pole as revealed in a comparison of EEG spectra. The former infants, who are less fearful of strangers and separation, are likely to smile to unfamiliar stimuli, while the latter are more fearful and more irritable. It is possible that the excitability of the central nucleus of the amygdala has a special relevance for this variation in mood, for it projects to the hypothalamus. Infants who show high levels of motor arousal and distress to unfamiliar stimuli have high heart rates and perhaps lower thresholds of arousal in the circuits involving the basolateral as well as the central nucleus of the amygdala. This small group of infants are most likely to become inhibited one-year-old children. Infants who show low motor arousal, minimal distress, and low heart rates are most likely to become uninhibited children. Although our current data are in accord with this idea, future research will have to determine the fruitfulness of this speculative suggestion.

Kindling and Inhibition

A third speculation is prompted by the fact that there was a noticeable change in the consistency of inhibited and uninhibited behavior between 5½ and 7½ years of age. Children who remained inhibited at 7½ years were much more consistent across all assessment contexts than they had been two years earlier. And it was these consistently inhibited children who showed the physiological signs noted earlier. Some theorists have reported a more robust preservation of personality characteristics after age 6 than before school entrance (see Kagan and Moss, 1962). This fact invites the hypothesis of biological changes occurring between 5 and 7 years of age that mediate stabilization of the qualities of inhibition and lack of inhibition. It is likely that the children who are still extremely inhibited at school entrance are at risk for the later development of panic or agoraphobia.

One of the processes that might contribute to the stabilization of inhibited behavior involves the concept of *kindling* (Adamec and Stark-Adamec, 1986; Post, Rubinow, and Ballenger, 1986). Briefly, a short daily burst of electrical stimulation to the amygdala of rats or cats eventually leads to permanent sensitization of this structure. After 30 to 60 days of daily one-second bursts of stimulation, animals begin to show spontaneous limbic convulsions, even though the electrical stimulation has ceased. Consider a speculation based on generalizing these facts from the animal laboratory to inhibited children. If inhibited children possess a more excitable circuit from the amygdala to the ventromedial hypothalamus, a frightening environmental event might function as a kindling stimulus. The anxiety-arousing events might include thunderstorms, marital quarrels, attacks from a sibling or older child, or violent television shows. Such events, occurring several times a week over five to six years, might

kindle the limbic system of inhibited children and make them susceptible to spontaneous attacks of anxiety.

The children who had remained behaviorally inhibited at 7½ years
were the only ones who displayed unprovoked bouts of anxiety. On a
particular day one child might refuse to go to school or to a party, or
be reluctant to go upstairs to the bedroom at night. Many adult panic
patients report that they were shy, timid, inhibited children, and a
sudden panic attack in a department store might be regarded as analogous to a spontaneous limbic seizure in a kindled animal.

I do not suggest that all newborn infants born with an easily excited
amygdala-hypothalamic circuit will grow up to be inhibited children.
As noted earlier, a vulnerability to the display of inhibited behavior in
the second year of life seems to require environmental stressors in
order to actualize the temperamental disposition. Being a later-born
sibling is one such stressor. First-born children who possess the relevant temperamental characteristics but who live in a minimally stressful environment may be less likely to become behaviorally inhibited
during later childhood.[1]

One reason there are not more robust generalizations from many
years of study of the relation between family practices and child
behavior is that some psychologists have been indifferent to the infant's temperament and have failed to evaluate the interaction between the infant's temperamental qualities and parental behavior
with respect to some delimited behavioral profile. The suggestion that
later-born status is associated with inhibited behavior only for children born with amygdala-hypothalamic excitability is one example of
this principle. Human infants react differently to the same potentially
stressful events. As psychologists begin to assess the interaction between experience and temperament, they will come closer to their
version of a synthesis of inherent biological states and environmental
events that has been so productive in evolutionary biology.

The research on attachment provides a nice example of this suggestion for, as I noted in Chapter 2, the differences between inhibited
and uninhibited children are relevant to the work on infant attachment for two reasons. First, the bases for the original classifications of
secure and insecure attachment come from the child's behavior in an

---

1. Adamec and Stark-Adamec report that a kitten that is potentially vulnerable to becoming a defensive cat is unlikely, as an adult, to be fearful with rats if it
witnesses the killing of rats during the final months of the first year.

unfamiliar context. Second, recent reports attempting to relate the one-year classifications to behavior five or six years later have implicitly assumed that sociability and emotional spontaneity—the salient characteristics of the uninhibited child—are also characteristic of securely attached children, even though there is no empirical evidence for the latter assumption. There is only the intuition that the ego ideal qualities of the American child—outgoing and emotionally spontaneous—must be derivative of another desired quality, namely, a secure infant attachment.

Thus, when investigators find that securely attached one-year-olds become outgoing, emotionally spontaneous six-year-olds they conclude that a secure attachment must have been maintained over the interval to produce that outcome. However, it is equally parsimonious, and just as reasonable, to argue that a one-year-old who is soothed easily by the mother upon her return to an unfamiliar room because the child is not exceptionally anxious is more likely to be an uninhibited infant than an inhibited one. The data summarized in this chapter indicate that uninhibited two-year-old children become spontaneous, outgoing six- and seven-year-olds. The empirical basis for that conclusion is more robust than the evidence for the assumption that infants who are securely attached at one year should behave like uninhibited six-year-olds.

Consider an analogy. Parents play more often with attractive infants than with unattractive babies. An investigator who assumes that infants who are played with often develop a firm expectation that others will be friendly predicts that these children will have many friends when they enter school. If the prediction is affirmed, the scientist will conclude that popularity is a function, primarily, of early parent–infant interaction. But because physically attractive children are likely to have more friends than unattractive ones, the child's attractiveness may have been an important, stable personal quality mediating the prediction.

I suspect this analogy applies to the current literature on attachment. The endogenous contribution of the temperamental qualities of inhibition and lack of inhibition to the attachment classifications at one year and to the behaviors observed at school entrance is being ignored. Continuing indifference to these influences on a child's social relationships will delay the synthesis the sciences of human development owe to the future.

The Advantage of More Evidence

Scientists come increasingly close, but never attain, an appreciation of the family of related events as it exists in nature. The slow progress toward this idealized goal is marked by a continual titering of words and observations, each with its own inherent flaws. The words distort by implying more coherence, unity, and completeness than exists. The empirical data distort in the opposite way by revealing only a small part of the coherent event in nature. As additional features of an event are discovered, it is often the case that new constructs are needed or the name of the existing construct is changed. When Becquerel discovered in 1896 that the crystals of a uranium salt wrapped in dark paper exposed a nearby photographic plate, he assumed that rays emanating from the crystal were the causal entities. The succeeding generation discovered additional features of this phenomenon, and the contemporary construct is called radioactive decay.

Jung noted that some adults prefer solitude and thought to social interaction and action, and he named a person possessing these qualities an introvert. Eysenck and his students added new evidence on the autonomic functioning of these adults and suggested that introversion referred to a combination of shy behavior and cortical arousal. Our research group has added behavioral observations and information on the acceleration and variability of heart rate, pupillary dilation, vocal tension, and cortisol level in infants and young children and invented the concept of an inhibited temperament, with the additional implication that this type of child is characterized by a lower threshold of arousal in limbic sites. I am not suggesting that our concept of inhibited temperament is a more correct construct than Eysenck's introversion, only that the additional evidence we gathered revealed features of a family of phenomena not implied by the older term.

Restriction of inquiry to a narrow set of variables reduces the probability of discovering all of the critical features of complex phenomena and, therefore, postponing a deeper understanding of the relevant mechanisms. The most serious problem in contemporary research on temperament is the habit of gathering only one source of evidence, most often a self-report questionnaire. Because it is improbable that all subjects with a given score on such instruments are similar in other relevant features, continued reliance on a single, self-report index of a temperamental category is likely to slow theoretical progress.

Part Three

Cognition

5

On Cognitive Development

In every society, a small number of Platonic ideas are surrounded with mystery and awarded such extraordinary significance that no one would ask why a contemplative adult was trying to understand them and their most direct actualizations more completely. The Greeks awarded such status to morality; early Christians tried to comprehend God; seventeenth-century Europeans sought to discover the laws of heat and planetary motion. Contemporary natural scientists seek insight into the essence of matter and the forces that will explain the origin both of the universe and of life, by assuming that a small number of special instantiations provide the clearest picture of the idea. The outputs of a linear accelerator, for example, presumably reveal optimal understanding of the idea of atomic particle.

For contemporary psychologists, human thought, but oddly enough not motor skill or repentance, is imbued with an equivalent aura of mystery. Some of the indirect signs of thought are believed to be captured by event-related potentials, solutions to logical problems, and, in infants, differential attentiveness to familiar and unfamiliar pictures or sounds. A century earlier, reaction time and sensory acuity were equally preferred sources of evidence. A large part of the history of each scientific discipline is captured by just such changes in the referents of the longer-lasting ideas. Stated differently, an important basis for change in a science, in addition to new theory, is invention of a new source of information.

Thought, which we know how to use but do not understand, poses as formidable an enigma as the origin of the universe or the evolution of vertebrates, but deep *a priori* presuppositions about the nature of thought retard progress in the same way that Ptolemy's idealized conception of the proper relation between earth and sun influenced inferences about the cosmos. That is why a philosophical analysis of cognition and cognitive development can be useful. This essay is a constructive critique of our assumptions about the development and measurement of cognitive processes.

The Need for a Baconian Frame

The constructs that name the basic units of a scientific domain originate in informed intuitions, dominant theoretical prejudice, and empirical observations. Early theories in biology and chemistry began with units that had their roots in theistic ideas, while the extraordinary progress following the Enlightenment was facilitated by a Baconian mood insisting that evidence, not a pleasing idea, was to be the source of units. The idea of the cell, biology's most fundamental unit, provides an exemplar case. It is doubtful if the most imaginative sixteenth-century naturalist could have imagined a diverse class of irregularly shaped structures bounded by a partially permeable surface membrane, dotted with chemical receptors, containing a nucleus of interlaced chromosomes embedded in a cytoplasm studded with tiny factories manufacturing a variety of proteins. This Rube Goldberg conception would have been rejected by the scientific community because of its asymmetry, structural heterogeneity, and uneven assignment of functional responsibilities.

Despite the fact that a few areas of psychological research have matured to a stage where data are the major source of constructs, this advance is less complete in the cognitive sciences and its subfield of cognitive development. Titles of chapters and essays continue to be abstract dictionary terms that do not stray very far from the comprehension vocabulary of the educated community. The use of such a small number of terms—perception, language, memory, symbolic representation, problem solving, and intelligence, to name the diverse set of events comprising cognition—is reminiscent of the Greek's parsing all of nature into air, water, fire, and earth. For reasons that are not clear, many psychologists are reluctant to accommodate to robust observations that challenge the utility of these overly abstract constructs.

For example, the correlation among performances on a battery of procedures assessing recognition or recall memory for verbal or pictorial information is relatively low, especially in children. This fact suggests that memory is not a unitary process and that a more constrained construct combining recognition or recall memory with a particular class of information would be more powerful (Kagan, 1981). Further, recent neuropsychological studies of memory processes suggest that connections among association cortices, limbic structures, thalamus, and pre-frontal cortex contribute to the memory performance observed (Mishkin and Appenzeller, 1987). Thus, the memory of a person's name, the place where you put your keys, and the shape of a vase appear to be emergent from different relations involving varied parts of the brain rather than a unitary process occurring in a particular place.

About six years ago Michael Moore and I studied 29 eight-to-twelve-year-old boys diagnosed as dyslexic and 29 matched controls. We found that although the recognition and evaluation of simple perceptual events were as efficient and accurate for dyslexic boys as for boys who had normal reading ability, about one-quarter of the dyslexics were much less competent at evaluating the meaning of orally administered sentences composed of familiar words (Moore et al., 1982). A small group of dyslexic boys displayed long response times, between one and two seconds, before they affirmed or denied the validity of single, orally presented sentences like "Black is the color of coal," or "A watch is bigger than a football," compared with about one-half second for the controls and most of the other dyslexics. However, all the children performed similarly when they had to detect 15 different occurrences of the word *to* embedded in a long tape-recorded story which also contained the words *two* and *too*. These data suggest that the evaluation of meaning is specific to a class of information and is not a unitary process. Otherwise, the dyslexic boys who took so long to evaluate a sentence like "Orange is the color of cucumbers" should have also required a long time to decide whether the word *to*, rather than *two* or *too*, was being read to them.

Equally important, even though the 29 dyslexic boys were as pure a group of dyslexics as could be found—each had been diagnosed as dyslexic by a professional and each was under special remedial therapy—this group contained at least two qualitatively different types of children. Three-quarters of the dyslexics responded as quickly as the controls when they had to decide on the meaning and validity of the sets of oral sentences administered. Only a special subset of seven boys out of the 29 took dramatically longer to make these decisions. In addition, these special seven dyslexic boys showed signs of lower central nervous system arousal during these tasks. The index of arousal we used was spontaneous blinking, which often occurs when one is working on an intellectual problem. The blink reflex, due to contraction of the orbicularis oculi, is mediated by efferents of the trigeminal nerve, which originates in the pons, and is influenced by the state of the reticular activating system. Higher levels of arousal in the reticular activating system typically occur while solving cognitive tasks, and the blink rate ordinarily rises. And, indeed, for the control group and most of the dyslexics, blink rate did rise during the first half of each of the test episodes. However, for these special seven dyslexics, blink rate was very low during all tasks.

These data suggest that the category *dyslexia,* even when applied conservatively, does not refer to a unitary group of children but contains at least two different types of reading-disabled children. Why is there such resistance among psychologists and educators to this form of analysis and to these more finely parsed constructs?

The Generalization of Process Predicates

One reason why psychologists write about human characteristics as if they reflected abstract qualities that did not change in important ways across time, place, or target of action is that the targets of their inquiry are usually processes rather than things. Many biologists study the characteristics of physical objects that can be observed either easily, like flowers and bones, or with difficulty, like bacteria and viruses. They summarize their observations with sentences that consist of a noun phrase referring to the entity followed by a predicate that describes some of the entity's features. Because most objects in nature are unique in some way, many advances in the natural sciences consist of discovering a feature that makes it necessary to discriminate between two classes of things that had been regarded as belonging to the same class—for example, between viruses and retroviruses.

The targets of inquiry for psychologists, on the other hand, and especially cognitive scientists, are processes like thought, memory, or perception that are generalized across context and information rather than parsed into finer categories. Consider the following three short sentences:

1. Trees grow.
2. Insects grow.
3. Children grow.

Despite the extraordinary differences in the details of growth in the three objects, the same predicate is used, tempting readers to conceive of the growth process as consisting of the same core set of events for all living organisms. Because most constructs in cognitive development refer to mental processes, there is more resistance to differentiating them into finer classes than to differentiating among the agents—children, infants, monkeys—who use these processes.

The practice of generalizing terms for cognitive processes across agents and information leads scientists to write as though the nature of memory or representation did not change when the age of the organism and the informational context did. Frege (1979) recognized this problem and attributed it to the tendency to treat the separate syntactic elements of the sentence as basic units, as some linguists do, rather than treat the entire sentence as a unit. Frege argued that the basic unit in scientific description is the proposition, not the noun phrase representing a topic or the predicate describing it. Frege suggested that propositions assume the form of function or argument. A function states a general abstract relation among variables, while the arguments are the references that give different meanings to the function. A psychological example, which Frege would not have used is:

(1) Organisms experience internal states to unexpected events.

The function in sentence 1 obtains its truth value by taking on specific arguments. Hence,

(2) "One-year-old infants experience a state of fear to strangers" is true. But,
(3) "Newborn infants experience a state of fear to strangers" and
(4) "One-year-old infants experience a state of guilt to new toys" are both false.

Although the theoretical meaning of psychological processes and, therefore, their truth value require specification of context and the characteristics of the organism, these constraints are typically ignored in most psychological studies of cognitive development. Reports are written as if there were only one argument for a function, implying that perception, memory, and reasoning are, like paint colors, autonomous essences that transcend time and location and can be applied to any object that happens to be near the brush.

Kenneth Livingston (unpublished) has found that when six-year-old children were tested with four different procedures designed to assess their knowledge of the concept *animal* or *living thing*, almost every child understood both concepts when asked to name a set of animals or living things; all children could name at least a half dozen of each type. However, when the assessment contexts were an inference test, clustering words in recall memory, and proactive inhibition, a large number of children failed to show evidence of possessing the same two concepts, suggesting that conclusions about whether six-year-olds understand the concept *animal* require specifying the procedure used.

As a final example, consider the fact that a three-day-old infant will recognize a previously presented novel auditory stimulus (an English word) following a two-minute delay if it hears a stimulus on postnatal days two and three, but a three-day-old infant who hears the stimulus for the first time on day three fails to show recognition if the delay is two minutes long (Zelazo, personal communication). This fact means that *recognition performance* is a function of both the strength of the trace (or the familiarity of the event) and the delay between familiarization and test. There is no absolute length of delay an infant of a particular age can tolerate; that value varies with the familiarity of the stimulus to be recognized. Thus, precise generalizations about infant recognition memory will be, at the least, propositions describing interactions of event familiarity and duration of delay, and perhaps other factors as well. The most robust generalizations about recognition memory the future owes us will refer to specific members of a family of processes now called simply *recognition memory*. (I suspect that the medical construct *allergy* is at the same epistemological level as recognition memory, for the most powerful generalizations are for specific allergies, like hives or asthma; few involve the superordinate concept *allergy*).

Although it seems obvious to me that the popular function terms in cognition are too broad, our intuition is jarred by the suggestion that the units in cognitive theory should be as restrictive as *recognition memory for familiar photographs with GSR as the index of recognition* or *concept of animal when clustering is the source of evidence*. Yet, in one sense, the results of these studies reflect an accepted state of affairs in quantum mechanics. One of the axioms of modern physics is Bohr's statement that scientists cannot know which aspects of their evidence reflect the entity in nature they wish to understand and which parts reflect what the procedures (or apparatus) have done to the entity. So, too, with experiments in cognition. When a subject in a proactive inhibition procedure cannot remember any of the three animals presented in the third trio of animal words, we cannot say precisely which part of that performance reflects the structure of the concept *animal* in the subject's mind and which part the procedural probe. That is why a statement declaring that most six-year-olds do or do not possess the concept *animal* must stipulate explicitly the procedural source of the data.

Constructs Should Represent Units cum Processes

If biology is taken as a fruitful guide to the study of cognition—and I acknowledge that there may not be consensus on that suggestion—a theoretical construct for a cognitive process should refer explicitly to the type of cognitive unit that participates in that process. For example, the biological process of meiosis applies to gametes, not somatic cells, and the process of synaptic transmission refers to neurons, not glia. I believe psychological theory will be advanced if we assume that the to-be-discovered generalizations about the processes of recognition, recall, or transformation of information when applied to schemata will be different from the generalizations that involve concepts, even though Rumelhart and McClelland (1986) reject the idea of schema as a basic unit.

I view schemata as partially veridical representations of experience that need not be part of a complex meaning network (for example, representations of 100 unfamiliar faces or 100 different melodies played on a lute). I view concepts, however, as networks of related symbols. Thus, a person *recognizes* a face as familiar or unfamiliar through assimilation of that face to a schema, but *understands* the meaning of a frown or a shrill voice by relating the event to a network of symbols. Obviously, many events can be represented either as schemata or as a network of symbols, or both. Frege would have approved of this suggestion, for he argued that a sentence has a sense meaning (*Sinn*) derived from the meaning of its component concepts, while a perceptual experience may not. That is why the predicates *understand* and *recognize* have different theoretical meanings. There is empirical support for this claim.

First, the fact that interference effects in recall memory are much stronger for concepts than for schemata is one bit of evidence for their separate status. Second, one-year-old infants, most of the time, will look longer at an unfamiliar than at a familiar event when both are presented simultaneously. But if the experimenter should say the name of the familiar picture—for example, cup—the child is likely to look longer at the cup than at the unfamiliar object. Third, the meanings of sentences in an orally presented short story, which are defined by a set of related concepts, are retrievable after a much longer delay than the representations of specific words or the tone of voice of the person reading the story. Fourth, concepts have contrasting complements (good-bad, boy-girl), while most schemata do not. And finally, violation of a conceptual expectancy (reading an incongruous word at the end of a sentence) is accompanied by a negative wave in the event-related potential at about 400 msec, but violation of a schematic expectation is accompanied by a positive wave in the event-related potential. If the functions that describe the recognition of a prior experience mediated by schemata turn out to be very different from the functions that describe the understanding of the meanings of a prior event, we should not use the same predicate *(recognition)* for both cognitive activities. No biologist uses the word *birth* as a technical predicate to describe both the division of an amoeba into two cells and a human mother delivering twins.

If investigators who study cognition were to add information that reflects the motivational and affective processes that accompany perception, memory, and inference, they would invent new concepts. For example, most subjects show a dilation of the pupil and a small rise in heart rate when storing information in short-term memory for later retrieval. But there is a great deal of variation in the frequency and magnitude of these sympathetic changes. This extra evidence adds information about the processes accompanying the mental work of the subject. Two identical recall performances—two subjects recall 40 percent of the words presented—could have different profiles of pupillary and cardiac change. The construct that explains the performance should take this fact into account. As cognitive scientists become more friendly to new classes of evidence they will see the necessity of new constructs. When that happens, the split between hot and cold cognition will vanish for all cognition is warm, some a bit warmer.

The Metric Used

Metrical considerations also favor differentiating between the processes that involve schema and those that involve concepts. Schemata are described as patterns, while concepts are described as a composite of their separate dimensions. A schema can be likened to a member of a set of structurally related steroids—each a unique pattern—in which the various members differ from each other in the arrangement of only one or two chemical elements. Chemists do not apply the metric *degree of steroidness* to describe or to quantify the structural variation in members of the set. Rather, the value assigned to a particular member is based on its biological consequences with respect to some target tissue (for example, potency to produce muscle growth in the larynx). Because schemata, too, are patterns, it is difficult to invent a metric that refers to a continuous characteristic that is inherent in the pattern, even though a quarter-century ago psychologists tried, unsuccessfully, to quantify visual patterns as varying in complexity.

However, many investigators describe concepts as a combination of a set of differentially weighted dimensions (for example, the concept *stone* has fewer dimensions than the concept *weather*). J. Maynard Smith (1985) has suggested that nature uses two basic strategies in creating phenomena—jigsaws and waves. Jigsaws are the result of putting smaller pieces together; a construction of a protein from amino acids is an obvious example. Waves, however, are holistic events that cannot be constructed by fitting together a set of smaller elements. Concepts seem to be more like jigsaws; schemata are more like waves.

There are, of course, occasions when a phenomenon can be viewed as a jigsaw or a wave, depending upon the question asked. For example, the ability to process speech syllables as adults do is a competence that has been recently awarded to the infant (Miller and Eimas, 1983; Kuhl and Meltzoff, 1982). An additional claim is that the processing of speech is context dependent. Eimas and Miller (1980) have reported that perception of the speech syllable *ba* or *wa* depends not only on the duration of the initial formant transition but also on the transition duration in relation to the duration of the entire syllable (Eimas and Miller, 1980; Miller and Eimas, 1983). There are two ways to interpret the data upon which this inference rests. The interpretation preferred by Eimas and Miller is that because no percept is fully determined by the information in the signal, the stimulus is referred automatically to a larger frame, a conclusion reminiscent of the early Gestalt writings on perception. The mind evaluates the stimulus with reference to the larger frame in which the signal is embedded.

However, a somewhat different description of these data is possi-

ble. When the syllable *ba* is described as an event composed of variations in the durations of initial formant transitions and completed
syllables, and investigators manipulate each of these dimensions sepa-
rately, they find that the infant's perception of the syllable *ba* or *wa*
under one formant transition duration depends upon the duration of
the syllable, and they conclude that there is context-dependent perception. This is a proper inference. But the infant's central nervous
system may not analyze the stimulus *ba* in the way the experimenter
intended. Therefore, it is also proper to state that the infant perceives
ba as a unitary event under one set of conditions and perceives *wa* as
a unitary event under another.

The physicist Pierre Duhem (1906), writing on the distinction between qualities and quantities, stated that if a new value on a dimension can be formed by addition—like loudness—the dimension can
be regarded as a quantity. But if a new phenomenon cannot be
formed by adding the separate values on a selected dimension—like
the syllable *ba*—it should be regarded as a quality. Every event contains many different dimensions, some of which can be conceptualized as continuous quantities, others as discrete qualities. The
preference for conceptualizing an event as a quantity or a quality
depends on the question being asked and, therefore, the theoretical
interest of the scientist.

Eimas and Miller are interested in how the central nervous system
might discriminate among the sounds of human speech. It is useful,
for that question, to view the stimulus events as continua. But for
investigators interested in the infant's schematic representation of
events, it may be more useful to regard the entire syllable as unitary,
with a distinct quality. A pathologist seeking the causes of a new viral
disease looks for the unique qualities of that pathogen; but a geneticist interested in classifying pathogens into their proper categories
often searches for continuous characteristics among a group of related viruses.

Maturation of Cognitive Functions

The last two decades have been witness to an increased concern with
the maturation of cognitive talents that appear to be separate from
language. When we say a cognitive competence matures, we mean
that structural and neurochemical changes in the brain have made
possible the processing and transformation of experiences that permit

a particular cognitive product to be actualized. It is assumed that the "product" is derived from the experiences acting in combination with an altered brain.

Infancy

The growth of the central nervous system during the first year, especially covariations among sensory association areas, the frontal lobe, and limbic structures, is accompanied by an increase in the ability to recognize an event over delays of 30 to 60 seconds by three to four months of age, and enhanced recall memory at eight to twelve months of age. The former talent is accompanied by the appearance of the smile to the human face, the latter by object permanence and stranger and separation anxiety.

Eight- to nine-month-old human infants exhibit a behavior that is called the "A not B" error. The error can be characterized in the following way. After two successful retrievals of a toy hidden under one member of a pair of covers the infant will return to that place on the next trial even though it saw the examiner hide the toy under the other cover on the third trial. In a comparison of human and monkey infants, Adele Diamond (1987) has shown that one-month-old monkeys and eight-month-old infants make the "A not B" error if the delay between hiding and permitting the infant to reach is more than a few seconds. Further, both monkey and human infants improve dramatically in the next few months, so that four-month-old monkeys and one-year-old humans do not make the "A not B" error. Maturation of the connections between the dorsolateral prefrontal cortex and parietal cortex provides a basis for the improved ability. Bilateral lesions of the principal sulcus of the dorsolateral prefrontal cortex of the adult monkey destroy the ability to solve the "A not B," as well as other delayed-response problems. Thus, the phenomenon that Piaget has called the *object concept* requires brain maturation. I suspect that the contribution of sensorimotor manipulation of objects, which is treated as absolutely necessary in Piaget's explanation of the object concept, may be less critical than most psychologists assume.

It is of interest that changes in behavior on a very different task also occur during the same developmental era. Infants were shown an attractive object inside a rectangular transparent box that was open on only one side—top, front, right, or left side. Adult monkeys with frontal lesions fail to retrieve the object because they always reach for it on a line corresponding to their direct line of sight. Seven-month-old infants, like lesioned monkeys, also fail to retrieve the object from an open side if they see it through a closed side because they cannot inhibit reaching in the direction corresponding to their sight of the object, even if one hand is touching an opening in the box on the right side. But over the next five months infants show a sequence of changes that is so predictable it fits a Guttman scale with a reproducability coefficient of 0.93. By eight months, infants will begin to look at the toy through different sides of the box; they may lean over to see the toy through the top of the box. However, they still reach only toward the locus they are fixating. At 9 months they first begin to succeed and will reach into an opening, even though they were looking through the closed top of the box. By 10 to 11 months infants will reach successfully through an opening, sometimes without even looking at it, because tactile information informed them of the open side. By one year, performance is close to perfect. Infants will now use the tactile information to guide them, and they rarely return to a side that touch told them was closed. Infants are now able to retrieve the information indicating that a particular side is closed and can integrate visual and tactile information (Diamond, 1987).

The emergence of the ability to retrieve the immediate past and to integrate two sources of perceptual information may be the result of growth in prefrontal cortex, hippocampus, and connections between these areas and the diencephalon and association cortex (Mishkin and Appenzeller, 1987). Manipulative experience with objects may be less important in these victories than some psychologists have surmised. It is also likely that the ability to integrate information originating in two different modalities over a period of a few seconds requires maturation of the connections between prefrontal cortex and amygdala (Mishkin and Appenzeller, 1987). Hence, the claim for intermodal schemata in infants under six or seven months may be suspect. The ability to retrieve schemata established in the immediate past and to relate that information to the present also may be necessary for display of separation anxiety (Kagan et al., 1978; Kagan, 1984). That is, separation anxiety appears as a result of the new ability to retrieve the schema of the mother's former presence in the room and to compare it with the fact of her absence. The inability to resolve the discordant representations generates a state of uncertainty which is often followed by overt distress.

The next 12 months contain other maturational victories, one of the most important being the appreciation of symbols and, soon after, comprehension and expression of language. Although the use of objects as tools by chimpanzees was hailed as evidence for a less disjunctive relation between the psychology of hominids and apes, the human addiction to the application of symbols must be one of our most distinguishing qualities. The earliest stone carvings reveal how easy it is for humans to consider a single perceptual feature as representative of a complex idea or concept (for example, a circle as representative of the sun's beneficial effects on the earth). And two-year-olds from different cultures have no difficulty in selecting the larger of two pieces of unpainted wood when asked, "I have a mommy and a daddy, which one is the daddy?" indicating that they treat relative size as a feature of the concept of gender. A year or two later, simile and metaphor emerge. The profound difference between apes and humans can be seen if ballpoint pens and paper are given to both. The children typically create a pattern of lines that symbolizes some event. The apes scribble a few unclosed, irregular curved lines in the middle of the paper (Boysen, Bernston, and Prentice, 1987).

The Transition at Five to Seven Years

The fact that important cognitive changes occur between the fifth and seventh years of life was recognized by mothers in rural societies, the Catholic church, and English common law long before Piaget and Freud tried to analyze the essence of these changes. Piaget has come closest to articulating the nature of the new talents. The most important are the abilities to relate two concepts and to appreciate that their relation can change with context and, therefore, is relative. Consider the robust fact of conservation of liquid. When the liquid from one of two beakers is poured into a tall, thin cylinder and the examiner asks the standard conservation question, the seven-year-old with an introduction to the arithmetic idea of equality has two conceptual appreciations of the array. One originates in perception, the other in the recently developed concept of equality between two perceptually dissimilar events. The concrete operational child appreciates the related meanings of the question "Which has more liquid?" and infers the one intended by the examiner. But at a birthday party, the same child might make a different choice. That is the implication I take from the work of Tversky and Kahneman, who claim that college students do not always apply statistical rules that they know when they are in a laboratory setting. However, they are likely to do so when they are buying a house or selecting a surgeon.

The ability to infer the mind of another is also present in class-inclusion problems, for the child must appreciate that the examiner has made the improbable and counterintuitive request to relate a part and a whole. Few adults expect to be asked "Which act has more virtue: Saving a drowning child or acting morally?" Or "Are there more insects in the world or more living things?" Hence, when five-year-old children are shown an array of four red and two white balls and asked "Are there more red balls or more balls?" they unselfconsciously choose the former because they assume the question is about the relative numerosity of red and white balls. But by seven years of age, when children can both monitor questions more carefully and can relate a part to the whole, they realize the possibility of two answers and offer the correct one (see Flavell, Spear, and Green, 1981). A nice example of this claim is found in a study of 30 normal children, three-and-a-half to six years of age, who were administered a procedure that neurologists often use as an index of integrity of cerebral functioning. The procedure is called the face-hand test.

If young children are touched simultaneously on one cheek and the hand on the opposite side (for example, the right cheek and the left hand) and are asked "Where were you touched?" the children typically report being touched only on their face. But if the same children are told: "I'm going to play a game with you. Sometimes I am going to touch you only on the cheek, sometimes I am going to touch you only on the hand, and sometimes I'm going to try to fool you and I am going to touch you in two places," 80 percent report being touched in two places. This simple, clear result has important implications, namely, young children usually do not try to infer the mind of the other. Four-year-olds do not consciously reflect on whether the examiner in this test might try to trick them and touch them in two places. The young child takes the instruction literally and ingenuously. The seven-year-old, by contrast, reflects on the other's intentions; that is one important reason why older children give more intelligent answers to our questions.

In another study, a group of four-, six-, and eight-year-old children were told that they were going to see some photographs of familiar objects—40 pictures in all—and they had to remember them. Some of the children were told they would only have to remember the photographs for only a few minutes, others were told they would have to remember them for a day, and the third group was told they would have to remember the photographs for a week. All children were first tested to see if they understood the significance of the difference between a few minutes, a day, and a week. Those who did not were eliminated.

The response of interest was how long each child took to examine each of the photographs during the familiarization phase. The four- and six-year-olds behaved as if they did not appreciate the fact that a day and a week were very long times, for they studied the photographs for a short period of time. But the eight-year-olds used that knowledge and examined each picture for about five seconds if they had to remember the photos for the longer time, but for less than three seconds if they were told they only had to remember the information for a few minutes. I interpret this finding to mean that the older children actively related the task demands implied by the instructions to their behavior, while the younger children did not.

Winner (1988) has suggested that appreciation of irony does not appear before six or seven years because the younger child cannot infer the intention of a speaker who, on a hot July day declares, "Isn't it cool today?" The ability to detect the relation between or among categories also permits the child to nest hierarchically ordered categories properly and, therefore, to know that dogs, pets, animals, and living things form a nested set of concepts. This is one reason why it is not until age seven that American children begin to worry about catastrophes, like war, kidnapping, and vandalism, for such apprehensions require the child to be able to relate the abstract concept of environmental danger to the concept of self. Additionally, the concrete operational child who can seriate (that is, apply a magnitude dimension to a set of events that reflects their differential size, number, or depth of color) can compare self with others on qualities like relative beauty, strength, and intelligence. As a consequence, important new components of the self-concept that could not be established earlier begin to grow.

Formal Operations

Piaget's suggestion that adolescence is marked by the emergence of fundamentally new cognitive competences is one of the most original ideas in any theory of human nature and provides insights about adolescent behavior that challenge traditional explanations. The abilities to deal with hypothetical situations, to sense the inconsistency in a set of related beliefs, and to know when one has exhausted all solution possibilities are generally absent from the repertoire of the average nine year old. These abilities help to explain the rise in suicides during the adolescent years, for in order to develop a state of depression deep enough to provoke a suicide attempt, the person must hold the belief, whether valid or not, that all attempts to solve a personal problem have failed and, further, no constructive action is possible. Second, the ability to detect inconsistency among a set of personally held and related beliefs contributes to some of the rebellion, anger, and anxiety characteristic of adolescents, especially in modern societies with pluralistic philosophies. Among modern adolescents, some important pairs of inconsistent themes include: (1) Illicit sex is morally wrong yet pleasant. (2) Dependence upon parents brings security, but one should strive to be independent of one's family. (3) Parents are wise and potent but have flaws of character. Recognition of these and other inconsistencies demands a resolution—either rejection of one of the two beliefs or synthesis of a compromise belief. During the period when this mental work is being accomplished, the adolescent can experience serious dissonance and uncertainty. I interpret these insights from Piaget, as I did the earlier competences of infancy, to mean that many of the major milestones in emotional growth follow the maturation of cognitive processes. This view is not only the reverse of Freudian theory, it is, in a real sense, a fresh discovery about human nature.

Awarding influence to maturation of the brain does not imply a friendliness to reductionism or a commitment to the assumption that eventually all statements in cognitive science will be translated into sentences with biological words. I remain loyal to the philosophical position which claims that although natural events are a unity, scientists parse them into conceptual domains, each in a different language and at a different level of generality. In addition, it is often the case that phenomena at one level are emergent from those at another. This position implies that although knowledge of the physiology of the brain can aid understanding of cognitive functions, it is not necessary to translate all psychological sentences into physiological ones. Further, it is not possible to do so without some loss of theoretical meaning. The elegant laws of planetary motion illustrate emergent phenomena which have not been replaced with statements in which the atoms comprising the planets are the basic entities.

So, too, with statements in cognitive development. The one-year-old's ability to tolerate a one-minute delay in an object permanence context is an emergent phenomenon derived from the growth of the brain and some experience with objects. It is difficult to imagine the replacement of a function that has, on the ordinate, the duration of delay on which successful reaching occurred and, on the abscissa, the child's age with a different function that relates discharge patterns in motor neurons to density of synaptic connections among visual, frontal, and limbic areas. Even if such a figure were possible at some time in the future, I doubt if it would be preferred to the one with psychological labels on the axes.

It is odd that some biologists and even some philosophers—Patricia Smith Churchland (1986) is an example—are insistent on the reduction of psychology to biology. No one today would claim that theoretical statements in evolution can be replaced with propositions that only have biochemical terms, like gene, protein, or amino acid, because unpredictable environmental events—like climate changes—must be included in an explanation of evolution. The expansion of mammals 60 million years ago was an event emergent from adaptive mutations in small rodents combined with alterations in ecology that eliminated large reptiles.

It is unlikely that we will be able to translate the descriptions of psychological growth into biological sentences, even though the biological knowledge enhances understanding in a major way. Perhaps that is why Stent (1987), in reviewing Churchland's book, writes, "I doubt that a complete reduction is de facto possible. My cardinal hunch is that a significant residue of unreduced psychological as well as neurobiological theory will remain with us long into the future" (p. 992).

Of course a major lacuna in theories of cognitive development is our inability to state explicitly the critical environmental conditions that are necessary to actualize the cognitive competences made possible by growth of the central nervous system. No child locked in a closet would become operational. Consider, as an example, the conservation of mass. The fact that the earliest age of conservation is about five years, regardless of environmental context, suggests some maturational changes are absolutely necessary for this performance. But the fact that unschooled children in many isolated communities do not achieve conservation until adolescence—if at all—suggests that certain experiences that are not part of daily life are also necessary. School instruction, which emphasizes categories and classes, is one contributing factor; exposure to counting and the varied ideas of amount are others.

It is likely that some competences will appear in almost any environment with people and objects, even though the appearance of the ability is delayed by several years. Mayan Indian children living in northwest Guatemala, who have no radios, televisions, books, or pencils, develop some of these universal competences, even though their appearance is delayed. These isolated Indian children were able to solve a culturally fair version of an embedded figures test despite no familiarity with pictures, paper, or crayons (Kagan and Klein, 1973); were able to perform as well as American children on a test of recognition memory for photographs of unfamiliar objects (typewriters and golf clubs); and, at adolescence, were able to generate reasonable replies when asked what would happen if the large lake they see every day were to dry up. But when the cognitive tasks become difficult and implementation of special strategies is necessary, these isolated Indian children do not display the performances seen in seven-year-old Americans until late adolescence.

Three different groups of children were administered a series of memory tasks (Kagan et al., 1979). One group was composed of 59 children between six and thirteen years of age living in Cambridge, Massachusetts. A second group of 126 children, between six and thirteen years of age, lived in a town in Northwest Guatemala which had occupational specialization and moderately good schooling. A third group of 152 subjects, six to twenty years of age, were living several kilometers away from the town in an isolated village that provided minimal schooling. Each child had to remember the order of a set of 12 chromatic drawings of objects that were familiar to them (the objects included a picture of a boy, house, chicken, cup, and chair). The child's task was to reproduce the exact order of the pictures first demonstrated by the examiner. The examiner began by laying two pictures on the table face up in front of the child. The examiner named the pictures from the child's left to right and allowed the child to study them. The pictures were then turned face down, the child was given two identical pictures and asked to place them directly under the pictures the experimenter had just turned over. This procedure was repeated, increasing by one the number of pictures present on each successive trial, until the child could remember the order of 12 pictures or until he made two consecutive errors. All children were given the same sequence of pictures. Interference from trial to trial was minimized by adding only one new picture to a series that had just been successfully recalled.

When the child had reached his or her maximal memory span on this task, he was seen on a different day for a more difficult task. The same drawings were used with the same serial order. However, in this more difficult task the child had to remember the order of the pictures after the examiner had altered the sequence. For example, the examiner first presented the pictures face up and asked the child to name them in sequence twice so that they were well registered in memory. The pictures were then turned face down and the examiner moved one or more of the pictures laterally, changing their relative location. The child was then given a set of identical pictures and asked to place them in the new order created by the examiner's alterations. The test was administered in steps of increasing difficulty, from two pictures with one shift to a maximum of six pictures with three shifts.

The Cambridge children reached high levels of performance by the time they were eight or nine years of age. The Indian children in the larger town with good schooling began to approach the performance of the Cambridge children by ten and eleven years of age. But it was not until eighteen years of age that the subjects in the isolated village began to approach the performance of the seven- or eight-year-old Cambridge children. In general, the slopes for rate of improvement in performance on retrieval memory for familiar pictures and words occurred at about seven to eight years of age in Cambridge, eight to nine years of age in the modern Indian town, and ten to eleven years of age in the isolated Indian village. We interpret this fact to mean that the processes that mediate the organization of information, rehearsal, and the expectation that reflective thought can aid memory performance mature at different times as a function of everyday experience. Since the extent and the quality of schooling were very limited in the small Indian village, it is unlikely that the improvement shown after ten or eleven years of age was a function of school experience. Rather, the belief that generating knowledge and activating strategies in difficult problem situations aids performance did appear eventually. I suspect this competence is fundamental to formal operational thought.

It is necessary, therefore, to differentiate between highly prepared and less prepared cognitive competences. The former set seems to require only the experiences that are part of living in the natural world. The less prepared competences—multiplication and conjugating verbs—require special tutoring. Linguistic contrasts provide an example. Children find it easier to learn the contrasts between *one and many* than between *several and many;* between *up and down* than between *right and left;* between *in and on* than between *near and far*. Preparedness does not imply a rigid schedule of times when structures will develop; it only implies that some structures-cum-processes are easier to acquire than others. Nature gives to the young organism the potential for acquiring a large number of abilities and lets experience control the small number that will be actualized.

This selected review of some of the obvious maturational milestones has listed only cognitive talents and, thus, contrasts with the milestones described by Piaget and, more recently, by Fischer, both of whom award major importance to the maturation of sensorimotor structures in the first year and less to enhancement of recognition and retrieval memory. Fischer's ontogenetic schedule assumes a deep connectedness in a sequence that begins with the coordinated acts of infancy and moves, in turn, to representations of events, coordinations of representations, propositions for abstract ideas, and, finally, coordinations of abstract ideas (Fischer and Silvern, 1985). The basic premises in this frame are, first, that implementation of motor skills is necessary for the later cognitive competences and, second, that the appearance of a new class of cognitive unit is followed by the emergence of the ability to coordinate and relate other members of that class. Although both premises are reasonable, the former remains in more dispute than the latter.

Final Speculations

As I wrote in the introduction, as well as in the first essay in this volume, the meaning of theoretical propositions about cognitive functioning depends upon the source of evidence. The reader will recall that when simply naming animals was the evidence, all children possessed the concept; but when clustering in recall or proactive inhibition provided the evidence, many of the same children did not seem to possess the same concept. One rebuttal to this statement is to insist that all ten-year-olds possess a similar conceptual representation of *animal,* but some will not display that knowledge in every assessment context. After all, persons with focal lesions of the temporal lobe do not display signs of that lesion on every relevant diagnostic test. But it is fair to ask if the referential and, therefore, the theoretical meaning of the concept of focal lesion is the same for two patients if one experiences difficulty remembering dates and the other does not, even if both have similar size lesions in the same place. This question leads to a second, more abstract point.

Contrasts in Description

Most descriptions, whether in scientific journals or in newspapers, have an implicit contrast class. When I point to a table laden with Thanksgiving delicacies and say "That's a pie," I am likely to imply a distinction between the pie and the other foods. But should I say, "That's a pumpkin pie," I am more likely to imply a distinction between two forms of pie. Current theories of cognitive development typically contrast, implicitly, biological preparedness for certain competences with a position that emphasizes the necessary contribution of certain experiences to acquisition of the competence. Piaget's genius was to unite the two by making action on the environment necessary for actualizing a universal cognitive process. When Jensen writes about Level 1 memory skills, he intends a contrast with Level 2 reasoning abilities and, thus, awards salience to the rote quality of a memory task rather than to the transformations that are part of metamemory. But when our research group describes the performance of two-year-olds on a procedure in which the child has to remember the location of a toy placed under one of six cups, our intended contrast is language competence, not reasoning ability. Thus, we make the capacity for sustained attention a primary feature of memory, not its rote-like quality.

When J. J. Gibson theorized about the autochthonous nature of the perception of motion, the implied contrast was learning the cues for motion. As a result, Gibson emphasized the structures of the stimulus arrays that produce a perception of motion. However, when the neuropsychologist Robert Wurtz writes about the perception of motion, the implied contrast is the neural basis for the perception of space, and Wurtz focuses on the brain sites that mediate motion perception. Wurtz and Gibson emphasize different features of the construct *motion perception,* even though both use the same descriptive construct and are interested in similar phenomena.

Jean Piaget contrasts the infants' sensorimotor actions on objects with representations of those objects, while our research, which is concerned with the same developmental period, contrasts the ability to recall a past representation with the ability to anticipate a future event. I do not suggest that one of these contrasts is theoretically more useful than another, only that all theorists bring to their observations a small set of *a priori* contrasts from which description and explanation derive.

Presently, the cognitive scientists interested in artificial intelligence are introducing a totally novel contrast into discussions of mental functioning. When they use terms like *remember, learn,* or *perceive* for the output of a program, their contrast is the human mind. But, historically, the contrast for a human cognitive process has always been another human cognitive process (for example, sensation versus perception, perception versus memory, memory versus evaluation). The wholesale borrowing of constructs that have always been used to describe human mental events and applying them to the propositions in computer programs leads to a final idea relevant to the dramatic rise of interest in the field of artificial intelligence.

Equivalent Explanations

Most developmental psychologists take biology, not physics, as a model for explanation because the historical conditions that mediate biological phenomena are always critical to the preferred explanation. If two qualitatively different conditions lead to the same observable phenomenon (for example, a lesion of the optic nerve and cataracts both produce an inability to see), the two forms of blindness are not regarded as theoretically equivalent, despite the fact that both patients have 20/200 vision. However, the concept of equivalence in physics holds that if the same mathematical description applies to a phenomenon that is produced by very different sets of conditions, the two phenotypically identical phenomena are considered equivalent theoretically. The classic example is the concave surface of the water in a bucket that is rotating on a table. However, if one imagines the universe rotating and the bucket standing perfectly still, the surface of the water in the bucket will also appear concave. Because the mathematics that describes the concave surface is the same for both a rotating bucket and a rotating universe, the two instances are considered equivalent.

Theory in cognitive development has not been friendly to this view. Most investigators have favored the biological premise that surface identity does not imply identity of mechanism. For example, the unconditioned nictitating membrane reflex (NMR) in the rabbit to a puff of air involves different brain structures than does the conditioned NMR, even though the reflex appears identical under the two incentive conditions (cerebellar nuclei are necessary for the conditioned reflex but not for the unconditioned one). Thus, no psychologist or physiologist would regard the two phenomena as equivalent. However, increasing numbers of cognitive scientists are showing signs of attraction to the physicists' equivalence. Scholars in artificial intelligence assume that if there is no detectable difference between a solution produced by a program and one produced by a human mind, the two solutions should be considered equivalent, despite the obvious differences in mediating conditions. Thus, the rise of artificial intelligence has created a tension between formalists, who treat identity of outcome and imposed explanation as primary, and empiricists, for whom identity of mediating, historical conditions is primary. Consider an example of this tension from a study on infants.

Starkey et al. (1983) reported that infants under one year look longer at a picture containing three objects than at one containing two objects when they hear a trio of drum beats, but look longer at two objects than at three objects when they hear a pair of drum beats. The investigators concluded that young infants possess cognitive structures that appreciate number. In the older child and adult, possession of the concept of number implies the knowledge that numerosity is a feature of every array of objects and that two arrays of physically different objects can have the same numerosity. Because the infants in this experiment (which, incidentally, has not been successfully replicated; see Moore et al., 1987) behave as if they treat two sounds and two visual objects as equal, the investigators concluded that some component of the infant's cognitive structure was similar to a component in the older child's representation of number.

The basis for this argument about number representation is use of the same construct (that is, the idea of *number*) to explain the phenotypically different, but presumably analogous, behaviors of infants and older children. This is reminiscent of nineteenth-century theorists who believed that the psychological derivative of the grasp reflex in the newborn could be seen in the adult desire to acquire and retain money and property. Those who are not persuaded by the conclusion of Starkey and colleagues will point to the very different cognitive structures and functions of infants and ten-year-olds, that is, historical facts that imply different mediating conditions. I argued earlier for a distinction between generalizations that involve schemata and those involving concepts. Unlike a majority of behavioral biologists, many cognitive scientists prefer ahistorical explanations that ignore important differences among infants, children, and adults as long as a feature of a cognitive performance is common to the behavior of persons of varied ages.

At present, most students of cognitive development remain empiricists rather than formalists, and they use similarity in mediating conditions resulting from prior history, not similarity of outcome, as primary bases for theoretical advance. It is reassuring that Piaget sided with the empiricists, despite his penchant for formalism, for he insisted that a child who conserved because he was tutored in a special way was not the same as one who answered the conservation problem spontaneously, because the mediating conditions were different. It will be useful for students of cognitive development to remain acutely self-conscious of this theme as formalists begin to invade a territory that has been dominated by empiricists committed to historical explanations.

This is not an innocent tension, nor is it limited to the social sciences. A similar theme can be detected in evolutionary biology in debates between pheneticists, who argue that the number of contemporary similar features should be the only guide to correct taxonomy, and cladists, who insist that an animal's evolutionary history must be part of the taxonomic decision. Scholars who describe contemporary Mexican society would never treat Japan and Mexico as belonging to the same category, even though both societies are characterized by an authoritarian relation between husband and wife, avoidance of confrontation in social encounter, and loyalty to the family, because each society acquired these characteristics in different ways. The biology of newborns provides a final example. It is not possible to detect any important differences between newborn mammalian infants conceived naturally and those conceived through artificial insemination. However, theoretical propositions about long-term population trends in animals or humans that contain the concept *reproduction* as a predicate will have very different meanings and validities under the two forms of conception.

Put simply, if a programmed robot's performance on a specific set of problems cannot be distinguished from that of a human adult, is it useful to assume that the two performances are equivalent theoretically? The influence of twentieth-century pragmatism is obvious when the question is phrased in this way. The answer will depend on our purpose. Yes, if we wish to use machines to replace humans on selected tasks, but no if we wish to understand how each form reached its goal. To a pragmatic skeptic who might ask why understanding of mechanism is important, my reply is simply that although coherence is one defensible definition of truth, correspondence between propositions and events in nature remains an equally useful and, I might add, essential second definition.

Scholars in artificial intelligence believe psychological statements about mental functions can be replaced with propositions in a program simulating a cognitive performance. The source of vulnerability in that position differs from the one we noted earlier in the discussion of biological reductionism. One of the most sophisticated attempts at computer simulation of cognitive processes is called PDP—parallel distributed processing (Rumelhart and McClelland, 1986). The basic assumption in this effort is that the units that are activated and inhibited become linked through frequent co-variation of certain input events, a premise that does not stray far from David Hartley's eighteenth-century treatise on associationism. Because no executive process is represented in the program, knowledge is extremely specific. For example, the program requires just as many trials to learn to recognize the letter *s* in the second position in a word as it takes to recognize the letter *s* in the third position. Further, there is no unit in the program that corresponds to a lexical structure. Thus, it is unlikely that the program would predict pro-active interference—one of the most robust phenomena in cognitive functioning.

Investigators in both artificial intelligence and biology, but for very different reasons, want to replace statements containing concepts like act, representation, symbol, feeling, motive, and self-consciousness with a different language. These claims are motivated primarily by a desire for the greater certainty provided by the logical coherence of a program and the reliable empirical facts of modern biology. The language of modern psychology does rely too often on metaphor and analogy to persuade. For example, the assumption that cognitive development consists of a series of stages in which structures characterizing earlier stages persist into later ones derives neither from impeccable data nor coherent argument but rather from intuitions about the growth of a tree. For those who believe that computer programs and neurobiology will advance the behavioral sciences, the best help developmental psychologists can offer is to tell these scholars what it is they have to explain.

6

Creativity in Science

Every language contains a small number of words referring to events which can generate the brief pulse of feeling we call awe. *Creativity* is one of the select words that has gained access to that privileged category.

The status of creativity was far less secure in the centuries before the Renaissance. The Middle Ages treated ideas that were original transformations of existing beliefs with respect only as long as they were actualized in cathedrals, poems, and philosophical essays that supported Christianity, not if they revealed a fault in that philosophical system. Bronowski (1958) notes that the Middle Ages did not revere the cathedrals but the acts of worship which they served.

The status of creative people has been enhanced with each succeeding century since the Renaissance, but the reasons why intellectual creativity inspired reverence are not easily understood. I suspect that the enigmatic nature of creativity represents yet one more example of the Western delight in giving to the human mind a special ontological status that differentiates it from the body in order to maintain an ideological moat between the material world and human spirituality. Remember that Descartes concluded that his thoughts, not his perception of the rosey fingers of dawn, were the only irrefutable evidence of his existence. But the high place of creativity in our value system required secular events also.

Two important facilitating conditions were a pluralistic society and the rise of empirical sciences, with their pragmatic implications for the larger community. When a society is relatively homogeneous in its primary beliefs, there will be minimal ideological conflict and, therefore, no need for anyone to invent arguments that are Hegelian syntheses of two opposing positions. In contrast with many Oriental cultures during most of their history, European cultures have been composed of a larger number of opposing religious and linguistic groups and, most important, a tension between the antirealist, absolutistic philosophy characteristic of European Christianity and the materialist, but relativistic, philosophy that has developed from half a millennium of empirical science.

Anyone who could ease that tension with essays, discoveries, novels, or paintings was valued, and a grateful society was eager to express its thanks by awarding the person the special title *creative.* Newton removed some of the religious mystery from cosmic phenomena; Kant rescued the idea of a universal moral capacity from a value-free natural philosophy that was treating benevolence as the simple consequence of hedonistic desires. Kant's essays helped to mute the growing skepticism toward gentle acts that had been regarded for centuries as moral.

When creative ideas began to supply bases for commercial progress, especially after 1700, Europe had even better reasons to reward intellectual originality. Many acknowledged that the position of economic and military power held by the West was due, in part, to the products of creative minds. As a result, more talented European youth than Chinese and Japanese youth wanted to be creative.

Meanings of Creativity

Before analyzing the psychological conditions that make it possible for some individuals to generate creative products, we must first settle on the meanings of a creative product. The meaning we normally rely on in conversation is the set of related ideas that members of a language community agree upon—Frege's "sense meaning." The sense meaning of the word *good,* for example, includes ideas like "benefitting another," "kindness," "charity," "honesty," and "love." This family of ideas can exist as an ensemble in individual minds without the need to think of any particular person. The sense meaning of a *creative product* includes ideas like "original," "novel," and the implicit notion that it is an aesthetically pleasing transformation of an existing thought, solution, or form. The "Eroica" was regarded as creative because of its unique transformation on Mozart's music. But St. Augustine would not have regarded Beethoven as creative because his music would not have been an assimilable transformation on Gregorian chants. As with the word *good,* one can understand sentences that contain the word *creative* without thinking about any particular individual.

The sense meaning of a *creative product* —not a *creative person* or the *creative process*—is also silent on its form, the historical era in which it was generated, and its implications for the society. It is simply a definition, not unlike saying "Fruits are pleasant things to eat," without specifying a specific plant and the conditions surrounding its growth, harvesting, shape, color, or taste. Thus Frege argued that words have a second meaning which specifies the thing in the world to which the word refers. This referential meaning allows us to decide if the word is being used correctly and whether the sentences in which it appears are true or false. If someone claimed that Bishop Wilberforce's arguments were creative, we could decide if that sentence were true by applying the sense meaning to his views on evolution.

Psychologists more often study the referential meaning of a creative product, not the sense meaning, for a very good reason. A central contemporary feature of a creative product is the fact that it is aesthetically pleasing to one community, usually the one for which it was intended, but not necessarily to another. A creative product, unlike a person's heart rate or running speed, is defined not only by its inherent structural qualities but also by the relation between the new ideas and those of the audience. Remember that many Europeans did not believe Freud's hypotheses, even when they became popular, and most physicians in India, China, and Japan have been indifferent to psychoanalytic theory. That is why we must specify the context of an idea that is a candidate for creativity and use the referential meaning in talking about this class of phenomena. Although a tree in a virgin forest exists even if no one is present, an idea we call creative requires the reaction of another, not just the judgment of the inventor or of history. Gunther Stent has noted that Avery's discovery in 1944 that DNA was the key to heredity was premature and, therefore, unappreciated because geneticists were not able to build upon it. We can say that Avery's hypothesis proved to be true, correct, or insightful, but, in the frame of this essay, it was not creative. I am restricting the word *creative* to refer to products that generate a specific cognitive and emotional response in an audience; hence, many valid ideas will not be judged creative while some invalid ones will be so judged.

The remainder of this essay is about the conditions that permit a small number of talented scientists working in specific settings at specific times to produce creative ideas. Many contemporary European and North American youth who have chosen science as a career want to be creative. But, as we shall see, only a small number achieve that goal. The different conditions that must come together at a particular time and place to produce a creative product include, minimally, special talent in a domain, the motivation to be creative, which is influenced by childhood experiences, and, finally, chance events that permit the talent and desire to be actualized.

Specific Talents

A majority of the creative persons most of us admire seem to have been creative in very specific domains. Leonardo da Vinci was an exception. Some have been inept in areas outside their sphere of excellence. That is why I do not favor the suggestion that a basic intellectual competence, or general intelligence, is a useful concept in explaining a creative product. Einstein failed foreign language at the Gymnasium and had great difficulty learning English as a second language; Rabi managed to be absent from the laboratory when a new piece of apparatus was being built because, his biographer notes, Rabi was not clever with machines. Thus, the first claim is that creativity is usually local to a domain of inquiry.

I also share the popular belief, although it has not yet been proven beyond doubt, that each unusual talent requires some special biological configuration of brain structure and chemistry that favors a specific competence, be it with numbers, images, words, notes, machines, or brush and oil. Mark Kac once wrote that all physicists are smart, a smaller number are geniuses and a rare few are magicians. A magician is able to perceive at once the deep and simpler structure of a complex physical problem. He regarded the late Richard Feynman as a magician.

Sources of Motivation

An unusual talent will not be actualized unless it is wed to a motive to use it. Our society currently provides several different incentives for applying a special competence to generate a creative solution to a difficult problem. One of the most obvious is to gain recognition from colleagues or fame from the larger community. One reason why the Japanese fret about not being sufficiently creative is that their society does not award enthusiastic acclaim to those who generate novel ideas. Indeed, people who are too original are apt to experience subtle social rejection. Susumu Tonegawa, an MIT biologist born in Japan who won the Nobel Prize in physiology and medicine in 1987, told reporters that he could not have done the research that led to the prize had he remained in Japan. His superiors would not have permitted him the space, funds, or psychological freedom to test what turned out to be creative hypotheses.

A second, less common, motive for applying talent in a creative way is hostility to peers. The aim of hostility is to cause physical or psychic distress to another. Adolescents will taunt those they dislike with statements that imply that the other is dumb. Such an accusation can provoke strong anger in the accused. Some scientists who produce a creative idea anticipate that their less creative, but hardworking, peers will be threatened by their originality. Therefore, a chronic hostility to peers can find gratification in creative work. James Watson irritated his biological colleagues when he suggested that this motivational dynamic was present among some scientists.

A related, but different, motive is the desire for psychological power over others. Intellectual communities in the West award a degree of psychological authority to their most creative members. Those with a strong urge for this form of power can gratify it by being creative. Biographical records imply that this motive was more salient for Newton and Russell than for Einstein and Whitehead. François Jacob (1988) describes a day-long seminar at the Pasteur Institute in which Martin Pollock and Jacques Monod argued about a theoretical point. Jacob describes the two men, "two trained roosters beak to beak, vying with humor and sarcasm. Not because of nationalism, but through a will to power, through a desire for intellectual domination" (p. 218). Jacob admits later in the memoir to his own strong need for glory and the sense of power it brings.

There is some modest empirical support for the hypothesis that the desire for fame and power blended with a hostility toward peers can facilitate creative work. Donald MacKinnon compared the life histories of creative mathematicians and architects with those of very successful, but far less creative, professional peers. A frequent distinguishing feature between the two groups was that the creative adults had experienced as adolescents a degree of peer rejection that generated anger and resentment toward others and, subsequently, a motive to be in a position of power over them.

A second source of evidence is the historical scholarship of Frank Sulloway, who has examined a large number of creative revolutions in science from Copernican theory to Wegener's hypothesis of continental drift. Using the *Dictionary of Scientific Biography* as his principal source of data, Sulloway found over 800 eminent scientists who either supported or opposed one of 16 different revolutionary ideas within ten years of its original publication. Significantly more scholars who favored or promoted the creative hypothesis were later-borns (they had one or more older siblings), rather than first-borns (82 versus 18 percent). By contrast, more scientists who opposed the novel idea were first rather than later born. This result is in accord with the claim that a motive for enhanced power and a resentment against those with power can, on occasion, catalyze a talent into a creative idea. First-borns generally enjoy higher status in their family and identify more deeply, first, with parents and, later, with legitimate authority than do later-borns. As a result, first-borns experience a greater reluctance to oppose the views of authority. Later-borns, by contrast, find it easier, and perhaps more gratifying, to challenge those in power. In the sciences, such a challenge often takes the form of looking for opportunities to replace established beliefs with fresh ones. There is a special delight in thinking of novel hypotheses that are critical of those that are consensual.

A fourth incentive for creative work is found in the private standards each adolescent extracts from the maelstrom of childhood. Most adolescents believe there is a best way to act and a best set of standards to guide life choices. This conviction grows out of a universal moral sense that emerges in all children by their third birthday. The Swedish novelist Lagerquist once had God reply to a soul who asked what His purpose was in creating humans with, "I only intended that man would never be satisfied with nothing."

Although every adolescent has an idea of what his perfect self should be, the specific content of that ideal is a constructed synthesis of past experiences. For some, the Kantian imperative that emanates from the ideal is "be helpful"; for others, "be loved"; for others, "be strong, rich, or respected." For a much smaller number, the imperative is to "be intelligent." I do not understand all of the conditions that lead a child to pick one of these standards rather than another to guide a life itinerary. But an adolescent who is trying to prove to self that he or she is intelligent will regard a creative product as the acme of that personal standard. It also helps if the person is just a little uncertain over meeting the standard for highly creative work. A child who is slightly unsure of his or her intellectual status has an additional spur to strive to meet the standard. The novelist Flannery O'Connor once told an interviewer that in order to write a great novel one should not understand the plot too completely. The uncertainty over the final form of the piece supplies the psychic energy needed for the creative process. Jacob writes of his alternating moods of euphoria and nagging anxiety as he began his scientific career and of "the fear of having no talent; of being good for nothing."

If the youths who experience a moral directive to be intelligent select natural science as the domain of actualization, they are likely to show an unusual degree of curiosity about nature. All children are curious about events in the world, and all adults prefer knowing why to remaining ignorant. Hence, we do not have to posit any special motive to explain a scientist's desire to understand nature more fully. But we do have to explain why that universal motive is so much more ascendant in creative scientists than in the rest of the community. Consider an analogy to risk taking. It is natural for all adults to take some pleasure from the resolution of temporary uncertainty. Most of us, on occasion, will place ourselves in conditions of mild to moderate risk. But the small group of mountain climbers, sport parachutists, and hang glider enthusiasts who consistently put themselves in situations of high risk because they derive so much pleasure from the activity must have had a set of childhood experiences that differentiate them from the rest of us.

I believe there may be two different psychological bases for the special pleasure—some would call it a "high"—scientists experience when their curiosity has led to an original discovery. The essence of the first explanation is captured by Rabi's confession that his discoveries made him feel closer to God. Each of us wishes to regard self as good and virtuous. We want to believe that we are something more than animals concerned only with our hedonistic pleasure, but, in addition, are moral agents with a touch of spirituality. For most adults, the ordinary acts of kindness, empathy, honesty, and love toward family members and close friends are sufficient proof of our moral status. A small proportion, however, because of life history, is less certain and needs more evidence. Growing up in a home where religious values are taken seriously can produce an unusually high standard for one's moral status. Jean Piaget was raised in such a home and, as a late adolescent, wrote a prose poem called, "The Mission of the Idea," in which he suggested that creative thought is linked to the idea of Jesus. Piaget wrote, "The Idea surges from the depth of our being" and "Jesus is the Idea made flesh." A large number of creative scientists, more than one would expect by chance, grew up in homes where a parent, grandparent, or close relative was a professional clergyman. Pavlov, Millikan, Wegener, and Alvarez are four examples from this century.

A different basis for a link between creative scientific work and moral status is present when children believe they have characteristics that the majority regard as less virtuous. Membership in a minority group that experiences community prejudice provides a frequent example. A disproportionate number of twentieth-century Nobel laureates, including Axelrod, Einstein, Luria, Bohr, Loewi, Lederberg, Rabi, Yalow, Jacob, and Levi-Montalcini, were members of a minority group. The latter two, in recently published autobiographies, comment on the sense of difference and anxiety they felt as Jews in Catholic countries with a strong streak of anti-Semitism. Similarly, being Catholic in Great Britain or Protestant in France, which represented minority status during the eighteenth and nineteenth centuries, significantly increased the probability of achieving eminence in biology and geology (Sulloway, personal communication). Members of minority groups will be a little more uncertain about their state of virtue than others and, therefore, will be motivated to correct the uncomfortable perception the majority hold toward them. If the values promoted in the child's home environment lead the adult to treat intellectual inquiry as a morally virtuous activity, scientific research will serve a moral mission. Additionally, the selection of science has a special psychological meaning for the victim of prejudice who is convinced that the majority holds a false and, therefore, irrationally based belief. The replacement of incorrect beliefs with correct ones is the goal of science; hence, the investigator who is also a target of undeserved hostility always hopes that when the truth is known the community will replace the old ideas with more valid ones. Siding with Schopenhauer, Einstein wrote that "one of the strongest motives that lead men to art and science is flight from the everyday life with its painful harshness" (cited in Holton, 1988, p. 395).

The use of scientific inquiry to affirm one's moral virtue is captured in Rabi's reflections on the experiments that revealed the nuclear spin of sodium. "The world was young and I was young and the experiment was beautiful. It satisfied everything I wanted to see. There was an artistry in it or whatever it is called . . . It just charmed me. These atoms in spatially quantized states, analyze them in one field, turn your focus back and there it is. Count them! It was wonderful. There I really, I really believed in the spin, there are the states, count them! Each one, I suppose, seeks God in his own way" (cited in Rigden, 1987, p. 88).

A second, very different basis for a persistently searching curiosity about nature bears a superficial resemblance to Freud's belief that intellectual work could be a sublimation of sexual interests, but differs from it in fundamental mechanism. This argument rests on the premise that in most societies, including Western ones, the concept of nature is semantically closer to the category *female* than to the category *male*. Nature, flower, earth, moon, and ocean are often referred to with a female pronoun. Several years ago a group of my students found that among the world languages that mark nouns for gender there is a bias that favors a female morpheme for natural phenomena and a male morpheme for manufactured objects. Thus, I begin with the assumption that in the minds of adolescents most everyday, observable natural events lie closer to the idea of female than to the idea of male.

The second assumption, which is more difficult to support, holds that some boys develop an intense, affectively laden curiosity about females that rests on more than just the desire to know about the female genitals. It involves, in addition, a motive to penetrate the mysteries of conception, pregnancy, birth, nursing, and the unquestioning nurturance women show toward their children and other loved ones.

Jacob (1988) recalls his mother, "Tender, sweet perfumed, warmth. Safe harbor from all fears and all violence . . . Maman, who rocked me to sleep, bathed me, wiped me, blew my nose, disciplined me, tucked me in, caressed me, scolded me, watched over me . . . Maman, who for years launched me into the day each morning. And waited at her window to welcome me home from school each afternoon. Who, when I was a medical student and would get back late at night, always left a snack on the table with a note as tender as a kiss" (pp. 21–22). To a child, who is quintessentially self-interested, it must be puzzling to witness and to experience the unselfishness of mothers. The desire to understand this enigma in a child who is unusually talented could provoke an intense curiosity to discover nature's secrets. I am suggesting, however, that the mother is more mysterious to sons than to daughters, perhaps because the latter know they will, as women, understand the female mood. If this speculative hypothesis has any validity, it implies that one of the many motivations for scientific inquiry is more salient for men than for women. That suggestion does not mean that women are not curious about natural phenomena, only that for a large number of academically competent adults considering professional careers, a desire to understand why plants flower, birds migrate, or embryos develop may be a little more pressing for males than for females.

In *The World As I See It,* Einstein (1934) combined in one quotation the ideas of radiant beauty, penetration, mystery, cradle, and emotion.

> The most beautiful experience we can have is the mysterious. It is the fundamental emotion which stands at the cradle of true art and true science . . . It was the experience of mystery—even if mixed with fear—that engendered religion. A knowledge of the existence of something we can not penetrate, our perceptions of the profoundest reason and the most radiant beauty, which only in their most primitive forms are accessible to our minds—it is this knowledge and this emotion that constitute true religiosity; in this sense, and in this alone, I am a deeply religious man. (cited in French, 1979, p. 304)

Of course, most creative scientists did not begin their career with a burning curiosity that was specific to the domain in which they made their later, important discoveries. For some, the original motive was, more simply, a desire to participate in science. Jacob sought a position at the Pasteur Institute because it enjoyed a high reputation. Had Lwoff been studying pig embryos rather than bacterial enzymes Jacob would still have joined Lwoff's laboratory. The activity of doing science is the original incentive for a majority of investigators because the activity is morally virtuous or provides gratification for the motives of curiosity, power, or fame. A new motive, following a series of successes, can grow from the pleasures creative science brings. Gordon Allport called this phenomenon the "functional autonomy of motives."

The Role of Temperament

I also believe that temperamental factors can contribute to the tendency to seek the solitary life of the creative scientist or scholar. As I noted in Chapter 4, our research group has been studying a small group of children who are extremely shy and timid during the preschool years and avoid groups of peers when they enter school. If these children happen to come from homes that value academic work, they are likely to find a satisfying substitute for group activity in school achievement. After reading the biographies or autobiographies of T. S. Eliot, Kafka, Whitehead, Turing, and Levi-Montalcini, I am convinced that each provides an example of how an inhibited temperament can nudge a child toward a life of creative scholarship.

Levi-Montalcini remembers that she was much more timid and melancholy than her fraternal twin sister, Paola. "My tendency to seek solitude and to flee from encounters with either sex reminded her [Levi-Montalcini's mother] of the sad, reserved character of her own mother" (p. 14). Levi-Montalcini notes that the alliance she established with her sociable, extraverted sister "did not free me from the anxieties I suffered as a child. These had their roots in extreme timidity, lack of self confidence, and fear of adults in general and of my father in particular, as well as of monsters that might suddenly pop out of the dark and throw themselves upon me" (p. 15).

Levi-Montalcini, like many of our inhibited children, would regularly ask her sister to accompany her to her bedroom at night. "To reach our bedroom and bathroom in the apartment where we then lived, one had to walk the whole length of a long hallway . . . The moment dusk began to fall . . . I would ask Paola, who didn't suffer from these torments, to accompany me whenever I had to face the ordeal. This fear of the dark, and of malevolent beings who might take advantage of it to attack me, was not the only manifestation of my insecurity and anxious nature" (p. 16).

She also hoped that her father would understand why his young daughter, who he called "a shrinking violet," did not want to kiss him; she found his mustache psychologically aversive. Levi-Montalcini sensed that these psychological qualities were based on temperamental factors, for she notes that her father, too, had a sensitive and serious personality.

I suspect that if biographers awarded to temperamental processes the same degree of formative power they now give to the actions of parents and siblings, geography, and historical period, their interpretations would be enriched. Whitehead's biographer, Victor Lowe, who was puzzled by Whitehead's gentle, retiring nature, might have gained some clarity had he reflected on his knowledge that as a child Whitehead was a shy, later-born, blue-eyed boy—three salient characteristics of the temperamentally inhibited child I described in Chapter 4.

Chance

Finally, the contribution of chance must be acknowledged. One would like to believe that unusual ability and persistent motivation would be sufficient, but, unfortunately, conditions that cannot be predicted are necessary to bind the separate human qualities into a significant discovery. There are many more persons capable of creative products than there are such products. Chance often operates by placing a scientist in the right location at the right time. During the last decade of the nineteenth century St. Petersburg was the only city in Europe with excellent laboratory facilities for surgery on dogs. Had Pavlov been in any other European city, he probably would not have discovered classical conditioning. Mendel was admitted into the only monastery in the area that had a large garden, a herbarium, and an abbot who was interested in botany. Had Mendel's family been familiar with an abbot from any other monastery, it is unlikely he would have discovered the genetics of the pea plant. If James Watson had followed the instructions from the scientific committee supporting his fellowship and not gone to work with Crick in Cambridge, he would not have gained access to Franklin's crystallographic data, and another biologist would have been co-discoverer of DNA.

Perhaps the most extraordinary tale involves Fleming's discovery of penicillin, which required at least five independent events to come together in the summer of 1928. First, there had to be a scientist visiting the London hospital who was assigned a work space on the floor below Fleming's laboratory. Second, the visitor had to be working on penicillium molds. Third, the hospital had to be old so that the penicillium spores could rise through the cracks between the floor boards and permeate Fleming's work space. Fourth, Fleming had to be a less compulsive bacteriologist than most of his colleagues so that he would leave his plates of staphylococci uncovered at the end of the day. Finally, the temperature in London that summer had to be a bit warmer than usual so that the penicillium could grow on Fleming's cultures and kill bacteria in the places where it became established. Had only one of these factors been missing, Fleming may not have discovered penicillin. Yes, chance does favor the prepared mind, but every high-flying idea needs a place to alight. The joining of investigator to setting can be the throw of the dice that Einstein resented so deeply.

Form of the Creative Product

Finally, I consider briefly the factors influencing the form the creative effort assumes. I shall restrict the discussion to the sciences because I know them best and do not claim that these ideas are relevant for writers, artists, and composers. Perhaps others who know these fields better than I will find the division I am about to suggest applicable to these areas as well.

The essential idea is illustrated, extensionally, by comparing Gauss, Turing, and Einstein, whose contributions used the formal apparatus of logic or mathematics, with Wegener, Freud, and Darwin, whose insightful *a posteriori* inferences from observations were arranged in prose arguments that were persuasive but not logically necessary. Although more members of the former group work in mathematics and physics than in biology or the social sciences, both types exist within each discipline. I believe the scientists in the contrasting groups are different in a deep and lasting way.

The first group celebrates the human mind, treating it as a revered object to be probed in a quiet room until it reveals its abstract beauty. The joy comes from using one's mind to invent a set of logically coherent ideas that solves a conceptual problem. The second group celebrates nature, especially her interrelatedness, concreteness, and contextual relativism. For this group the satisfaction comes from discovering something new about real events in a real world. For the young Ernst Mayr it was birds; for Linus Pauling it was rocks. Unlike the formalists, who are excited by the freedom of playing with impossible ideas, most empiricists heed Peter Medawar's advice to work on soluble problems. The biologist Julius Axelrod (1981) writes, "The important thing is to ask a question that is realistic" (p. 27); Jacob notes, "Biologists abhor abstraction . . . I saw Nature as a good girl. Generous, but a little dirty. A bit muddle-headed. Working in a hit or miss fashion. Doing what she could with what was at hand" (p. 320). No natural phenomenon has the bright, pristine quality of a universal law woven from a logically commanding mathematical argument. The difference between the two types of scholars is captured in a comparison of Russell and Whitehead. In a passage from *Portraits From Memory,* Russell (1963) writes,

> It was Whitehead who was the serpent in this paradise of Mediterranean clarity. He said to me once: "You think the world is what it looks like in fine weather at noon day; I think it is what it seems like in the early morning when one first wakes from deep sleep". I thought his remark horrid, but could not see how to prove that my bias was any better than his. At last he showed me how to apply the technique of mathematical logic to his vague and higgledy-piggledy world, and dress it up in Sunday clothes that the mathematician could view without being shocked. This technique, which I learnt from him delighted me, and I no longer demanded that the naked truth should be as good as the truth in its mathematical Sunday best. (p. 39–40)

For reasons I do not completely understand, I derive more delight from discovering a secret of nature, even one that must be hedged with caveats, than from most formal, *a priori* arguments. I am suspect of the mind's susceptibility to settling on simple solutions. With Eugene Wigner, I have difficulty understanding how the mind/brain of *Homo sapiens,* barely a hundred-thousand years old and evolved primarily to keep us alive long enough to beget the next generation, could have inherited neural structures capable of creating accurate mathematical descriptions of phenomena that were present millions of years before humans appeared. I also confess to a flaw that may be fatal to empirical scientists. I so revere nature that sometimes I suspect I do not want to understand her too completely. If I am too successful, she will lose all of her mystery. I poke and prod her but, with e e cummings, smile privately in celebration of her perennial answer—Spring.

Part Four
Self

7

The Emergence of Self-Awareness

The products of every scholarly mission gain clarity if viewed against two reference sources—the dominant ideology of the period and the idiosyncratic intellectual history of the investigator. This essay on the emergence of self-awareness is no exception. Since the end of World War I most observers of human development, especially those in England and the United States, have awarded major formative power to social experience and have been loyal to the principles of gradual and connected growth. The young child's first word, first cry at maternal departure, and first sign of self-consciousness were assumed to be the visible result of a long and cumulative history of underground constructions built in small units from the many social interactions with family members. This was not the view of nineteenth-century scholars like Preyer or Stern, who believed that the early-appearing human qualities were more autochthonous and inevitable as long as the child met the minimal conditions of living in a world of objects and people. The data to be presented in this chapter seem to be in closer accord with these century-old views than with beliefs held by contemporary theorists.

The phenomena to be discussed should also be viewed as a continuation of a strategy I began to adopt about a dozen years ago. In earlier work my colleagues and I assumed the reality and theoretical utility of abstract constructs like passivity, sociability, hostility, achievement, reflectivity, and identification, and we made our observations accommodate to those ideas (Kagan and Moss, 1962; Kagan, 1971). Although these concepts seemed useful in integrating both naturalistic and experimental observations with older children, they were less appropriate to the behavioral repertoire of the infant. Gradually, almost unconsciously, I began to shift my empirical strategy and accommodate to the typical surface behaviors of the young child. During the first year, infants look, smile, and babble to stimuli, play with objects, and show imitation of or distress at the unexpected and the unfamiliar. I noted the developmental course of these behaviors in response to varied incentives and, after discovering regularities, invented constructs like *inhibition* and *enhanced retrieval capacity,* consciously resisting the use of constructs that implied a theoretical similarity to the behaviors of older children or adults (Kagan et al., 1978).

It seemed reasonable to extend this Baconian attitude to the second year of life. I began these studies without an overarching theoretical conception of the major milestones between 12 and 24 months of age. Piagetian theory is not a particularly useful guide to this era, and systematic research on this period is still sparse. But no investigator begins his work without prejudice. The selection of variables is the first demand of science, and selection always implies *a priori* ideas. The tasks we chose and the behaviors we selected for quantification were influenced by a central supposition about early development: namely, that the emergence of cognitive competences resulting from the maturation of the central nervous system is essential to understanding the changing profile of behavior during the early years.

The history of developmental inquiry contains a guide for the choice of procedures. The study of behaviors that dominate the repertoire during a particular phase of development often leads to inferences about processes that are occasionally concealed when the reactions to experimental procedures are assessed, especially if the situations require responses less natural to that stage.

Young children are uncertain in most experimental situations, and this state is often a major cause of their reactions. Thus we devoted a great deal of time to observing behaviors that are prominent during the second year in the laboratory as well as in the more familiar home setting with the mother present. These included symbolic play with toys, imitation, speech, and reciprocal social interaction. The explicit assumption was that these are universal behaviors whose time of appearance reflects the rate of maturation of more basic psychological functions, as the age of appearance of pubic and axillary hair indexes the times when important changes are occurring in the hypothalamus, pituitary, and gonads. Indeed, the changes of puberty provide a useful model for our work. As reproductive fertility is established, there are surface changes in the distribution of hair, size of the genitals, pitch of voice in males, and breast size in females. It is not obvious that these diverse phenomena have their origin in an endocrine mechanism that is triggered by an alteration in hypo-thalamic sensitivity to circulating sex hormone.

Method

We evaluated five classes of behavior that emerged during the second year: intelligible speech, concern with parental prohibitions and violations of parental standards, avoidance of tasks that are difficult to implement, patterns of social interaction with adults and children, and, finally, symbolic play.

The research passed through three stages. During the first, we followed two cohorts of children for about 10 months. The younger cohort of 14 children was observed twice a month every month from 13 to 22 months of age. The older cohort of 16 children was observed on the same schedule from 20 to 29 months and again at 30, 32, and 34 months. All the children were Caucasian, from middle-class families. The investigation revealed two facts of importance. First, there was a major change in cognitive performance around the second birthday. Second, and of more significance, obvious distress appeared in the months before the second birthday when an examiner modeled some acts in front of the attentive youngster. The need to understand this phenomenon more deeply led to the second phase of the project, which involved study of two cross-sectional samples of children in order to eliminate alternative interpretations of the anxiety we noted. Reflection on these results suggested a need for a richer corpus and led to the final set of studies. One was a detailed examination of the growth of six children who were observed in their homes longitudinally every three weeks for close to 10 months. A second was a comparable investigation of 67 Fijian children growing up on isolated atolls in the Pacific (Katz, 1981). A third was a longitudinal study of seven Vietnamese children who, with their parents, had recently arrived in California (Gellerman, 1981). I shall now summarize the phenomena that were seen in these children during the last half of the second year.

Results

The Appearance of Standards

Around 17 to 20 months of age, children display an obvious concern with a special class of events and actions whose attributes deviate from what adults regard as normative. Children now point with trepidation to small holes in clothing, tiny spots on furniture, dolls with chipped paint, missing bristles on a broom, or an almost invisible crack in a plastic toy and utter, with dysphoric tone, phrases like "Oh-oh." Hundreds of events, many of them subtle and instrumentally irrelevant, capture the child's attention and, on occasion, elicit a special facial reaction and verbal comment. Some one-word utterances have the qualities of a conceptual category. One of the 22-month-old children consistently called a "boo-boo" any place where an upholstered button was missing on a chair or sofa, a bowel movement, dirt on the floor, and a broken toy telephone. These events share no common physical quality. What they do share is that each is a variation on a normative experience which presumably has been associated with a communication from parents indicating that the event is disapproved.

In one of the cross-sectional studies, 14- and 19-month-old children were allowed to play for 20 minutes with a set of 22 toys. Ten toys were unflawed, without irregularities or tears—for example, a fire engine, a car. Another set of 10 toys was purposefully flawed in some way. Examples included a boat with holes in the bottom, a doll with black streaks on the face, a broken telephone. Additionally, two of the toys were odd-shaped, meaningless wooden pieces that were unflawed. We inserted these two toys to test whether special concern with the flawed objects was due to the fact that their integrity was violated rather than to the fact that they were discrepant. No 14-month-old child behaved in any special way towards the flawed toys, while 57 percent of the 19-month-old children showed unambiguous signs of concern with one or more of these objects. They would point to one of the flawed toys and vocalize, bring the toys to their mother, or say explicitly that something about the toy was unusual—"Fix it," "Broke," or "Yukky." No child behaved this way toward the meaningless forms.

Almost fifty years ago Charlotte Bühler (1930) also noted a sensitivity to parental standards during the second year. In her experiments, one-to two-year-old children were forbidden to touch a toy in the room by an adult. But when the adult left the room briefly, many touched the toy. When the adult returned, all of the 18-month-olds showed behavior that Bühler regarded as embarrassment or a frightened expression.

The language protocols from the six children we saw at home revealed that between 19 and 26 months the speech of every child contained reference to standards (*broken, boo-boo, dirty, wash hands, can't, hard do*). Similar data gathered by others (the sources are both English and German and include a 1928 diary by Stern and Stern) indicate that by 20 months most children are using words that refer to standards. The remarkable agreement in the time when children first use evaluative language implies the maturation of a new cognitive function (Bretherton et al., 1981). It is unlikely that all children decide by 24 months that a dirty blouse is a violation of a norm: they must first be exposed to some information which leads them to classify certain actions and associated outcomes in a special way. The most likely possibility is that certain events have provoked adult reactions which generated in the child a state of uncertainty. These reactions can be as subtle as an unexpected change in the timbre of the parent's voice or shape of her eyes, or as salient as a verbal reproof or spanking. The associations among the event (the norm violation), the unexpected parental reaction, and the subsequent state of uncertainty lead the child to award salience to the violation. Interviews with the Fijian parents revealed that the three most frequent behavioral categories regarded as "wrong" (*cakava cala*) were the destruction of property, acts potentially dangerous to the child's physical welfare, and aggression.

Because 18-month-olds can generate prototypic representations of events, detect deviations from those prototypes, and react to the detection, there is reason to believe that they are able to generate the ideas of a proper and improper event, which they will eventually come to call "good" and "bad." One two-year-old became visibly upset because she held a small doll but a large toy bed and could not find a small toy bed, which she indicated was more appropriate for the doll. She had a representation of the proper object. What is required for the actualization of an evaluative frame are certain cognitive talents attained during the second year and experiences that permit children to associate some events with signs of adult displeasure.

I suggest that one critical function that emerges by the middle of the second year is the tendency to make inferences regarding the causes of an event. The child now expects events to have antecedents and automatically generates cognitive hypotheses as to their cause. Thus, when the child sees a crack in a toy, he infers the flaw was caused by someone's action. Because that action is associated with displeasure, the child responds emotionally. The data from a linguistic inference task indicate that by the middle of the second year most children also are able to infer that events have names, and hence an unfamiliar word must name an unfamiliar object. The examiner first presents the child with a trio of known objects (a toy cat, car, and cup). After allowing the child to play with the toys for a bit, the examiner asks the child to hand her each of the objects on three separate questions. If the child is correct, the examiner then proceeds to the critical test trial. The examiner places two nameable objects (a doll and a dog) and one unfamiliar object that has no name (a wooden or styrofoam form) in front of the child. The examiner then says, "Give me the zoob." By 18 months the majority of children gave the unfamiliar object to the examiner. It is of interest that children learning sign language rather than oral speech first combine two signs in the middle of the second year. I suggest that the ability to combine two ideas is the essence of the inferential talent.

A second competence that matures in the second year is the ability to appreciate the psychological state of another. This competence permits empathy—what Hume called sympathy—and facilitates in a major way the control of aggression and excessive dominance toward another child, even without punishment for those acts. There is persuasive evidence for the two-year-old's ability to appreciate the perceptual and feeling states of another person. Novey (1975) visited children 18 and 27 months of age at home and invited them to play with either a pair of ski goggles that permitted vision or a pair that was opaque and gave a sense of blindness. A day later each child came to a laboratory setting and, after a period of play, watched the mother put on the opaque goggles. The 27-month-olds who had had previous experience with the opaque goggles behaved as if they had inferred that their mothers could not see. They tried to remove the goggles, asked the mother to remove them, and made fewer gestures toward her, in comparison with the children who had been exposed at home to the transparent goggles.

Longitudinal observations provided by mothers specially trained to record their children's reactions to the distress of others revealed a major change in behavior during the latter half of the second year.

The two-year-old children behaved as if they were inferring the state of the victim, and accordingly, they issued appropriate responses. They hugged or kissed their victim, gave him a toy or food, and requested aid from an adult. Those behaviors were absent or infrequent responses to the same incentives during the early months of the second year (Cummings et al., 1981).

The combination of the ability to infer cause and to empathize with the states of another, combined with a preparedness to associate signs of disapproval with certain actions, permit the child to move into an evaluative frame. I view this preparedness as analogous to the suggestion that rats are prepared to associate gustatory stimuli with unpleasant visceral states, while birds are prepared to associate visual stimuli with the same internal states. This supposition is affirmed by interviews with the Fijian mothers, who commented that children naturally become more responsible after their second birthday when they have acquired *vakayalo* (sense). As a result of this new competence, parents hold children more responsible for their actions. The recognition by the Fijians of a sudden appreciation of right and wrong is in accord with the belief of nineteenth-century observers that young children are innately moral.

James Sully (1896) suggested that the child has an "inbred respect for what is customary and wears the appearance of a rule of life" and an "innate disposition to follow precedent and rule, which precedes education" (pp. 280–281). For "there is in the child from the first a rudiment of true law abidingness . . . the day when the child first becomes capable of this putting himself into his mother's place and realizing, if only for an instant, the trouble he has brought on her, is an all-important one in his moral development" (pp. 289–290). Sully believed all children must, because they are human, realize that causing harm to another is immoral. Such knowledge can never be lost, regardless of any subsequent cruelty the child might experience. The child does not have to learn that hurting others is bad; it is an insight that accompanies growth.

In a popular text written at the turn of the century, two Americans, Tracy and Stimpfl (1909), asserted that the child is born with a disposition to be moral: "Moral ideas do not require to be created or implanted in the minds of children by their elders. Nothing is more certain than that the child is born potentially a moral being, possessing a moral nature which requires only to be evoked and developed by environmental conditions . . . An empirical account of the derivation of the moral nature out of conditions in which no germs of it are to be found, fails utterly when tested by observed facts or by logical criticisms" (p. 179). After 1915, this theoretical view vanished from American texts in the wave of enthusiasm for social learning.

Because the concern with standards seems to be an inevitable event in the second year and one that appears long before linguistic or reproductive maturity, we might ask about the evolutionary advantage of this competence. Humans have the capacity to harbor resentment of other people and a desire for personal property, together with the ability to plan acts based on these emotions. Hence, it may have been necessary in human evolution to make sure that inhibitory functions would emerge early in development to curb these disruptive dispositions. An appreciation of proper and improper behavior facilitates the inhibition of aggression toward siblings, especially toward young infants. The importance of this inhibition is reflected in a rare event which occurred in 1980 in Boston, when a two-year-old boy killed his six-month-old younger sibling by stabbing him repeatedly with a kitchen knife. We are horrified by this event, in part because it is a freak phenomenon. But since all two-year-olds have the ability, the occasional motivation, and the opportunity to commit this action, why is it not more frequent? I suggest that one reason is that most children around the world have begun to establish standards on aggression by the second birthday.

Anxiety over Potential Failure

Perhaps the most significant new phenomenon my colleagues and I observed was the appearance of obvious signs of anxiety after the examiner modeled some acts in front of the child. After the child had played for about 15 minutes—in the laboratory or at home—the examiner and the mother joined the child on the floor and the examiner modeled three different acts with appropriate verbalizations while the child was watching. The acts became more complex as the child matured. For the children 22 months of age, the model made a doll talk on a telephone, made a doll cook some food in a pan and then had two dolls eat dinner, and made three animals take a walk and hide under a cloth in order to avoid getting wet. After she modeled the three acts, she simply said "Now it's your turn to play." She did not ask the child to imitate her actions. The child was then allowed to play for an additional 10 minutes. Distress was defined as

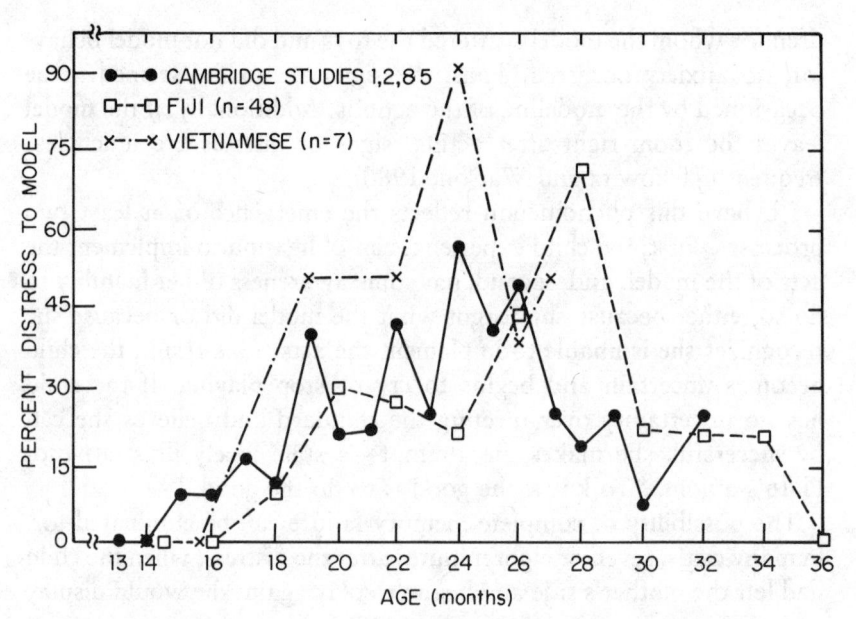

Figure 1. Proportion of children showing distress to the model.

the occurrence of any one of the following behaviors during the minute after the model completed her actions: fretting, crying, clinging to the mother, absence of any play with the toys during the entire minute, and protestations indicating the child did not want to play or wanted to go home. The most frequent reactions of distress were nonverbal and included clinging to the mother, inhibition of play, and crying. As shown in Figure 1, the behavioral signs of distress appeared first around 15 months, grew with age, and reached a peak around the second birthday in all the samples. This display of distress in specific to this incentive and is independent of fearfulness to novelty. The Fijian one-year-olds, who had never seen a doll, showed extreme upset when the examiner showed them a doll. But fear of this stimulus waned during the second year, while signs of fear to the model increased in frequency, and at no age was there a correlation between fearful behavior toward the doll and distress following the model's behavior (Katz, 1981).

In order to eliminate alternative interpretations of this distress, we surmised that perhaps the child did not expect the adult to interrupt her play and, therefore, was upset by the unexpected interruption. But when we repeated the experiment with two other groups of children for whom the model scattered the toys and did not model behavior, no anxiety occurred. Thus, the signs of anxiety seemed to be occasioned by the modeling of the actions. Additionally, if the model leaves the room right after acting, signs of distress are much less frequent (Jackowitz and Watson, 1980).

I believe this phenomenon reflects the emergence of at least two processes. First, the child experiences an obligation to implement the acts of the model, and, second, has some awareness of her inability to do so, either because she forgot what the model did or because she recognizes she is unable to implement the acts. As a result, the child becomes uncertain and begins to cry or stop playing. If the child has no uncertainty over meeting the standard and believes she can be successful, she makes the attempt—a state nicely illustrative of Plato's axiom, "To know the good is to do the good."

The possibility of complete memory failure can be eliminated for, in many cases, seven or eight minutes after the distress, when the child had left the mother's side and begun to play again, she would display an exact or fragmented version of one of the model's prior actions and smile. There may have been a temporary forgetting of the model's behavior, but it was not permanent.

Slightly fewer children showed distress when the mother rather than the less familiar examiner was the model. Because the child had a less familiar relationship with the model, it is possible that she felt a stronger press to display the acts modeled by the examiner. Uncertainty in the social relationship could motivate the child to be concerned with the model's possible reactions toward her. If the child felt no obligation to imitate the model, she would not pass to the second stage of uncertainty over her inability to duplicate the acts she saw. These data reveal the exquisitely sensitive dependence of this behavior on subtle dimensions in the social relationship.

Smiles of Mastery

A third phenomenon of this era is the occurrence of a smile after the child has attained a goal through effort—when she completes a tower, puts a final piece in a puzzle, or fits a dress on a doll. These are not social smiles but private ones. The protocol for the seven Vietnamese children included the presentation of a puzzle and an invitation to the child to build a block tower on each visit to the home. Smiling upon mastery was rare at 17 months, increased after 19 months, and peaked at 25 months of age, when six of the seven children smiled privately upon completing one or both tasks. These private smiles that accompany mastery can be interpreted as signifying that the child had generated a goal for an external action sequence, persisted in attempts to gain that goal, and smiled upon attainment. The response is released when the child perceives that she has attained the cognitive representation of a previously generated goal following investment of effort. This assumption awards the child not only a disposition to generate goals but also the ability to know when that goal has been reached.

It seems useful, therefore, to posit one class of standards, called *normative,* which contains representations of actions and events that have been linked with adult approval and disapproval. The familiar list of aggression, destruction, and cleanliness is prototypic. The second class, called *mastery standards,* contains representations of goals to be attained through actions that have not necessarily been associated with adult displeasure or praise. I recognize that I am reinventing the distinction between the two components of the Freudian superego: the violations of a community's values and the representations that define the ego-ideal. I did not have that distinction in mind as I observed the children's behaviors; the data invited it.

There is a relation between the two classes of standards. Recognition of standards on aggression leads to inhibition of these behaviors. But recognition that one's behavior might not meet a private standard of mastery can lead to a reluctance to attempt problem solution or to deal with challenges that might be within the child's sphere of mastery. Hence, timidity to challenge might be the price we pay for the socialization of disruptive acts. Some evolutionary biologists might argue about the relative advantages of withdrawal in a mastery situation compared with voluntary checks on aggression. But both properties may be packaged as a unit; the child cannot have one without the other.

Directives to Adults

A fourth phenonenon of this era is the emergence of behaviors that reflect the desire to influence the behavior of adults through requests or directives. The most frequent instances of this category include attempts to change the behavior of an adult or requests for help with a problem. Common examples include putting a toy telephone to the mother's ear and gesturing or vocalizing in a way to indicate that the child wants the mother to talk on the telephone, pointing to a place in the room where the child wants the mother to move, or giving the mother a doll and toy bottle and indicating, through gesture, that she wants the mother to feed the doll. The growth function for this behavior for the longitudinal sample of six American children studied at home is almost identical to the growth function for the seven Vietnamese children who displayed peak occurrence of this behavior at 21 months.

I suggest the child would not have begun to direct the behavior of an adult if she did not have an expectation that the request would be met. The enhancement of this class of response can be viewed as evidence that the child expects he can influence the behavior of others. It is true that eight-month-olds also point to desired objects and may whine, as if they are communicating that they want an object. But I believe that at this earlier age infants have no conscious conception that the cry or gesture will change the behavior of the adult. The response simply follows their seeing the desired object or their frustration at not having it. The pointing of the eight-month-old may resemble superficially the request for help with a puzzle seen in a 20-month-old. But the two responses are profoundly different with respect to the underlying cognitive competences. The monkey, the four-month-old baby, and the two-year-old can be operantly conditioned to make a motor response when it is followed by a reinforcement consisting of a change in visual stimulation. But this similarity does not mean that the accompanying cognitive processes are necessarily the same in all three organisms.

Self-descriptive Utterances

The speech of the six American children studied at home provided additional evidence for the growth of a function related to self-awareness. All of the utterances and associated contexts during the play session were recorded by one of the observers. Over 90 percent of the utterances were spontaneous remarks. As others have reported, when speech first emerges, the vast majority of one-word utterances name objects in the child's visual field. The next most frequent class of utterance during the first stage of speech is to communicate a desire for an object or event, or to point to an object and say its name with a tone of voice that signifies a frustrated need. I am concerned here with a type of utterance we called self-descriptive utterances. These were defined narrowly as utterances that occurred while the child was engaged in an action and referred to that action (*climb*, as the child was climbing up on a chair; *up*, as the child tried to get up on a box), and utterances containing the words *I, my, mine,* or the child's name with a predicate (my book, I sit, Mary eat). Once the child began to speak two- and three-word utterances, there was little difficulty in deciding whether a phrase was self-descriptive. The average reliability for coding this variable was 0.95. Self-descriptive utterances were absent at 17, 18, and 19 months, increased dramatically around the second birthday, and were sophisticated by 27 months, including phrases like "I do it myself," or "I can't do it." All the children showed similar growth functions for this class of utterance, with a major increase between 19 and 24 months. Lois Bloom and her colleagues (Bloom et al., 1975) have collected a similar set of protocols from four children over the course of repeated visits to their homes. When I coded her data for self-descriptive utterances, the proportion was remarkably similar to that found for our children: namely, about 35 percent. It is important to note that the proportion of self-descriptive utterances was relatively independent of the child's mean length of utterance. I believe that when the child becomes aware of his ability to gain goals through his actions, he feels pressed to comment upon his behavior. The child's actions have suddenly become a salient incentive for linguistic description, or at least more salient than the activities or qualities of other people. The child does not begin to talk about himself because he is able to utter predicates, but rather because the child is suddenly aware of a fresh experience. He is aware of what he is doing.

The Replacement of Self in Symbolic Play

Finally, there is a significant qualitative change in the child's symbolic play with toys during the months before the second birthday. During these months the child substitutes a toy for the self in pretend sequences. The child now puts a telephone to a doll's head rather than her own, a bottle to a toy animal's mouth rather than her own mouth. This transformation implies that the child is playing the role of director and distancing herself from the simple sensorimotor play that is seen near the first birthday.

The studies implemented by Lewis and Brooks-Gunn (1979) are

most relevant to this work. They administered a variety of procedures to children between 9 and 24 months of age in order to determine the time when those children showed signs of self-recognition. They concluded, "Between 18 and 21 months of age a large increase in the number of infants demonstrating self-recognition abilities is seen across a wide range of representative modes . . . Clearly, self-recognition is well-established by 21 months of age" (p. 215). Their most dramatic evidence involves a procedure originally reported by Amsterdam (1972) in which infants are first allowed to look at themselves in a mirror. Their noses are then unobtrusively marked with a spot of rouge, and they are brought back to the mirror to observe their reflection. The behavior of interest is whether the child reaches for the place where the rouge has been put. Although no 9- or 12-month-olds touched their noses, this behavior increased dramatically from 15 to 24 months of age, and over 60 percent of the 21- and 24-month-olds touched their noses. It cannot be a coincidence that this is the time when distress to the model, directives to adults, and mastery smiles also show a sharp increase in frequency.

The appreciation of standards on proper behavior and awareness of one's competences to meet these standards imply that children should now show a major improvement in performance on tasks presented by adults. The data affirm that prediction.

Memory for Locations

The children in most of the studies showed a major improvement between 17 and 23 months in performance on a memory for locations task. The child was seated on the mother's lap, facing the experimenter and a stage. The child watched the examiner hide a prize (a raisin or a cheerio) under one of many receptacles. The receptacles were screened by an opaque screen for delays of one, five, or ten seconds. The screen was lifted and the examiner asked the child to find the prize. The child was first tested under one-second delays, using two, four, six, or eight receptacles of different colors, shapes, and sizes. After the child solved this problem, the examiner proceeded to four, six, and eight containers, with the hardest problem being eight receptacles at a ten-second delay. Figure 2 shows the growth function for this performance. Children showed a major improvement in the months before the second birthday, the same time

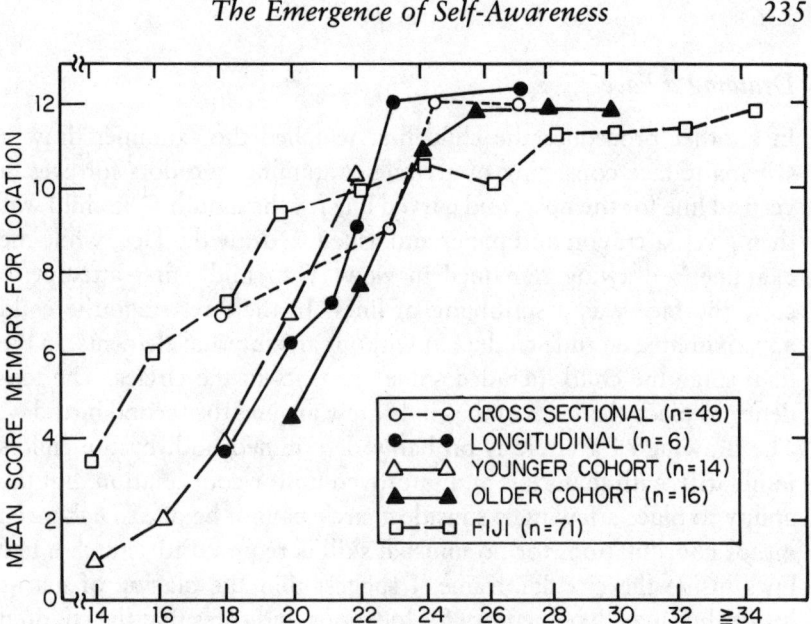

Figure 2. Mean score on memory for locations task.

when other indexes of self-awareness and of standards were growing. By two years of age, almost all the children in all the samples solved the problem of eight different receptacles with a ten-second delay. Even though the task requirements and materials were probably less familiar to the Fijians than to the Americans, the Fijian children showed enhanced performance at the same time. I view this improvement as reflecting increased motivation to meet a standard of competence, rather than a fundamental change in memory capacity.

This suggestion is supported by the fact that many three-year-old American children, especially those being reared in families encouraging autonomy, perform less well than two-year-olds. I believe this is because the increasing enhancement of self that occurs during the third year provokes the older child to resist accommodation—or conformity—to all adult requests. After the third birthday the child is made uncertain by contemplation of violation of adult standards. He will occasionally violate them in order to resolve and control the disquiet. Because modern Western parents do not want a fearful or timid 10-year-old, they tolerate these violations, which we have come to call the disobedience of the "terrible twos."

Drawing a Face

In another procedure the child first watched the examiner draw a schematic face consisting of a circle containing two dots for eyes, a vertical line for the nose, and curved line for the mouth. The child was then given a crayon and paper and asked to draw the face, while the examiner's drawing remained in view. The child's first attempt to copy the face was a scribbling of lines. In the next stage the child approximated a crude circle, but without any internal elements. In the final stage the child included some elements in the circles. The tendency to place elements in the circle grew around the second birthday. The drawing of a circle is probably determined both by the child's familiarity with materials and improved motor coordination, but the ability to place a few marks inside a circle cannot be due to enhanced motor coordination, for no unusual skill is required to scratch a few lines inside the circular frame. I suggest that the placing of marks inside the circle, like memory for locations, indicates that the children were reflecting more seriously on the standard posed by the examiner and had an expectation of meeting that standard. Hence they made the attempt.

Discussion

On the basis of the evidence summarized, I suggest that the central psychological victories of the last half of the second year are (1) an appreciation of standards of proper behavior and (2) an awareness of one's actions, intentions, states, and competences. I have chosen the phrase *self-awareness* to name this second set of related psychological functions, because the term seems consistent with the types of evidence collected—mastery smiles, directives to adults, distress to the model, and self-descriptive utterances. Other observers, focusing their attention on different aspects of the child's development, have used different names for the psychological changes that characterize this era of growth. Tiedemann (1787), for example, remarked that the child develops *Eigenliebe* (love of self) during the same period; Preyer (1888) suggested that *Ichheit* (selfhood) emerges during the second year. But the Utku of Hudson Bay believe the child develops *ihuma* (reason), and the Fijians say the child has now acquired *vakayalo* (sense).

Important premises are hidden in each of these phrases. Although

Tiedemann and Preyer assumed that the behavioral changes indexed a new appreciation of individuality, the Utku and the Fijians, like most non-Western societies, emphasized the child's ability to appreciate the difference between right and wrong (Briggs, 1970). It is understandable, after the fact, that urban Europeans would wonder about the origins of the narcissistic, autonomous, and actualizing ego, while small, isolated hunting or agricultural communities would be more concerned with the child's adherence to social norms. The name chosen for a complex phenomenon has significant connotations for empirical work. If the complex event that geneticists call "mutation" had been named "replacement," different experiments might have been performed. Self and self-awareness are very popular ideas in the West: hence the contemporary scholar's mind leaps to these words quickly. If these same data had been discovered by a seventeenth-century Chinese observer, he would doubtless have used a different term.

Changes in the quality of the child's play during the second year suggest a slightly different and more speculative way of describing the victories of this era. One of the most striking changes is the increased duration of a play epoch. Brenner and Mueller have reported a major increase in the duration of social interaction sequences among boys observed longitudinally during the second year. I believe that a central change of this period is the ability to sustain ideas and action plans. The psychological stage on which schemata interact and guide action does not collapse every half-minute or so as it did previously. As a result, the child does not forget the goals he is pursuing, asks his mother for help if he is unsuccessful, and smiles upon attaining a self-generated goal. Perhaps what I have been calling *self-awareness* is better categorized as the "capacity to hold cognitive representations on the stage of active memory." Maturing central nervous system structures and functions permit schemata to remain in consciousness for a longer period of time. This argument is appealing, because available knowledge about the relation between brain function and psychological phenomena implies that damage to specific frontal and temporal areas of the brain is often accompanied by a loss of ability to retrieve past memories or to hold ideas on the stage that is called *active memory*. Retrieval, maintenance, and operation upon information seem to be yoked to central nervous system functioning in a fundamental way.

The suggestion that the enhancement of the behaviors we have considered is a direct consequence of brain growth finds persuasive support in data on histological changes in the young cerebral cortex. The length and degree of branching of dendrites in the human cerebral cortex do not approach adult magnitudes until two years of age. And Rabinowicz (1979) has concluded that neuronal density (the number of neurons per unit volume) decreases very rapidly until birth: "From birth to between three and six months the decrease is slower and it ceases at about 15 months . . . one has to deduce that a very important moment in cortical maturation appears to be the period between 15 and 24 months, a period when almost all the layers reach, for the first time, a similar state of maturation" (p. 122).

I do not think it a coincidence that this period corresponds to the interval when the child displays the behaviors that are regarded as indicative of self-awareness. If the changes I have described are inevitable psychological consequences of maturational events in the central nervous system, as long as the child lives in a world of objects and people, both current and traditional descriptions of the emergence of a sense of self may be misleading. Theorists in the psychoanalytic tradition, like Margaret Mahler (1968), have assumed that initially self was merged with another person and the infant gradually differentiated itself from the parent. But perhaps there is no self prior to the second year, as there is no frog in the tadpole and no morphemes hidden in the babbling of a three-month-old.

The most popular view, supported by theorists with diverse agendas, insists that a sense of self develops gradually, as a direct consequence of action. Preyer (1888) was reluctant to attribute the "I"-function only to endogenous changes in the central nervous system and, in agreement with the associational beliefs of his period, declared that it was through the child's actions and sense experiences that the I-feeling emerged.

Guillaume (1971) suggested that the first phase of self was dependent upon imitation of others. The pragmatist George Herbert Mead (1934) made social interaction a mandatory requirement for the first stage of self, and wrote that the self "arises in the process of social experience and activity . . . It is impossible to conceive of a self arising outside of social experience" (pp. 135, 140).

Charles Cooley (1902) was closer to nineteenth-century suppositions in awarding more influence to the perceptual and affective components of the self than to the action sector. Nonetheless, he too insisted that acts informing the young child of her effectiveness are prerequisites for the feeling of self, which "appears to be associated chiefly with ideas of the exercise of power and of being a cause" (p. 177). Piaget (1976) wrote on the relevance of interaction: "The subject only learns to know himself when acting on the object and the latter can become known only as the result of progress of the actions carried out on it" (p. 353). Lewis and Brooks-Gunn (1979) also argued that the child's awareness of self "has as its source the interaction of the young organism with others—both people and objects . . . it is from action that knowledge develops" (p. 241), in a connected, stage-like sequence. Although these psychologists did not explicitly deny that the maturation of a new competence lies at the root of self-recognition, they awarded to accumulated interactions with objects and people the major bases for the appearance of self-awareness and self-recognition.

The British psychologist Crook (1980) is unusual among modern theorists in his emphasis on cognitive maturation as an element in the emergence of consciousness: "The child's emerging sense of self is dependent upon the growth of its cognitive abilities in categorization, its experiences of contingency and agency in interaction with care-givers, and its experience of the emotional quality of its own conscious states" (p. 254).

I, too, believe that a child isolated from all people and objects will not develop self-awareness. But I am less certain that these processes and their attendant structures are necessarily created out of specific forms of feedback from imitation of others, play with parents, and the directing of adults. It is possible that the American children in Cambridge, the Fijians, and the Vietnamese refugees all displayed signs of apprehension to the modeling of acts during the last half of the second year because their patterns of social experience were similar. However, the remarkable temporal concordance for the appearance of distress to the model, across all samples, exceeded that for the onset of speech, which most scientists acknowledge depends in part on the maturation of new capacities. Perhaps no special class of social interaction is necessary for these competences to develop. Perhaps all that is required for the capacities called "self-awareness" to appear is any information resulting from the child's actions and feelings. The neurons of the visual cortex require patterned stimulation in order to mature and permit the psychological competence of discrimination. But almost any form of patterned stimulation will do. Similarly, certain species of birds living in isolated cages will sing their characteristic song at maturity if they only hear a tape-recorded version of it at the proper time; interaction with other birds is irrelevant.

Rhesus monkeys raised only with an inanimate object and isolated from all contingent interaction with any living creature showed signs of fear when put in a novel environment at four months. The fear reaction—as evidenced by higher heart rate and distress calls—was an inevitable consequence of the maturation of the central nervous system in these isolated animals (Mason, 1978).

Similarly, it is of interest that one species of macaque—crab-eaters—displayed normal patterns of social behavior despite the fact that they spent the first six months of life in complete isolation. The investigators wrote, "Extended social experience is not necessary for the development of species' typical social behavior in crab eating Macaques . . . Whether early social experience is or is not necessary seems to depend on genotypic differences—a sorry state of affairs for the generality of social development theories based on environmental factors" (Sackett et al., 1981, p. 316).

By contrast, rhesus and pigtail monkeys raised in isolation showed more serious disturbances in social behavior. Obviously, social interaction contains a rich and complex source of information and probably hastens the development of these processes. But it is neither theoretically obvious nor empirically demonstrable that a child who has few material encounters with people will fail to develop the behaviors reflective of self-awareness, though he may develop them at a slower rate. It is useful to take a strong skeptical stand, if only to stimulate relevant research.

Most Western scholars have been reluctant to posit endogenous mechanisms, relatively independent of specific external events, which might be responsible for the emergence of new behaviors such as self-awareness. For example, during the last decade of the nineteenth century and the first decade of the twentieth, biologists were generally opposed to the idea that spontaneous mutation in genes, rather than the cumulative effects of natural selection, was the major force in evolution. After the geneticists gained power around World War I, natural selection was given decreased potency. It was not until the 1930s that the modern synthesis of discrete endogeous genetic forces and natural selection became acceptable doctrine.

Similarly, many physiologists during most of this century have resisted the idea that the central nervous system did not require feedback from sense organs in order to generate coherent sequences of rhythmic movement during repetitive behavior, locomotion being the classic example. Most physiologists wanted to have sensory processes control basic movement patterns. But experimental evidence has led Delcomyn (1980) to argue persuasively that "isolation of the nervous system from all possible sources of sensory feedback does not abolish the normal pattern of rhythmic bursts in motoneurons . . . Timing of the repetitive movements that constitute any rhythmic behavior is regulated by intrinsic properties of the central nervous system rather than by sensory feedback from moving parts of the body" (p. 493).

Both physiologists and psychologists have wanted to believe that external events, potentially quantifiable, are the primary causes of action, because this premise is more in accord with an epistemology of mechanism and a philosophy of logical positivism than with a presupposition that awards potency to invisible entities that seem to have direction and structure from the beginning. The latter view leaves the investigator frustrated in his search for the chain of manipulable causes for the observed event.

Additionally, these data speak to the premise of gradual growth, for there is a deep prejudice against postulating significant entities that can arise with a short history. Western scientists prefer to impose gradualism on all instances of change. T. H. Huxley warned Darwin that his insistence on gradual evolution represented "an unnecessary difficulty" in the theory, and both Gould and Stanley (Eldredge and Gould, 1972; Stanley, 1981) have argued that, on occasion, speciation can be rapid—a phenomenon called *punctuated equilibria*. It has been suggested that most of the mammalian species now present on earth are descendants of a small rodent-like animal and that this burst of speciation occurred in a relatively brief span of about 12 million years—only 20 percent of the interval since the extinction of the dinosaurs 60 million years ago.

Increasingly sophisticated studies of morphological embryogenesis are verifying Weiss' (1968) suggestion that the differentiation of cells "produces a definite number of discrete, distinct, discontinuous and more or less sharply delimited cell types which are not connected by intergradations" (p. 212). Biologists now describe aspects of organ development in terms that explicitly assume abruptness of change. Newman and Frisch (1979) suggested that in the early formation of the chick limb there appear to be sudden structural changes in the conditions surrounding developing cartilage cells. If the morphological growth of the embryo provides a useful model for early psychological growth, then a relatively sudden change in central nervous system function may be more important for selected psychological competences like self-awareness than the amount of time the child has spent in a particular class of interaction. New developmental forms can occur without long periods of transition. D'Arcy Wentworth Thompson has noted, "We cannot transform an invertebrate into a vertebrate nor a coelenterate into a worm by any single and legitimate deformation . . . Nature proceeds from one type to another . . . To seek for stepping-stones across the gaps between is to seek in vain forever" (in Gould, 1980, p. 193).

I believe that the growth of the functions I have called self-awareness is composed of the maturation of at least five competences: recognition of the past, retrieval of prior schemata, inference, awareness of one's potentiality for action, and, finally, awareness of self as an entity with symbolic attributes. The degree of connectedness among these five functions is obscure. Although the first four are all presumed by awareness of the self as an entity, it need not emerge from them. That is, awareness of the self as an object with attributes is not an inevitable process: some new processes must be inserted into the developmental sequence if it is to appear. Once again we encounter the ancient enigma in historical sequence. What propositions must we invent to describe how novel properties use and subsume earlier ones, but are not produced by them? The biologist who wishes to explain morphological changes in phylogeny faces the same problem. The convolutions of the cerebral cortex depend on the prior existence of a forebrain. But without the mutations that were a part of evolution, no convolutions would have occurred. Unique endogenous changes are required if the novel structure is to appear. Thus recognition, retrieval, inference, and self-awareness are necessary for awareness of the self as an entity with attributes, but they are not sufficient. The half year that begins with the first smile following completion of a puzzle and ends with the embarrassed statement, "I can't do that," contains one of the most significant sets of competences to appear in our species.

8

Measuring the Concept of Self

The idea of self has at least three different meanings. The meaning discussed in the previous chapter refers to the universal emergence in the second year of an awareness that one can have an effect upon people and objects, together with a consciousness of one's feelings and competences. Preyer (1889) called this process the *I-feeling,* and this meaning was of central importance to nineteenth-century observers of children. The diaries of Preyer (1889) and Hogan (1898) as well as the influential texts of Baldwin (1895) and Stern (1930) were concerned, in a major way, with the time when the child was first able to act self-consciously. Preyer believed that the child's reflections on his sensations and actions gradually led to the information of the I-feeling. "Only by means of very frequent coincidences of unlike sense-impressions, in tasting-and-touching, seeing-and-feeling, seeing-and-hearing, seeing-and-smelling, tasting-and-smelling, hearing-and-touching, are the intercentral connecting fibers developed, and then first can the various representational centers, these 'I'-makers, as it were, contribute, as in the case of the ordinary formation of concepts, to the formation of the corporate 'I', which is quite abstract" (Preyer, 1889, p. 205).

The persistent concern with the emergence of self-consciousness by nineteenth-century observers was understandable because they were preoccupied with the important human quality of morality. No attribute of childhood, not even keenness of reasoning, was as important as good character. Self-consciousness was the basis of an autonomous conscience, and the first signs of this function announced the child's potential capacity to select morally proper actions from alternatives.

A second meaning of self refers to a set of properties the child believes applies to her and is usually called a *self-concept*. Among the most obvious are intrinsic dimensions such as physical characteristics, gender, and ethnic-group membership. The concept of self also possesses a set of comparative qualities. Although a dog is a mammal with four legs and fur, it is also less aggressive than a wolf, stronger than a canary, and less poisonous than a snake. The concept of self, too, has both intrinsic and comparative dimensions. Although a particular child is a female, Canadian, Catholic, with brown eyes, she is also prettier than her sister, smarter than her best friend, and more fearful of animals than her brother.

A third meaning of self, consisting of the private evaluations of the qualities of the self-concept, has become synonymous with the idea of *self-esteem*. Self-esteem was of little interest to nineteenth-century investigators who believed that temperamental qualities, not a history of habits or ideas shaped by experience, were the major sources of individual differences among children. But when adjustment to society replaced character as the criterion for mature growth in the 1930s, emotional security and intellectual competence quickly occupied central places in the definition of adjustment. The child's confidence in his ability to demonstrate to self and to others that he was valued, attractive, and talented became as important as character. This private confidence rested, in part, on a comparison of the self's properties with those of others.

The writings of Cooley (1902) and Mead (1934) were seminal in the elaboration of the self-concept and self-esteem. Cooley argued that the person's concept of self was created from interpretations of other's reactions; hence, Cooley is given credit for the phrase "looking-glass self." Mead refined Cooley's views and suggested that a person's concept of self was determined largely by social experiences that permitted the individual to understand how others reacted to him; that is, to view the self as an object with properties as others did (see Wells and Marwell, 1976, for an excellent review of the history of the self-concept, and Smith, 1979, for a more personal history).

However, as I noted in Chapter 3, ideas like self-concept and self-esteem derive their intuitive validity from introspection and the conscious reports of others. The utility of these concepts is less obvious when we use different evidence. The most successful members of a society do not always regard themselves as more confident than the less successful. Recall François Jacob's conscious feeling of intellectual inadequacy when he joined Lwoff's laboratory. Further, the replies of inhibited and unhibited children to our interview questions about their concept of self were much less predictive of their behavior than our knowledge of their prior actions with strangers and their physiology. Freud's most important concepts—libido, repression, anxiety, defense, id, ego, superego—were inferences from his patient's descriptions of their feelings and motives and his own introspections. I suspect that the selective appeal of Freud's ideas was a function of the phenomenology of his varied audiences around the world. When the source of evidence changes dramatically, as is true today when biochemical data are used to diagnose phobic patients, the theoretical constructs become very different. Thus, it is not obvious that *self-concept* will remain a useful idea indefinitely.

Methodological Issues

The knowledge structure that defines a child's self-concept is less amenable to direct inquiry than the child's knowledge of the external world; hence most measurement procedures have generally been subject to criticism. When psychoanalytic theory made ego processes popular, projective methods were used to provide scientific indexes of this construct (Murray, 1938). It is fair to say that this mission failed, and empirical, but not theoretical, interest in self-concept waned for awhile. But the indomitable empirical spirit in American psychology, which is eager to get on with the work, denied what it knew and attacked the problem directly. Investigators asked subjects, using relatively undisguised procedures, to describe their psychological properties. Because the answers produced significant correlations with some other quantifiable property, the pragmatic spirit prevailed and doubts about the validity of the original data were put aside.

The interest in children's beliefs about their attributes has been accompanied by a proliferation of self-report instruments (Wylie, 1961; 1974; 1979). Some investigators simply ask the child directly whether he agrees or disagrees with a particular statement (such as, "I feel useless at times"). Coopersmith's (1967) self-esteem inventory asks subjects to indicate whether a particular sentence is or is not descriptive of their personality (for example, "I am pretty sure of myself"; see also Piers and Harris, 1964). Other commonly used rating scales ask a subject to indicate the extent to which particular descriptors apply to her. Rosenberg (1979) had subjects indicate (on a four-point scale) whether they agreed or disagreed with a particular item ("On the whole I am satisfied with myself"). Other investigators have asked the subject to describe the self (Livesley and Bromley, 1973) or write answers to the question "Who are you?" (Bugental and Zelen, 1950). Some investigators ask the subjects to compare the self with others, either by rating themselves with reference to some group norm or by rank-ordering themselves and members of the group in terms of particular characteristics (Wylie, 1974, 1979, and Wells and Marwell, 1976, contain a review of these scales).

Although most psychologists recognize that the validity of these self-report instruments is flawed because some children report favorable characterizations of themselves which they know are either inaccurate or are inconsistent with less conscious evaluations, most investigators continue to use these methods. As a result, questionable conclusions are drawn. Regular pleas by Wylie (1961; 1974) that scientists should worry about the validity of these procedures, and warnings that the methodological bases for current work are fragile, have gone largely ignored, as have the criticisms of self-report data I presented in Chapter 1.

The data to be presented in this essay come from studies whose aim was to address some of the methodological issues that surround the assessment of the self-concept through direct questioning of the child. This phrasing of the question may appear to be inconsistent with my earlier argument that investigators need not assume that each child possesses a unitary, most essential concept of self. Different measurement procedures reveal different, but legitimate, meanings of the concept, as I noted in Chapter 1. I remind the reader, however, that a particular meaning of self-concept tells us nothing about its validity in propositions intended to be theoretical. A desirable evaluation of the self with respect to popularity has one meaning if self-report supplies the evidence and, as we shall see, a quite different meaning if empathic identification with an unpopular figure in a film is used as the evidence. However, psychologists who use the construct of self-concept to explain the relation between a child's current behavior and his or her life conditions need a valid index of self-concept.

For the propositions in most current theoretical writings self-report is not a valid source of evidence, although it might be more valid in, as yet, unrealized theoretical contexts. Suppose, for example, one wanted to relate a child's concept of self to aggressive behavior when frustrated or threatened. It may be that children who claim they are competent or popular, although peers, parents, and teachers disagree, are more likely to react with anger following frustration than those who acknowledge this pair of undesirable qualities. However, most of the theoretical writing that relies on the construct of self-concept tries to explain the relation between earlier life experiences and current behavior. In this particular theoretical context the validity of self-report information appears flawed.

Study 1: Self-Evaluation and Triads Sorting

The first study was a preliminary attempt to explore the validity of one self-report method—the ranking of self in comparison with same-sex peers in the child's classroom. The 70 children (35 girls, 35 boys), 8 to 10 years old, belonged to eight different same-sex groups from four classrooms in two public schools in Cambridge, Massachusetts. The groups ranged in size from 6 to 10 children. One school was located in a middle-class neighborhood, the other school in a working-class neighborhood.

Methods

Children were asked to rank themselves and all the same-sex members of their classroom on five attributes of concern to preadolescent children: academic skill, popularity, physical attractiveness, dominance with peers, and athletic ability. The ranking was performed with the aid of a game board that had 15 squares, each a different shade of blue, arranged in a linear sequence from very light to dark blue.

The children were given cards with their name and the names of same-sex peers in their classroom written on them (the examiner confirmed that subjects could read the names of their peers). The children ranked themselves and all the same-sex peers on one attribute at a time. The dark blue end of the board represented the positive pole of the scale for all dimensions. When the examiner was assured that the children understood the meaning of the attribute, she asked the children to place the card representing the names of the same-sex peers as well as the self on appropriate squares. For reading, for example, the children were told that the very best reader in the classroom belonged on the dark blue square and the child who is poorest in reading belonged on the lightest square. The children were discouraged from placing two cards on the same square. Whenever the experimenter felt the child was answering too quickly, she asked direct questions about all adjacent children in the ranks, such as "Is child A better at reading than child B; is child B better at reading than child C?" In addition, each of the classroom teachers was asked to rank the children within same-sex groups on each of the five attributes at the time the study began.

Because the eight same-sex peer group varied in size, it was necessary to standardize the ranks. Each child's ranks were converted to deciles. The score of 1.0 always signified the first rank (such as the best in reading). A score of 10.0 signified the last rank, and a score of 5.5 the mean rank, regardless of the group size. The distribution of each set of ranks was rectangular. All statistical manipulations of the rank data were performed on these standardized scores.

In a second procedure—the triad sorting of self and peers—the child was asked to sort groups of three children into the pair of children that were most alike, leaving out the one who was most different from the other two. The child's repeated sorts of trios of same-sex peers, some of which included the self, was used to generate a similarities matrix which could be scaled in several dimensions and analyzed in relation to the dimensions surveyed in the self-ranks. If children who were regarded by their peers as possessing undesirable qualities gave a positive evaluation on the self-ranking procedure, but sorted themselves in the triads with peers who they regarded as not possessing those desirable attributes, the triad method would be useful in separating the valid from the less valid self-rankings.

Most children were presented with all possible triads of the same-sex peers in their classrooms (including themselves in some triads) and asked to decide which two acted most similarly and which one acted differently. No specific behavioral quality was mentioned, but children were told explicitly not to answer on the basis of a child's physical size or hair color. The names of the children were written on small pieces of cardboard which a child could sort. The number of times a particular pair of children was grouped together was the index of a similarity for that pair of children.

Characteristics of Self-Evaluations

The mean ranks assigned to the self for each of the five attributes were significantly lower than 5.5, indicating that most children ranked themselves above average. Further, the child's self-evaluations were only moderately related to the peer evaluations of them for four of the attributes (r ranged from .24 to .39), and unrelated for physical attractiveness ($r = .08$). Although the lack of a strong relation between the self-ranks and the ranks of peers does not automatically invalidate the self-rankings, it does lead one to question whether the self-reports are a valid index of a child's beliefs about self when the self-rankings are intended to explain the relation between the child's current behavior and his past history.

The Scaling of Triad-Sorting Data

Data from each subject's responses to the triad-sorting procedure were converted into a similarity matrix in which the cell values were the number of times a subject sorted particular pairs of children together. Matrices were also generated from the group data; cell values represented the number of times all children in the same sex groups sorted particular pairs of children together, after eliminating triads in which the child who was sorting was also a member of the triad.

Multidimensional scaling (MDS) solutions can be obtained in any number of geometric dimensions. The goodness of fit of a solution increases as the dimensionality of the solution increases. *Stress* is a statistical index which is inversely correlated with the goodness of fit. Stress values can range from 0 to 1.0, where 0 indicates a perfect monotonic fit. In the present study, stress values for two-dimensional group solutions ranged from .023 to .313, with a median value of .20.

The MDS configuration for one of the eight groups is displayed in Figure 3A. Vectors showing the results of the regression analyses described above have been plotted on the configurations. The vectors have the same slope as the line of best fit and are oriented so that the arrows point toward the positive, or desirable, end of the dimension. The length of each vector is proportional to the square of its multiple regression coefficient (that is, the degree to which the peer-rank attribute is represented in the MDS configuration).

In the group of middle-class boys illustrated in Figure 3A, the attribute vectors all pointed in the same direction (within a range of 45°). The configuration revealed a cluster of four boys (Bh, Kf, Mr, Mt) who are considered by their peers and teachers to be competent at reading and athletics and attractive, dominant, and popular. Chil-

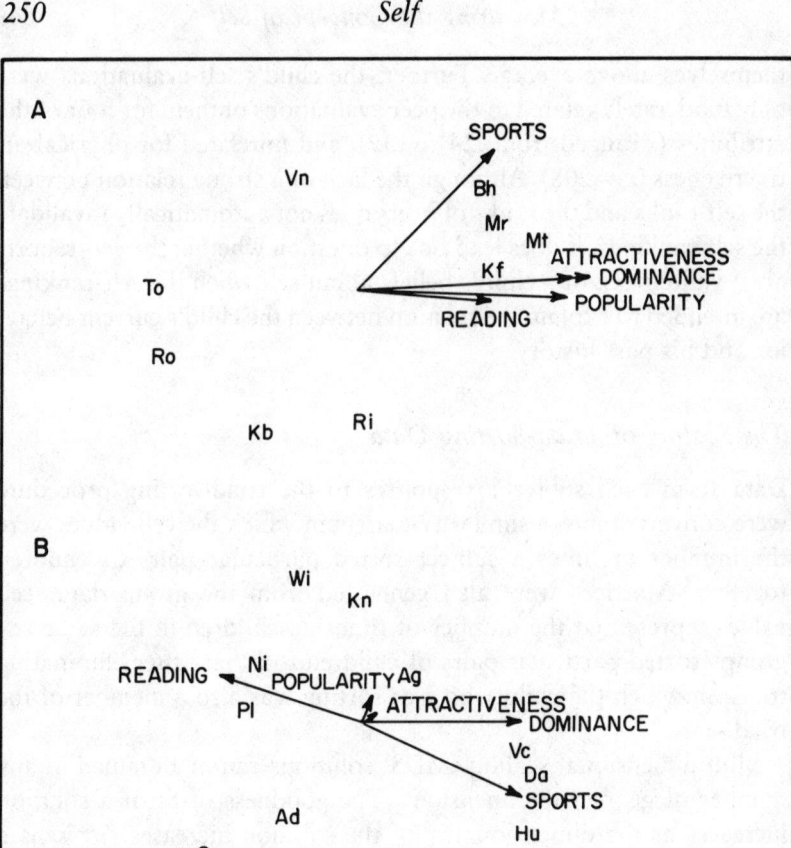

Figure 3. (A) Group configuration for boys in middle-class room. (B) Group configuration for boys in working-class room.

dren on the opposite side of the configuration (Ro, To) were ranked negatively on all five attributes.

Seven of the eight groups produced configurations similar to the one illustrated in Figure 3A. There was typically a small group of children at the positive end of the dimension, a group of two or three at the opposite pole, and two or three children in intermediate positions. For example, the boys in the other middle-class room produced a solution with five boys at the positive pole on all five dimensions and two boys clearly at the negative pole. The one exception to this generalization occurred for one group of working-class boys where some of the vectors formed a 180° angle with other attributes (the attributes were negatively correlated; see Figure 3B).

We now ask a simple question: What is the correspondence between the child's self-ranks, on the one hand, and the individual, multidimensional scaling solution of that child's triad responses? It will be recalled that the children who were ranked by peers as having desirable qualities acknowledged their positive status on their self-ranks. But a large proportion of the children who were ranked low by their peers also assigned themselves high ranks. There are several reasons why a child who was regarded by others as unpopular or incompetent at reading might say that she possessed these desirable properties. The most likely is that the child did not wish to acknowledge to the examiner her undesirable status. On the other hand, some children may have been unaware of their status, and still others might be using defensive denial. However, reading ability, popularity, and athletic skill are public qualities, and the child regularly receives information about them. Hence, we assume that most of the children were consciously aware of how they compared with their peers on these attributes. We used the triad-sorting procedure to test that assumption. If the positive self-ranks were a conscious distortion, some children might reveal their more private beliefs on the more disguised triads procedure.

We examined those children ranked low by peers (standardized peer-ranks were equal to or greater than 8.0 for four or all five of the attributes). This extreme group of 12 children included five middle-class boys, one working-class boy, three middle-class girls, and three working-class girls (17 percent of the group). Only one child, a middle-class girl, acknowledged on her self-ranks the low ranks given to her by her peers. The remaining 11 children gave themselves considerably higher ranks than did their peers on one or more qualities. How did these children place themselves in their individual scaling solutions based on the triads procedure? Consider two children whose self-ranks on all five attributes deviated significantly from the ranks assigned them by their peers.

Subject Ro, boy, middle-class school. Ro is the son of professional parents who, despite an average IQ score, was not performing well in school. He often disrupted the classroom by screaming, challenged the other children competitively, and was hostile to the examiner. In the triad-sorting procedure Ro placed himself spatially close to the boys whom the peers regarded as having positive attributes and maximally distant from To, who was the only other boy ranked negatively

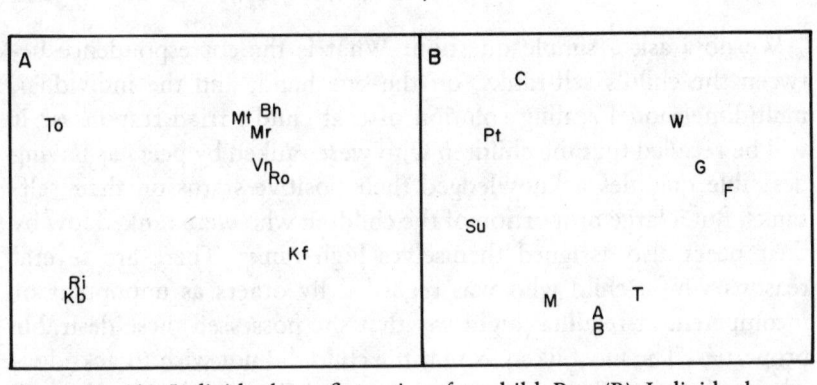

Figure 4. (A) Individual configuration for child Ro. (B) Individual configuration for child Su.

on all five attributes (see Figure 4A). Thus, Ro's triad sorting and self-report were concordant.

Subject Su, girl, working-class school. Su, who was labile of mood and often expressed her anger, also deviated significantly from the peer-ranks. But in contrast with Ro, Su placed herself closer to the other children who also had low status, especially Pt. Su acknowledged her undesirable characteristics on the triads procedure but did not on the self-ranks (see Figure 4B).

Of the 11 extreme children whose self-ranks deviated from the peer values on one or more dimensions, four placed themselves close to children with desirable characteristics on the triads procedure, while seven children did not, suggesting that, perhaps, their positive self-ranks were a distortion of their private beliefs. Three children placed themselves close to children whom the peers regarded negatively and four children placed themselves in isolated positions, close to neither desirable nor undesirable children.

Thus, the triads procedure added some information about the childs' self-concept for the two-thirds of the children whom the peers regarded negatively but who denied this peer evaluation in their own self-rankings.

Study 2: Empathy with a Model

The purpose of the next two studies was to explore the utility of a procedure involving empathic identification with a model. If the child's pattern of empathy were in accord with his self-conscious evaluations, investigators could feel more confident about their classification of a child. But if there were a serious inconsistency between the two sources of data one might question the validity of the self-report information.

The rationale for the procedure is simple and has some degree of phenomenological validity. Every adult has had the experience of responding empathically to a person to whom he or she feels psychologically similar. The idea that children and adults detect psychological and physical similarities between themselves and others and react affectively to people who share qualities with themselves is neither original nor of recent origin. It appears in the world's literature, as well as in the first psychological essays on self-consciousness. Additionally, identification with ethnic, religious, and racial groups is a common phenomenon (Kagan, 1958; Stotland and Dunn, 1963). If this experience could be captured in a laboratory, psychologists would have a useful tool for evaluating a person's private beliefs about herself, for empathic behavior is under less conscious control than evaluations given to an interviewer or answers to a questionnaire. There is some evidence that this process can be brought into the laboratory. Five-year-olds showed greater empathic involvement with their parent than with an adult of the same sex (Kagan and Phillips, 1964), and Maccoby and Wilson (1957) found that preadolescent children were more likely to identify with a child in a film who was of their own sex and similar social-class aspirations. Moreover, the children remembered more of the actions and words of the character with whom they identified in the film. In our studies we sought to determine if a child would show empathic identification with a film model who was described as possessing a salient attribute of the child. We wished to explore, as with the triads procedure, whether a child who did not acknowledge an undesirable attribute on direct questioning might, nonetheless, show empathic involvement with a model who possessed the less desirable attribute.

The sample was composed of 25 preadolescent Caucasian, middle-class boys who had been diagnosed as having severe reading disability and 11 control boys, each of whom was matched with one reading-disabled subject on age, social class, and ethnicity. The control boys were reading at grade level or above. The median age of the group was 10 years, with a range of 8–13 years; only two children were 8 years and three were 13 years.

The 25 reading-disabled boys were reading 2 or more years below their appropriate grade level, despite average or above average IQ scores. The diagnosis of reading disability was based on both standardized tests of reading skill administered by the research staff and test scores obtained from the schools. Each of the reading-disabled boys knew he had been classified by teachers as reading disabled.

Methods

Each boy came to our laboratory with a female examiner. This group of boys was accustomed to the laboratory environment as a result of several prior visits to the same building over the course of one year. After some conversation, each boy was shown a 12-minute experimental film in color made on Super-8 film.

The experimental film depicted a competitive contest between two Caucasian boys who were of similar physical appearance and age as our subjects. The contest was conducted by a woman. Each boy in the film was shown a drawing composed of a few lines and had to guess what the two objects in the picture might be if the drawing were completed. The film was edited so that each of the film models appeared alone on the screen for an equivalent length of time. The woman in the film would turn to one of the boy models as she administered a test item and that boy appeared on the screen alone both while he was working at the solution of the problem and immediately after being told the validity of his answer. The woman in the film rewarded each boy when he successfully identified the drawing and told him he was wrong when his answer was incorrect. The two boys in the film took turns in the contest (eight test items per film model), and the film was constructed so that each model was correct on four occasions and incorrect on four occasions. At the end of the film the woman declared a tie score and rewarded both boys.

The subject was told that he was going to see a film of a contest that involved two boys at a public school like his own. The examiner said that adults had judged the fairness of the contest but she wanted the child's judgment regarding its fairness. The examiner first showed the subject each of the incomplete and complete drawings that would appear in the film so that he would not be distracted from the film models' efforts by trying to solve the perceptual problem himself. Any of the child's questions were clarified at this time.

The examiner then added that the subject might want to know something about the two boys in the film, named Sam and Joe. It was at this time that the female examiner assigned a psychological trait appropriate to the experimental subject to one of the film models, and the opposite trait to the other film model. For the 25 boys with reading disability the examiner described one of the film models as having a serious difficulty mastering reading; the other film model was described as being a good reader. The control subjects were given information about the birthdays and number of siblings of the two film models, neither of which was characteristic of the subject. The children were asked to repeat the communication given by the experimenter (that is, to say what traits were assigned to each film model) in order to guarantee that each boy had assimilated the description of qualities assigned to the models.

For half the experimental subjects the boy that was called Sam was assigned the attributes appropriate to the subject; for the other half, the boy that was called Joe was described as having the traits that matched those of the subject. After the instructions and the child's repetition of the qualities ascribed to each model, the experimental film was shown. During the film each boy's behavior was recorded on audiovisual tape by a concealed camera of which the subject was unaware. After the film each subject was asked about his perceived similarity to each of the film models.

Some children on some occasions showed unambiguous signs of empathic involvement. They would openly cheer for and encourage one of the models or disparage or mock the other model. A second, slightly more ambiguous behavioral sign of empathic involvement was the occurrence of smiling following the success of his model or the failure of the alternate model, or smiling while his model was working on the problem. There were two slightly more ambiguous categories of behavior which could be regarded as indexes of affect. One was leaning forward to the screen when one of the models was present. This behavior might be regarded as an indication of interest. The other variable was an obvious change in facial expression— furrowing of the brow, grimacing, twisting of the mouth. Although it was not possible to name an emotion for these changes in facial expression (excluding smiling), these responses were clear and could be reliably coded. Because the face is regarded by many (Izard, 1971; Ekman, Friesen, and Ellsworth, 1972) as a muscle surface that is sensitive to changes in internal affective tone, we chose this variable as indicative of empathy. Finally, we used differential occurrence of talking as an index of emotional involvement.

The analysis of the film data revealed that 16 of the 25 reading-disabled boys (64 percent) showed greater empathy with the model described as having a serious reading problem, and none showed greater empathy with the model described as a competent reader. By contrast, only 2 of the 11 controls showed differential empathic behavior with one of the models ($\chi^2 = 4.70$, $p < .05$). Thus, it appears that when the child has a distinctive trait, even if it is undesirable, empathic behavior with one of the models does occur. The value of the empathic measure is evident when one compares it with the children's statements (given at the end of the film) as to whom they resembled. Of the 12 reading-disabled boys who did not admit to the examiner that they were similar to the film model with reading disability, 7 showed greater empathic involvement with the model described as having that handicap.

Study 3: Self-Evaluation, Triads, and Empathy

The purpose of the third and final study was to replicate the implications of the first two investigations. The fact that almost two-thirds of the reading disabled boys were likely to display empathy with the model, together with the fact that the data of Study 1 implied that denial of personal attributes was frequent among children with qualities their peers considered undesirable, led us to select a group of boys who, according to peers and teacher, were at the extreme of unpopularity and poor reading ability in their classroom. We wished to determine if the triads and empathy measures would add important information to the more conscious self-evaluations for children who were regarded by others as having undesirable attributes.

The sample consisted of 71 fourth-grade boys from 16 classrooms in 10 public schools located in working-class neighborhoods in and around Boston. The boys were 9–10 years of age; 36 were Caucasian, 13 were black, 9 were of Hispanic origin, and 13 were from other ethnic groups. All children were fluent in English, and all procedures were conducted in English. The experimental group consisted of 39 boys who were extremely unpopular in their classrooms, severely retarded in reading ability, or both. A group of 32 control children was chosen to be matched to the experimentals on ethnicity, language spoken in the home, and classroom or neighborhood. However, the control children were not in the bottom quartile of their class on reading ability or popularity. That is, the control subjects did not possess the undesirable qualities for which their matched experimental subject was selected.

Methods

Each of the 71 children was administered three procedures in the same order. They were (1) ranking of self and same-sex peers on popularity and reading ability, (2) sort by triads, and (3) viewing a film.

Ranking. Each experimental and control child was asked to rank all the boys in this classroom, including himself, on popularity and reading ability. The procedure used was identical to the one described for Study 1.

Triads. Unlike Study 1, we were not interested in determining the dimensions the children might use to organize their peers but wanted to see whether a child who was given a specific psychological dimension to use in the triads would place himself with children who did or did not possess the desirable attribute. The subjects who were in the unpopular or poor reading groups were administered the triads procedure only once. They were asked to make their grouping either on popularity or on reading. The subjects who were both unpopular and retarded in reading were asked to do the triads twice, once for each characteristic. The child was given trios of boys in his classroom and asked to say which two were most similar and which one different on either popularity or reading ability. Each child received 36 triads for each quality.

Film. The film was the same one described in Study 2 but two important changes were made in the procedure. First, despite the empathic identification with both Sam and Joe by the reading-disabled subjects, the data from Study 2 suggested that Sam was physically the more attractive model. More control children said they liked Sam on a postfilm interview and many subjects were less restless and more attentive when Sam was on the screen than when Joe was on camera. For this reason we made Joe the experimental model for all the subjects in order to avoid ambiguity over whether greater empathy with Sam was due to his attractiveness as a model. Second, in Study 2 the control children were given no basis for believing in any similarity between the model and themselves. In this study the control children were given the same basis as the experimentals. Thus the control child for the popularity group was told that Joe was popular and Sam was not. The control child for the reading group was told that Joe was a good reader and Sam was not. The control child for the experimental boys with both undesirable qualities was told that Joe was popular and good in reading while Sam had the opposite traits. By contrast, the experimental children were told the reverse. They were told that Joe was unpopular and that Sam was popular; Joe was a poor reader and Sam a good reader; or Joe was both unpopular and a poor reader while Sam had the opposite attributes. This strategy was based on the *a priori* expectation that the experimental subjects would be more likely to empathize with the undesirable model, the control subjects with the desirable model. Because Sam was inherently more attractive than Joe, we would have "helped" our prediction by making Joe undesirable for the control subjects.

The coding of the film data was exactly as described for Study 2. That is, if a child cheered or encouraged one model or sneered or mocked at another, that child was classified as showing greater empathic identification with the former model. If these behaviors did not occur, a child who showed more appropriate smiling to one model than to the other was classified as being identified with that model. If neither of these two behaviors occurred, but if the child showed more changes in facial expression, talking, and leaning forward to one model than to the other, he was classified as identified with that model. The reliability of the coding was 90 percent.

A significant proportion of the experimental children did not acknowledge their poor reading ability or unpopularity on the self-ranking procedures. Among the 11 boys ranked as extremely unpopular by their peers, 4 indicated that they were very popular; of the 16 boys judged by their teachers to be very poor readers, 6 ranked themselves as good readers. Among the 12 boys considered to be both unpopular and poor readers, 9 denied one or both traits. Indeed, only 14 of the 39 experimental boys ranked themselves consistent with the peer-ranks.

The utility of the triads procedure is apparent if one examines the number of experimental subjects who ranked themselves as possessing desirable qualities but whose triad scores were classified as ambiguous. Three poor readers who ranked themselves high on reading ability produced ambiguous triads, and four boys who were both poor readers and unpopular produced ambiguous triads for at least one of these traits. A total of 9 of the 19 children who denied one or both undesirable qualities in the ranking procedure did not place themselves with the competent children in the triads procedure, implying a self-concept that was, to some degree, in closer accord with the peer-ranks.

The empathy measure also seemed to be of value. Of the 19 experimental boys who had claimed they were good readers and were popular, one-third showed greater empathy toward Joe, the model who was unpopular and who read poorly. Six of the 11 children in the reading group who denied their inadequate reading skill on ranks or triads showed greater affective involvement with Joe, the model who was poor in reading. No child who acknowledged his poor reading skill on self-ranks or triads showed greater empathy with Sam.

Discussion

The results of these exploratory studies have two implications. First, children's responses to direct questions about their psychological qualities appear to be relatively valid indexes of the child's belief (if peer and teacher evaluations are the criteria) when the self-ranks admit to undesirable attributes. But positive evaluations are more suspect, for at least one-third of all children who did not possess the positive attributes, in the perception of their peers, evaluated the self positively. However, some of these children acknowledged their undesirable quality on the triads or film. It should not be surprising that positive self-evaluations are ambiguous in meaning; what is surprising is that some investigators have refused to acknowledge that fact. These data, when added to information gathered by others, suggest that investigators should stop using such instruments as the only measure of the child's beliefs about the self.

There are at least three possible reasons why preadolescent children might not admit to an undesirable quality. The simplest is that the child is not aware of his or her quality. A second interpretation claims that all children are aware of having undesirable qualities but refuse to admit them. A third interpretation involves the defenses of denial or repression. Some children do not recognize their undesirable attributes because of a defense against recognition of those qualities. It is likely that all three types of children are represented in our samples. But informal conversation with the children before and after the experimental procedures lead me to suggest that the majority were aware of their undesirable status but did not want to admit it to the examiner. That is why I believe in the potential utility of the triads and film procedures. The combination of self-ranks, triads and film are more sensitive than either method alone in diagnosing the child's self-concept. Of the 19 children in study 3 who ranked themselves high on reading or popularity (all of whom were ranked low by their peers), 7 acknowledged their low status on either the triads or the film. The use of these two more disguised procedures increased the probable accuracy of our classification of the child's private beliefs by more than one-third—a nontrivial gain in validity. Detection of complex psychological qualities requires complex procedures.

There is no single, best source of evidence that informs us of the nature of a child's self-concept. Rather, each datum adds a little knowledge to the family of processes implied by this term. Further, useful information can come from varied sources. On occasion, the art and literature of a society can be informative. The writings of Beckett and Grass reveal a conception of the individual self in twentieth-century Europe that is more isolated than the one depicted by Shakespeare or Hardy.

One afternoon in a Tokyo art museum I saw an exhibition of paintings by young Japanese artists that appeared to reveal a central aspect of the contemporary self-concept of the Japanese. A large number of paintings contained paired objects—women, animals, trees. Because such a pattern is unusual in European or North American art, I quantified this observation. I purchased a book that contained 173 paintings on display, by as many artists. All the works were completed after 1945. I compared these Japanese paintings with 90 paintings illustrated in *Contemporary Chinese Paintings*, edited by Hua Junwu, We Zuoren, and Zhang Anzhi (1983). With three exceptions, the Chinese paintings in this book were completed since the founding of the Peoples Republic in 1949.

I noted for each painting whether it contained one or more of the following three characteristics:

(1) Paired objects that belonged to the same class (women, men, birds, kites, houses, boats) or multiple pairs of the same classes of objects (three pairs of women, two pairs of sheep).
(2) A dominance relationship between two people, two animals, or a person and an animal, or an obviously aggressive person or predatory animal with a victim.

(3) A dominant horizontal plane (rather than vertical); paintings with single figures or objects were not coded for this category.

Even though the surface content of the Chinese and Japanese paintings was very similar—the majority of paintings from both societies were scenes of nature—a larger proportion of Japanese paintings contained paired objects (33% vs. 13%; chi square = 12.3, $p <$ .001). Additionally, the members of the pair were often complementary on a dimension—one member was dark and the other light, a part of one object was covered and the other uncovered, one was a reflection of the other, or one was more elaborated than the other. When paired objects appeared in the Chinese paintings, they were not so obviously contrasted on a complementary dimension.

One possible interpretation is that the frequency of complementary pairs reflects the contemporary Japanese concern with the public and private modes of interaction which are primary themes in contemporary Japanese novels. The two perspectives are called *tatemae* and *honne*. It is important for a Japanese to hide his or her true emotions and attitudes from those who, at the moment, are not in an inner group because they are neither kin nor colleagues or because one is in a public place. A Japanese social scientist notes, "Whatever his reason or his conscience might tell him he should do, if doing it would invite isolation he would be unwilling to take the risk" (Fukutake, 1982, p. 43). Lucian Pye (1985) adds that "Japanese tend to be keenly aware of the differences between a person's open statements (tatemae) and his inner thoughts and intentions (honne). Therefore the good leader will frequently discount the formal acknowledgement which would have certified a consensus and will probe instead into latent discontent" (p. 175).

The Chinese are less uncertain over the frame they should adopt in social situations. More like Americans, the Chinese are relatively open with strangers, and their modern novels reveal that they are more often concerned with each person's relationship to authority rather than with the tension between private and public behavior. It is of interest, therefore, that 16 percent of the Chinese paintings illustrated a dominance relationship, either between men and women, adults and children, a person and animal, or a predatory or aggressive animal (tigers and eagles were common) in a threatening posture. Only two percent of the Japanese paintings depicted this class of idea, and not one of the Japanese paintings illustrated an aggressive animal.

Inferences about the self-consciousness of members of a culture from its art or prose are always uncertain. Although Aries's inference concerning the European conception of childhood based on pre-Enlightenment paintings was regarded as valid initially, it is now questioned (correctly, I think) by both historians and social scientists. On the other hand, the Impressionists' concern with nature and the daily life of the average citizen was probably influenced by the growing egalitarianism in nineteenth-century Europe and the new view of man's relation to nature that followed Darwinian theory. That is why I suspect these contemporary Japanese paintings reflect a node of uncertainty in current Japanese consciousness that is muted among Europeans and North Americans.

A person does not reveal his or her private beliefs readily. Psychologists who are convinced that a child's conception of his attributes is an important determinant of behavior, as I do, should be prepared to invest as much effort in discovering those beliefs as was invested by the child in their establishment.

9

Self-Consciousness:
A Dialogue without Answers

The initial phase in the development of most empirical sciences relies on ideas whose presumptive validity is based on a broad intuitive appeal. Examples of concepts which seemed to earlier scholars to be obviously correct include the belief that all objects in the world have unchanging essences; that every event is determined by some prior causal force; that the infant's organs are present in miniature from the beginning of the embryo's growth; that the brain registers a veridical image of what the eyes perceive; and that women are weaker than men. Each of these ideas was treated as true because it seemed to match experience or was an obvious deduction from the premises underlying available knowledge.

The current understanding of the concept of self, which is phenomenologically compelling to Western minds, may also be flawed. Three reasons for skepticism include the assumption of an essential process containing some components that do not change over time, the practice of using introspective self-report as the major source of referential information about the self's characteristics, and the belief that an individual's voluntary actions are unpredictable because they are monitored by the self (hence, each person is morally responsible for his or her behavior).

A serious problem with the construct of self or self-concept is that it is not always treated in an objective frame of description. When most investigators write that children who are rejected by their family behave aggressively because of a poor self-concept, they are using the term self-concept to refer to hypothetical states that may or may not be available to the child's consciousness. This frame, which is appropriate, is identical with that of a sensory physiologist who explains the perception of color as due to opponent processes in the thalamus. This epistemological stance has consensual validity in the scientific community, whether or not the construct of self is valid. But some social scientists use the idea of self-concept in a subjective frame to refer to a person's conscious evaluation of his or her qualities. The most popular procedure involves direct questioning of children or adults about their personal characteristics and associated evaluations. This referent for the idea *self-concept* assumes that the theoretically most profitable meaning of the construct involves the person's subjective beliefs. A few psychologists go further and write as though the contents of consciousness should be a primary criterion for judging the validity of all procedures. If behavioral evidence indicates that a particular group of children have a weak or poor self-concept in the objective frame, but the children report a positive self-concept on a questionnaire, the former evidence is suspect. Recall the evidence described in the prior chapter in which many unpopular children denied this quality when asked directly. I believe this second view is mistaken. Human consciousness is a phenomenon to be understood in the same way we inquire into depression, separation anxiety, growth of retrieval memory, and learning sets in monkeys. Although each of us may feel that our consciousness is among our most significant characteristics and the most important determinant of our behavior, such an assumption is neither empirically proven nor logically commanding.

My own belief is that because consciousness is salient to each of us as acting agents, we have exaggerated its significance as an origin of action. Much of the time it is simply a commentator on the internal states that often are the more forceful bases for behavior. So many significant biological and psychological processes occur outside of conscious awareness, theorists would be extremely limited in their imaginative scope if they always had to accommodate to a person's consciousness. Adults are usually unable to describe how they solve a particular problem (computer programs that simulate human problem solving ignore consciousness). Second, consciousness is usually evaluated by asking a person to provide a symbolic description in the form of sentences that try to be grammatical. This procedure imposes serious constraints on the person's reply. Further, self-reports rarely contain inconsistency. No sane person would say, "I am afraid" and "I am happy" because the two concepts refer to inconsistent ideas, even if we, in the objective frame, had good reason to suspect that a person felt both anxiety and happiness because she was about to initiate an illicit rendezvous. Finally, there is usually very little relation between objective signs of feeling tone and a self-report. Thus, scientific statements about self-consciousness in the subjective frame must be treated with great caution.

Although this essay is not the place to consider philosophical views in any depth, I suggest that some of the paradoxes philosophers have encountered are due to a confusion of objective and subjective frames. Such confusion is common in philosophical essays on morality. G. E. Moore suggested that good and bad must be defined by each person's conscious attitudes and feelings. Years later John Rawls stated that each person's rational decision in moral situations should be the criterion for morality. But both Moore and Rawls have implied that elements of consciousness participate in a moral choice. However, these philosophers, along with many others, also believe they are writing rules for morality in the objective frame. Their essays were persuasive pleas to the community to adopt into their consciousness elements of the scholars' objective arguments so that subjective and objective frames would be congruent. Unfortunately, the behavior of most people in situations with a moral choice reveals the futility of this aim. Many terrorists who kill feel highly moral in their subjective frame, even though we, in the objective frame, may regard them in quite the opposite way. By contrast, when a mother offers unconditional love to her child we are prone to declare her moral, even though her private, conscious motive may have been to win the child's affection away from an estranged father. Despite the fact that on occasion the two frames coincide, they are often discordant.

I do not know if a concept of self-consciousness will survive the next fifty years of research, and I bear the currently popular idea no prejudice. Should it persist, however, I suspect its primary referential meanings will not be the self-report indexes that provide its current operational form, and its sense meaning will emphasize a family of processes rather than a unitary one.

The tightly reasoned essay is the preferred strategy for critiques of controversial themes. I have chosen to present the uncertainties that surround the concepts of self and consciousness in a different form— a hypothetical dialogue between a young philosopher and an older woman who is his tutor. I hope that this format will provoke a more attentive and pleasurable reading, even if it does not change many minds.

A Dialogue

Scene: A small lake in Northern Italy.

Participants: Simpliciter (S), a young student of philosophy who has just joined the Academy. Reflectiva (R), an older philosopher who has become Simpliciter's teacher and friend.

Time: A morning in May between past and present.

S: What a beautiful Spring morning we are able to enjoy.

R: What nonsense are you speaking?

S: What do you mean nonsense? Is this not a beautiful morning that gives each of us much pleasure?

R: How do you know this moment gives pleasure or the day is beautiful?

S: You are always such a skeptic. Consult your consciousness. If your consciousness feels it is beautiful, and you experience pleasure, then my statement is true.

R: But how do I know my conscious feelings are pleasant? All I know is that I feel something. Why are you so certain that pleasure is the proper word to describe these feelings?

S: There is no talking with you when you are in such a mischievous state of mind. Do you not believe that there is a difference between feeling good and feeling poorly?

R: Yes, of course. But tell me how I can know the difference?

S: By consulting your self-awareness, your consciousness. What would you suggest we do to determine if you felt good or poorly?

R: By deciding first what events defined feeling good and feeling poorly.

S: What would you pick?

R: Well, I might measure my pulse and see if it was different when I ate sweet foods than when I ate bitter ones. If my pulse rates were different when I ate the two kinds of foods, then at least I would have a clue as to which foods gave me pleasure and which did not. If my pulse always had a similar value when I was eating sweet foods, but was of a different value when I was eating bitter ones, I would know when I was feeling pleasure and when displeasure.

S: But your pulse has nothing to do with how you feel. Feeling is in your consciousness, not in your pulse.

R: I do not understand. You claim that there exists in my conscious mind some events that are properly called "feeling good." On the surface that seems like a reasonable idea. But shouldn't we first determine if these words refer to a similar class of events in all people? I am certain you agree that not all of the words people use have the same referent. I am told that in some islands in the far East when a person says he feels sad he actually intends to imply that he is wise. Surely we can't rely only on someone's verbal statement about how they feel to decide on the state of their consciousness. Both of us know many people living under conditions neither you nor I could tolerate for a moment who would reply that they felt good if someone asked them. Insane patients in our asylums tell visitors they feel happy on days when they look as pale as ghosts. Isn't that sufficient evidence for you to acknowledge that we cannot decide if a person is feeling good simply by asking, "How do you feel?" That is why I insist we need some other evidence.

S: What you say has merit and gives me pause. But your solution is obviously incorrect. Will you grant me that the state I call "feeling good" must be part of a person's consciousness?

R: In order to hear you out I will accept that premise, but I warn you, only temporarily.

S: Fine. Well, if feeling good is a property of a person's consciousness, that is where we must search for evidence as to its actualization, not in the beating of the heart.

R: But how do you know what is in a person's consciousness?

S: By asking, "What do you feel?" The coordination of the information that contributes to the feeling state is done by the self, and the only way to discover it is to ask the person to describe his state with the best words possible.

R: Why do you believe that the words a person uses to describe his feeling state correspond to the state of his consciousness?

S: It must. A person will not say he feels fine if the sensations in his consciousness do not match that feeling.

R: That is precisely why I gave you the earlier examples, which you agreed were reasonable. I do not think we can assume that a person's statements about his feelings, even if intended to be honest, are always in close correspondence with the state of his consciousness. People will say they feel calm when their hearts are racing, their muscles stiff as boards, and they show irritation to the slightest frustration. Some people will say they don't recognize

a familiar person although the muscles of their face and the per-
spiration on their palms reveal that they do. Some unfortunate
individuals with lesions in their spinal column whose brains and
consciousness are unable to experience any sensory feedback
from their body will say they feel as anxious as you and I when an
accident has occurred. I cannot believe that their statements are
faithful to their consciousness, unless you simply assert that the
state of consciousness is defined by the sentences a person speaks.
Let me try another approach. Please pick up that stick from the
ground. Now close your eyes and move the stick around in this
hole in the ground. Good. What does your consciousness feel?

S: I feel intermittent pressure on my hand as the stick hits the side of
the hole.

R: Good. Now put the stick in that opening in the tree. Keep your
eyes closed. What do you feel?

S: The same feelings, intermittent pressure on my hand.

R: One last request. Hold the stick loosely in your fist, with your eyes
closed, while I move it back and forth. What do you feel?

S: Well, the same sensation. I feel the pressure of the stick against my
hand.

R: In all three cases you reported that your consciousness experienced the same sensations, the intermittent pressure of a stick
against your hand.

S: Yes, that's true.

R: But wouldn't you have used very different words to describe the
three experiences.

S: What do you mean?

R: Well, if someone saw you poking a stick in a hole in the ground
and asked you what you were doing, what would you say?

S: I'd say I was exploring a hole.

R: But if someone asked you the same question as I was moving the
stick in your hand, what would you say?

S: I would say you were moving the stick in my fist.

R: So even though your conscious experiences were similar, you
would have used very different words to describe them. That is
my point. The words a person uses are not faithful to what consciousness is experiencing.

S: Then how shall we treat a person's statements about his feelings?
Shall we ignore them?

R: No. We should treat what a person says about his conscious experience as we treat his pulse rate. It is a fragment of information, a limited, fallible clue to help us diagnose the state of his consciousness. How do you feel at this moment?

S: Confused, a little troubled, and a bit peeved with you.

R: But you seem to me to be much more relaxed than you were when we first met. Your body is less tense, your voice lower in pitch and less strident, and your face almost has a smile. I am certain you are feeling much better now than you did earlier when you commented on the beauty of the morning.

S: You are a devil with words. Let's forget about feeling good or poorly and talk about the self which monitors the thoughts in our minds and the sensations from our bodies. Will you grant me that each person possesses a self that is aware of the quality of its feelings, the content of its thoughts, and contains some features that are continuous throughout life?

R: I'm afraid that, once again, I do not understand. My reply is the same I gave to your statement about feeling good. How can we know if such a unitary self exists? And even if such an idea referred to an event in nature, it is unlikely that its components would be constant from day to day, and certainly not from year to year.

S: Well, of course the self exists. What mental entity is it that is aware of pain, knows one's name, decides what sentences to speak, holds opinions about the world, and selects and reflects on actions. I trust you agree that we need to posit some entity that participates in and monitors these processes.

R: I only agree that those events you describe may occur. I am not certain that it is useful to posit a single hypothetical entity that is responsible for all of those functions. I grant you the utility of a word like self but I suspect that there is one self that monitors our feelings, a different self that evaluates our virtue, a third self that monitors actions; perhaps a few more selves are necessary to cover all the important domains of experience.

S: This time I shall win the argument. Look, you will acknowledge that each of us can relate what we know now with what we have learned in the past, and, in light of both sets of knowledge, decide to act in a particular way. If there were not a single entity, that sequence would not be possible.

R: I disagree. A computer in Rome contacts a terminal in Milan, via a mainframe in Florence, which transfers information to a machine on Lake Como that prints a letter. There is no unitary computer, just connections among separate entities.

S: But those are mechanical objects. You cannot invent a similar analogy for biological phenomena.

R: I believe I can. When I have not eaten for a day, I become hungry. But we know that my hunger is not a single unitary process. My hypothalamus reacts to the drop in blood sugar, the walls of my stomach to emptiness, the receptors in my mouth to dryness. Surely you will grant that the state of hunger is not a single event in a particular place. Why then assume that the self is any different?

S: If the self were not a single coordinated entity, how could you explain that a criminal act committed during adolescence will, 20 years later, lead the person to feel shame or prompt the self to do penance? If the self were many fragmented selves, we would not have access to despair from the deep past, fragrances of earlier springs, or the shiver of last winter's chill. You are simply not willing to acknowledge these facts we know to be true.

R: I do not understand why integration of experiences over time requires us to assume that there is a unitary self that does not change. I understand from some of our friends at the Academy that if white blood cells are stimulated to make antibody against measles during early childhood, 20 years later the adult will have white blood cells that have the potential to produce antibody to the measles germ. But the white blood cells that existed in childhood are gone; the adult has a totally new set of white blood cells. Even though the fragrance in a flower garden on a May afternoon can evoke the thought of a similar garden experienced 10 years earlier, that fact does not require us to assume that the two sensory experiences are part of a unity. You are being unduly influenced by your subjective intuition. Our subjective intuitions are often notoriously poor indexes of what is true in nature. My subjective consciousness tells me that the sun moves and the earth stands still, the ocean ends at the horizon, and water and ice must be composed of different substances. Moreover, new knowledge changes our intuition. For ten years when I met Bruno on the street he would smile and greet me with a warm voice, and my intuition told me he was my close friend. I then learned he voted against my brother for an Academy assignment. Now, although he greets me in exactly the same way, my intuition about the smile and greeting has changed. Further, before our astronomers discovered the distances of the sun and the moon, our intuitions were that both were equally far away. Now that we know the sun is much more distant, our intuitions have changed and we have the feeling that the moon is closer.

No, my friend, you are too trusting of your conscious intuitions. I suspect I have one self that talks to you, a different self that greets a stranger, and a third self that writes my diary at sunrise. You forget that Oriental philosophers assume that there are at least two selves. One monitors the encounters with strangers, the other with family and close friends. They even give the two selves different names. We smile to a neighbor whom we dislike. How can one entity mediate the two inconsistent moods? I appeal to your logic. There cannot be one self that is both friendly and hostile to the same person at the same time. When you are lecturing in the morning to students on philosophy, does your self believe it is wiser than the students?

S: Of course.

R: But you have told me that when you attend the seminars at the Academy, you feel intellectually inadequate when the older members are talking.

S: Yes, but they know more about the topic.

R: But how can there be one self that feels intelligent and wise in the morning but unintelligent the evening of the same day? Surely that is not logical.

S: But the context has changed. My self is comparing my qualities with those of others and comes to different conclusions, depending upon the target of comparison.

R: But look at what you have just admitted. You have said that you do not have any unitary idea of your wisdom. You have different ideas, depending upon the situation. That is exactly what I suggested. We have different selves in different contexts.

S: That conclusion does not follow. I do not have to assume one brain when I am talking and another when I am painting.

R: Watch out. We are told that the metabolism of the brain is different when we are engaging in different activities. There is no unitary brain state either, but many different states.

S: But there is one brain that is the site of these different states, regardless of the activity engaged in.

R: You forget that last month we heard a lecture describing the changes that occur in our brain over a lifetime. This unitary entity you call the self must derive its form, in part, from the synaptic connections in our brains. Yet these connections are not static. Over a twenty-year period they must change a great deal, and so the selves of today cannot be identical to the selves of childhood. If they were, they would be the only human qualities that never changed. Although nature is occasionally mischievous and creates unique exceptions to general principles in order to keep us humble, I am not persuaded that the self is that special exception.

Let me try a simple thought experiment with you. If your self were a single entity that integrated information from your feelings, thoughts, and actions, then you should be able to tell me how your body felt several minutes ago when you were arguing with me about the meaning of feeling good. Can you do so?

S: No I can't, but how is that question relevant?

R: It is relevant because if you had a single self, it should be able to know what you felt, as well as what you said. If you had several selves, however, and only one was executive at any moment, you might be able to report the question you had asked me but be unable to say how your body felt.

S: But I wasn't paying attention to how I felt when I asked the question.

R: But the entity that was not paying attention is one of the selves I am arguing for; it is the self that monitors your feeling states. These separate selves compete, and at the time your executive self was composing questions, this self was subordinate. This competition among the selves is not completely under your control, you know.

S: I am beginning to suspect that you secretly agree with the new radical philosophers who claim that humans do not have a self that is free to select an action. Do you believe that if a team of scholars measured all of my past experience and had access to all of my brain states, they could have predicted my decision to come and talk with you this morning? I don't believe so. That is one reason why we need a unitary concept of self.

R: You seem to be upset by the possibility that some observers might be able to predict your decision to visit with me. Why?

S: It is disconcerting because I have always assumed that one of the central attributes of self is the capacity to make conscious decisions that are not predictable by others.

R: Let us play a little. Suppose it were possible for some omniscient group of experts who had all the information on your past and current states to predict most of the time when you would walk, eat, play, or work. But you were completely unaware of these expert predictions. You would still experience a sense of choice and, in that sense, you would have a self with free will.

S: No, if my past were controlling my current behavior then, in actuality, I would be a partial prisoner of my past. I would not have free will. It isn't just what I believe to be true.

R: But each of us must be a partial prisoner of our past. I cannot help but get upset when a woman is treated unjustly, yet that is not true of all citizens. I cannot help but be polite to an old person, but not all are equally civil. These seemingly spontaneous reactions are determined by my past, even though I have the feeling that at the moment when I criticize someone who has been unfair, or offer an old man assistance in crossing the street, I issue those acts freely. I never feel that my self is coerced by my past.

S: But if your past influenced your behavior, then you are deceiving yourself. You did not have complete freedom of choice.

R: I think I see the problem. Consider a spider constructing a web. Do you agree that it has no consciousness of what it is doing?

S: Yes.

R: Because experts can predict when the spider will build a web and the form of the web, the act of web building is determined and the spider is not free.

S: Yes, that is true. But spiders have no consciousness. Humans are different.

R: Wait a moment. Let's move up to a chimpanzee, our close relative. We are told that chimpanzees are very similar to us in treatment of their young and how they feed, sleep, and mate. Do you agree that chimpanzees do not have freedom of choice for many significant behaviors?

S: Yes. But suppose they don't have self-consciousness either.

R: Now consider your nephew Damon who, I believe, is three years old. You agree that he has consciousness, don't you?

S: Yes, he does.

R: But can't you predict better than chance when Damon will get upset, what he will say to you when you visit, the games he will play, the length of his sentences, and on and on. Can't you predict a great deal of Damon's behavior, even though he has consciousness and free will.

S: Yes. But not all of his acts.

R: Wait a moment. Let us first agree that a person can have consciousness and yet a great deal of that person's behavior is determined in some way.

S: Yes, I see that. But what about the many times that Damon is unpredictable.

R: For example?

S: Well, last week he did something uncharacteristic. He went to his room, saying he wanted to play alone. He stayed there for three hours and he has never done that before.

R: Do you think he decided that act freely, with no incentive? Was there no information you could have gathered that would have helped you to predict that act, even though it was displayed for the first time?

S: I thought a bit about it the next morning. He had been punished for spilling honey over the table and felt ashamed. I think his decision to be alone was a reaction to the spilling of the honey.

R: Well then it was partially determined by the past, and was partially knowable, wasn't it?

S: Yes, I guess so.

R: Give me an example of an act Damon might issue for which you are certain that no information would allow you to predict it better than chance.

S: Well, if he suddenly put on his mother's shoes and took scissors and started to cut up curtains in the house. He is a good boy and would never do that.

R: But suppose he did. Do you believe he would have acted that way independent of any of his past experiences—a totally spontaneous act of free will?

S: No, I guess not.

R: Then you agree that no person can perform an act that is totally independent of the past.

S: I admit that. But why then do we have the compelling sense that we choose to behave the way we do?

R: You phrased it correctly. We have a *feeling* that our choices are free. It is not possible to predict every act a person might display; there is a window of unpredictability. But that is true of every natural event. No expert can predict exactly where a particular leaf in a forest will fall at a particular moment. But the expert can fairly well predict where most of the leaves will fall. We have partial freedom, while our consciousness has a sense of complete freedom. That is the critical point. Free will is an idea of subjective consciousness; from that perspective it is valid, even though no one has complete freedom of choice from the perspective of another.

S: Wait, I don't understand that last statement. What does it mean for you to say that from your perspective I do not have complete freedom of choice, yet I believe I do. How can both of those statements be true.

R: Let me explain. Each agent has a private consciousness that is not available to others, but others try to understand these private states of agents. Let us call each agent's consciousnesses his "subjective understandings," and the beliefs others hold about the agent "objective understandings." I do not claim that the objective understandings are more profound or more valid, only that the two understandings need not be consistent, and often are not. They have different meanings because of their separate origins. Do you agree with the zoologists who claim they know why female turtles bury their fertilized eggs in the sand several hundred feet from the shoreline?

S: They do so to protect the eggs from predators.

R: Good. Does that explanation have a clear meaning?

S: Yes.

R: Suppose we could enter the mind of the turtle and determine her consciousness. Do you agree that she would have no conception of the purpose of her behavior?

S: Yes.

R: So the objective understanding of the observer has no relation to the subjectivity of the turtle.

S: Yes. But you keep on using animals who don't have subjective consciousness. Use humans as examples.

R: I will. Do you remember that last month you told me that your wife was rude to your sister Penelope when she visited from Atlantis. Yet when you told her about her behavior, she said she did not realize she had been rude. She said she was tired and not feeling well and that is why she may not have been as friendly to Penelope as she is normally. Yet when you reminded her that she was peeved because Penelope had not sent a birthday greeting to you, she acknowledged that perhaps she had been irritated at her at the time, but claimed she had no awareness of anger when she visited.

S: Yes, I recall, and I am certain that my wife was rude because my sister forgot to send a note on my birthday.

R: That is a good example of the two perspectives. In your wife's subjective consciousness she was tired. In your objective understanding she was angry and, therefore, impolite. Do you see that the two understandings need not be in accord?

S: Yes, but in that case I was right and my wife's understanding was wrong. There may be two understandings, but one is correct.

R: Not so fast. How do you know you were right?

S: One explanation of an event has to be correct. We can't have two different, but correct, explanations of the same event.

R: But we can, if one is in the subjective frame of the actor and one in the objective frame of the observer. Only when both explanations come from the same frame must one be correct.

S: I don't see why the frame of understanding makes any difference.

R: Consider a person who believes he is unworthy of any happiness because he has failed at every important task he has undertaken and has tried to commit suicide. But his friends and family see him as a successful professional who is well liked by everyone. We know this is true of our friend Paulo.

S: Yes, that's true.

R: A man who tries to kill himself provides good evidence that he believes he is unworthy, or at least unhappy. Yet no one knew that was true about Paulo. For a man cannot be both sad and happy, worthy and unworthy at the same time. Because one source of unworthiness was in the subjective frame and the other in the objective frame the statements are not inconsistent. The two understandings are complementary. Each has a meaning, but each meaning is derived from its own frame.

S: Now you are going to say that the self's sense of free will has meaning in the subjective frame but not in the objective frame.

R: Precisely. Every Saturday I note that you will take a walk before lunch, but only if you have been reading for most of the morning. Yet you are certain your walk is a spontaneously chosen act.

S: I believe there is a significant exception to the separation of subjective and objective frames.

R: What is that?

S: The motive of self-interest. In the subjective frame, my self always protects its access to sensory pleasures and power first. And that idea is also regarded as true in the objective frame of our scholars who study human nature. They, too, say that humans have evolved so that they are always trying to maximize their pleasure, welfare, power, and economic gain.

R: I am not certain I agree. Haven't you picked up a piece of glass from a path because you thought that a person might not see it and step on it? Did you move the glass away because you were self-interested? I don't think so. Last night, around midnight, I took a walk before retiring and saw Ignatio looking at Michael's freshly painted fence. You remember that Ignatio is angry with Michael and has been so since the time Michael flirted with his wife at their anniversary party five years ago. Michael had left his purse on top of the latch by mistake, and Ignatio knew that Michael prized that purse very much. Ignatio looked at it and then to my surprise took the purse off the post and put it on the threshold of the door so that it would be less visible to passers by, and then left. That was clearly an act of charity. There was no one on the street, and he had the opportunity to get even with someone he does not like, yet he performed an act of kindness that took effort. He did so because he could not do otherwise.

S: What do you mean he could not do otherwise? Ignatio is a sane, mature person with free will. If he chose to, he could have done something to hurt Michael.

R: I suggest that Ignatio's feelings at that moment prevented him from doing so.

S: That makes no sense to me. Each of us controls our feelings every day. We are angry with someone and we greet them politely; we feel sad and yet are able to smile to a friend; we feel attracted toward a lovely woman we do not know, yet act with indifference. We have absolutely no problem controlling our feelings. So why do you say that Ignatio did not steal the purse because he could not control his feelings?

R: In every example you posed a person would have yielded to feelings that are violations of what he or she might view as proper behavior.

S: Yes, that's true, so what?

R: What emotion do we feel when we act improperly?

S: Self-reproachment. But that is a timid feeling compared with anger or sexual arousal. How could it overpower such strong competitors?

R: It does so because it is linked to the most important belief each of us tries to maintain.

S: What is that?

R: The belief of the evaluative self that it has virtue because the executive self has acted in accord with what is proper and right.

S: That is nonsense. How can you explain the violent or corrupt behavior of so many people who know that they are not acting in accord with what they believe is right and good? If your hypothesis were correct, most people would behave in a civilized way and thievery, lying, and corruption would be rare.

R: That is a forceful reply. Let me try to answer it. We have agreed that in the subjective frame each of us feels we can decide how to act.

S: Yes.

R: Will you also grant that our evaluative self wishes to be judged good?

S: I will for now, but I am not certain of the correctness or utility of that idea. Proceed.

R: If you grant those two assumptions, you may be forced to agree that most of the time we will behave properly, as Ignatio did. He knew that if he stole the purse, or let it remain prominent, he would later feel that he was not a good person. What I must explain, therefore, are the times, which are far less frequent, when people behave improperly.

   Let me begin with a stark example. A man kills a traveler in the woods and steals his gold. He knows he is acting immorally and knows he will suffer some guilt. He killed because he believed his emotions, be they greed, a desire for momentary power, or anger at the traveler, could not be suppressed.

S: That was my earlier point. Ignatio felt strong anger toward Michael, but we couldn't understand why that anger didn't influence him last night.

R: Anger did not dominate Ignatio's actions because at that moment the executive self was in control of Ignatio's behavior. The feeling self could not deceive the executive self into believing that the anger at Michael was so intense it was not responsible for his actions. If the feeling self could have done so, he might have stolen the purse. Moral behavior protects the evaluative self from reproachment. If the executive self decides it is not responsible for an improper act, no blame is imposed by the evaluative self and the improper act becomes more probable.

S: But what conditions allow a person to conclude that the self is not responsible?

R: Strong emotions. We give in to what we regard as immoral temptations because the feelings associated with the immoral urge are so strong the feeling self can persuade the executive self it is not responsible for the act.

S: I don't find that argument persuasive. I know many people, as do you, who are emotionally indifferent, cold as fish, who act immorally with ease and often on impulse. They seem to experience no struggle with responsibility for the act. How can you explain their behavior?

R: I fear you will accuse me of inconsistency. For reasons that I do not completely understand, their evaluative self uses different evidence to affirm its virtue than do you and I. Their acts, which seem immoral to us, symbolize a form of virtue to them.

S: Virtue! Stealing, corruption, murder—surely you are joking.

R: I realize that statement sounds ridiculous. But wait. Suppose your life history was such that you felt uneasy, anxious, unloved, afraid, or helpless much of the time. Throughout your youth some of these feelings dominated your consciousness. I suspect you would be tempted to do something to alter this dysphoric mood. Unfortunately, many of the acts you and I regard as immoral have, as a consequence, a temporary sense of elation, efficacy, or potency. An act of vandalism, corruption, intimidation, or murder is an assertion of temporary effectiveness. Through their display a person is able to mask, temporarily, the feeling of incompetence or impotence, and, as a consequence, the evaluative self feels some virtue.

S: That is a poetic statement. What evidence can you supply to support such a speculative and counterintuitive notion?

R: Just a little. Why is it that crimes are most common among the youth who failed in their early studies in school?

S: I don't know.

R: I suspect that their failure at this important assignment made them feel less effective and, therefore, less virtuous. But the major rationale for my position is a deduction from one significant fact. It is this. Do you agree that of the many, many opportunities people have each day to lie, hurt, insult, steal, or commit acts of destruction only a tiny number of such acts actually occur? Indeed, the ratio of such immoral acts committed to the total number of opportunities in the entire world on a single day approaches zero. It seems odd, but immoral acts that hurt another are statistically freak events.

S: I had never thought of improper behavior that way but, on reflection, I suspect you may be right.

R: Do you also agree that much of the time those who behave morally, despite an easy opportunity to commit an improper act, are not restrained by fear of being noticed or punished? Often the person is alone and no one could possibly know about the crime. This was true of Ignatio last evening.

S: Yes.

R: Well, then, it must be that, most of the time, human beings behave morally because they have a natural bias to do so. I suggest that this bias originates in the continuous wish to affirm the evaluative self's virtue. Why else would most people behave properly despite a temptation to immoral behavior without obvious risk? Our task is to explain the aberrant times when a person does act immorally. Take thievery. Let us exclude those who steal because their material needs are strong and consider only those who steal something they do not actually need. Why would they do so unless that act had a symbolic meaning? I suggest that one symbolic meaning is a sense of effectiveness or potency.

S: Why don't you say people steal because they enjoy it? Why do you have to bring in the idea of effectiveness or virtue? You are twisting words to serve your position, when it seems that we have a much less tortuous explanation. They enjoy stealing.

R: Why should anyone enjoy stealing? It is not a sensual act. If it is enjoyed it must be because of its symbolic value. I grant there are many symbolic prizes other than a feeling of effectiveness, but such a feeling could follow an act of thievery.

S: Why do you make feelings so important to morality? Such a position is not in accord with the writings of our philosophers who treat moral behavior as a consequence of logic and rationality. They claim that most persons do not steal because they do not want others to steal from them. Because each of us is compelled to be logically consistent, we do not steal for we have no right to ask of others what we do not demand of ourselves. Of course, these philosophers also have trouble explaining the habitual thief, for he is supposed to be logical, too. Although our philosophers say that thieves do not reflect upon the logic of their actions, that argument is not less credible than your claim about stealing in order to feel effective. It seems to me we have two weak explanations of the thief. Personally, I have always believed that the thief failed to learn that stealing was wrong or, perhaps, was not punished for stealing when he was a youth. Hence, he did not experience fear when he planned or executed his act. What is wrong with that simple minded, straightforward explanation of the thief?

R: The first premise in your explanation is clearly incorrect. Ask any thief if stealing is wrong and he will tell you so without equivocation. He knows that stealing is wrong. The second premise is harder to refute, but I appeal to your sense of reasonableness. Think of Aristo's upbringing. His father and mother were upstanding citizens who must have punished him for stealing; yet, he is serving two years in exile for stealing from his father-in-law. He knew stealing was wrong and he felt anxious about the act. He told us so when we were with him the night he was caught. No, your explanation will not work for him. A thief knows he is behaving improperly and knows his behavior is disapproved by his friends and society. He steals because it reassures self of a feeling of effectiveness which, in turn, permits the thief to feel some virtue.

S: You are using nonsensical words. Now I shall adopt your skeptical position. What do virtue, potency, and worthwhileness mean? How do I know if a person feels virtue, or the lack of it?

R: Yes, I have lapsed into loose talk. Mea culpa. We are told that humans are the only species with the symbolic categories "good" and "bad." Unlike the categories "furniture" and "food," whose exemplars I can point to in a room, I cannot point to anything in the world and say that it belongs to the category "good" or "bad." That is why some of our philosophers have concluded that morality belongs to aesthetics. Good and bad are evaluative terms whose meanings rest with our feelings, and one source of these feelings is part of our nature. I trust you agree that the emotion of empathy emerges in all children by the second birthday. A second source of these feelings is more complex and I am less certain of its origins. All children seem to appreciate the actions and qualities their community classifies as good or bad. If they act in a way that deviates from their understanding of the community's belief, the evaluative self feels a lack of virtue and the person will try to behave in a way that will enhance the sense of virtue. So each person looks for opportunities that will permit the evaluative self to come to the judgment that it is good. We celebrate Gando's birthday each year and erected a statue of him in the Common. You will remember that he was incompetent in school, a poor athlete, and he stammered at group meetings. I suggest that he had a sense of being ineffective as a young man and, therefore, felt minimally virtuous. He became our most moral citizen to enhance his virtue. He defended the rights of slaves against a vocal majority and fasted for three months to gain their eventual freedom. Our community was so moved by that act of sacrifice they insisted on legislation to honor him. I do not wish to minimize Gando's accomplishments, nor do I impugn his moral intentions when I suggest that those moral behaviors were attempts to persuade the evaluative self of its virtue. Perhaps he had to behave more morally than his peers because he was less effective than they in the domains that, as a child, he had learned were valued by our community. I am not suggesting that his moral actions were not issued out of honest care for others. He chose to help those in need because, like Ignatio in front of Michael's fence, he could not do otherwise. But he felt that strongly because his evaluative self demanded affirmation of its virtue.

Let me give you a second example. You must remember our revered scholar Wigetto, who confided to a friend that he had committed two crimes for which he felt guilty. As a school teacher in one of our rural districts he once struck a girl who was a pupil in his classroom. Initially he denied the act to the authorities and felt badly about that lie. More seriously, he let his friends believe that he had no barbarian blood, when he knew that one of his grandfathers had been a northern barbarian. He felt guilty over permitting that deceit to persist and experienced a lack of virtue. In order to relieve the guilt he gave away most of his money and worked without stipend for years. As you know, he wrote a long treatise about morality in which he attempted to place it on a transcendental plane. I suggest that his behavior during most of his adult life was an attempt to affirm the evaluative self's virtue.

S: But that argument makes the absurd prediction that the more effective, talented, or potent a person is the more virtuous he will feel and, therefore, the less moral he will be in a conventional sense. We both know that is not true. The peasant is not more honest or loyal than the successful artist or merchant. According to your argument, peasants should be our most moral citizens because they have minimal effectiveness in other domains we value.

R: And they may be. If we equated the opportunities to commit the same immoral acts for our peasants and our artists, I am not certain who would emerge as more moral. But you will recall that this discussion arose because you claimed that self-interest was an exception to my insistence that the subjective and objective frames should be distinguished. I am suggesting that the evaluative self has a continual desire to affirm its virtue. If that victory occurs in one domain of living, there is a less urgent need to affirm it in another. But this desire usually takes precedence over all other interests of our many selves. It is our most important interest.

S: I believe you choose words to suit your argument. I claim that the self's attempt to prove it is virtuous is simply a derivative of self-interest; self-interest is always primary. Reassuring the self of its virtue permits it to conclude that it is better than others and, therefore, entitled to more privilege.

R: Slow, you run too fast with that idea. I don't think you are right when you say people are always comparing their self with the self of another. We do not do so when we remove a piece of glass from a path. The idea that humans always act in the service of self-interest has created serious mischief. So many citizens have come to accept the truth of that assumption about human nature that the average person now treats it as a natural law. And because they believe they should not violate a natural law, they try to obey it. Indeed, some of our citizens feel uneasy when they do not act in self-interest, even at times when they do not wish to. This so-called law is simply an ethical statement with no more scientific validity than the proposition, "Poseidon rules the oceans." What worries me is that the presumptive validity of the law of self-interest is becoming a self-fulfilling prophecy. Let me remind you of a current problem in our society, where the desire among some citizens for virtue appears to undermine their self-interest.

S: I don't believe you can do so.

R: Many citizens in our community have become upset by the fact that some of our naturalists are doing experiments with small animals, usually rabbits, to find out how our bodies work and discover ways to cure our serious diseases. These discoveries will surely benefit the entire community. Yet this vocal group claims

that the work is cruel to the animals, and they insist that the
research be stopped, even though cessation of the work is opposed to their own self-interest for it will delay the time when
these common diseases will be cured.

S: Well, isn't it cruel to cut up a rabbit's body?

R: No more cruel than what our butchers do to prepare a holiday
meal. Why is it not cruel to kill a pig for a wedding feast but cruel
to kill a rabbit to learn more about human diseases?

S: Well, we must eat meat.

R: That is not true; you know we could survive on plants. It is
possible to live a healthy life and never eat animal flesh. No, I
don't believe these people care deeply about an animal's feelings.
Their deep motive, and I doubt they are aware of it, is to impugn
the moral authority of the naturalists. Those who study nature are
highly respected by most citizens in our community. They have
secure positions, are well financed, and each year many are publicized and receive state honors. But they talk to each other about
their work in technical language most of us do not understand,
and they are beginning to probe phenomena we believe are sensitive and private. As a result, the average citizen has become
threatened by their work and would like to reduce their power
and virtue. A good way to accomplish this goal is to challenge
their morality by accusing them of being cruel to animals. That is
a serious charge, for it implies that our naturalists have less virtue
than they and most of the community believe.

S: How can you be certain of that counterintuitive explanation? Do
you have another example?

R: I do, but it is even more speculative. You will remember from
your study of ancient history that the Brehwins were poor
shepherds in the desert, surrounded on one side by the Potomies
and on the other by the Tyleptians—two groups with much secular power and wealth.

S: Yes, I do remember.

R: Well, suppose the Potomies and the Tyleptians were like our naturalists and the Brehwins were the citizens attacking them. The
Brehwins were threatened by the power of their two neighbors
and, therefore, motivated to find a way to reduce their authority.
Unconsciously they looked for some accusation that would impugn their morality.

S: What did the Brehwins do? I forget.

R: You will remember that the Potomies and the Tyleptians believed in local gods—a god for the wind, a god for the sun, one for the earth. These gods were unpredictable and not always on man's side in times of crisis. Wouldn't it be clever to invent a god that was superior to all these local gods, a god who was in charge of the sun, the earth, the water—a god who controlled all the gods. It would also be wise to make this god a trusted, gentle being who was always man's friend. That is exactly what the Brehwins did. You will remember that they claimed their god was superior to the many gods of the Potomies and the Tyleptians. They even declared that the gaining of wisdom and honesty—two qualities they as shepherds could attain—were morally superior to the accumulation of wealth and power, which they felt they were unable to attain. They impugned the moral authority of the Potomies and the Tyleptians, as some of our citizens impugn the morality of our naturalists.

S: That is an extremely speculative argument.

R: I agree. But I believe in the principle it illustrates. The evaluative self is made uneasy by any person or group that has more of some quality it regards as symbolic of virtue. So it persuades the executive self to denigrate those people in some way. If it can't take away their secular signs of virtue, be they power, wealth, or status, it can suggest that they are immoral.

S: It seems now that you agree with my view of the primacy of self-interest. Since people in most societies believe that poverty, low status, or being dominated by others leads the evaluative self to feel a lack of virtue, doesn't it follow that in order to avoid judging the self as bad these less advantaged persons would seek to gain more wealth, status, and power. You must agree that such motives and actions are self-interested.

R: That is very clever of you.

S: And since more, rather than less, wealth, status, and power bring better health and the ability to resist exploitation and coercion, it is unlikely that any society would, for very long, hold the belief that these qualities were bad. And if I am right in that assertion then self-interest would be universal in both the objective and the subjective frames.

R: You catch me without an immediate reply, but your argument holds only for societies with variation in wealth, power, and status.

S: But you will acknowledge that such variation exists in all societies we know anything about.

R: Will you accept a compromise? If self-interest refers to desires for sensory pleasure, power, wealth, and status, then can we agree that self-interest is only a primary preoccupation of human beings when there is variation in these prizes? However, the preoccupation of the evaluative self with affirmation of its virtue is salient under all societal conditions. You and I can imagine conditions in which self-interest was not a foremost concern but cannot imagine conditions in which affirmation of virtue was not.

S: Yes, in a mood of wild fancy I might imagine such a hypothetical community. But because its realization is impossible, for all practical purposes my claim that self-interest is a universal characteristic of our species is true. Do you appreciate that this is the first time in our many discussions that you have become the idealist and I the skeptic? How did that happen?

R: Yes, I did note that change in our positions, and my feeling self is troubled. My executive self shall brood on it this afternoon and give you a reply when we meet tomorrow morning.

References

Introduction

Boyd, J. P., ed. 1955. *The Papers of Thomas Jefferson,* vol. 12. Princeton, N.J.: Princeton University Press.

Briggs, J. 1970. *Never in Anger.* Cambridge: Harvard University Press.

Carr, E. H. 1961. *What Is History?* New York: Vintage.

Edgerton, R. B. 1971. *The Individual in Cultural Adaptation: A Study of Four East African Peoples.* Berkeley: University of California Press.

Eibl-Eibesfeldt, I. 1974. Phylogenetic adaptation as determinants of aggressive behavior in man. In J. De Wit and W. W. Hartup, eds., *Determinants and Origins of Aggressive Behavior,* pp. 29–57. The Hague: Mouton.

Holton, G. 1988. The roots of complementarity. *Daedalus* 117:151–197. (Originally in *Daedalus,* 1970.)

Janik, A., and S. Toulmin. 1973. *Wittgenstein's Vienna.* New York: Simon and Schuster.

Jencks, C. 1972. *Inequality.* New York: Basic Books.

Kagan, J., and R. E. Klein 1973. Crosscultural perspectives on early development. *American Psychologist* 28:947–961.

Ludmerer, K. M. 1972. *Genetics and American Society.* Baltimore: Johns Hopkins University Press.

Mayr, E. 1977. Darwin and natural selection. *American Scientist* 62:321–327.

McCloskey, R. G. 1967. *Introduction to the Work of James Wilson,* vol. 1, pp. 132–133. Cambridge: Harvard University Press.

Sperry, R. W. 1977. Bridging science and values: a unifying view of mind and brain. *American Psychologist* 32:237–245.

White, M. 1972. *Science and Sentiment in America.* New York: Oxford University Press.

Wilson, E. O. 1975. *Sociobiology.* Cambridge: Harvard University Press.

Chapter 1: Meaning and Procedure

Ackermann, R. J. 1985. *Data, Instruments, and Theory.* Princeton: Princeton University Press.

Adams, A. E., S. N. Haynes, and M. A. Brayer. 1985. Cognitive distraction in female sexual arousal. *Psychophysiology* 22:689–696.

Atkins, P. W. 1984. *The Second Law.* New York: Scientific American Books.

Beach, F. A. 1950. The snark is a boojum. *American Psychologist* 5:115–124.

Bridgman, P. W. 1927. *The Logic of Modern Physics.* New York: Macmillan.

Cairns, R. B., and B. D. Cairns. In press. The developmental-interactional view of social behavior. In D. Olweus, J. Block, and M. Radke-Yarrow, eds., *Development of Antisocial and Prosocial Behavior: Theories, Research and Issues.* New York: Academic Press.

Cairns, R. B., D. J. McCombie, and K. E. Hood. 1983. A developmental-genetic analysis of aggressive behavior in mice. I: Behavioral outcomes. *Journal of Comparative Psychology* 97:68–69.

Campbell, B. A., and M. Ampuero. 1985. Dissociation of autonomic and behavioral components of conditioned fear during development in the rat. *Behavioral Neuroscience* 99:1089–1102.

Carnap, R. 1956. The methodological character of theoretical concepts. In H. Feigl and M. Scriven, eds., *Minnesota Studies in the Philosophy of Science,* vol. 1: *The Foundations of Science in the Concepts of Psychology and Psychoanalysis.* Minneapolis: University of Minnesota Press.

Churchland, P. M. 1979. *Scientific Realism and the Plasticity of Mind.* Cambridge: Cambridge University Press.

——— 1984. *Matter and Consciousness.* Cambridge: MIT Press.

Ciochon, R. L., and R. S. Corruccini, eds. 1983. *New Interpretations of Ape and Human Ancestry.* New York: Plenum.

Creel, D. 1980. Inappropriate use of albino animals as models in research. *Pharmacology, Biochemistry, and Behavior* 6:969–977.

Crews, F. 1986. In the big house of theory. *New York Review of Books,* May 26, pp. 36–42.

Delaporte, F. 1982. *Nature's Second Kingdom.* Trans. by A. Goldhammer. Cambridge: MIT Press.

Dyson, F. 1979. *Disturbing the Universe*. New York: Harper and Row.

Ekman, P., W. V. Friesen, P. Ellsworth. 1972. *Emotion in the Human Face: Guidelines for Research and an Integration of Findings*. New York: Pergamon.

Ellis, B. 1966. *Basic Concepts of Measurement*. Cambridge: Cambridge University Press.

Fagan, J. F. 1984. The relationship of novelty preferences during infancy to later intelligence and later recognition memory. *Intelligence* 8: 339–346.

Feigl, H. 1956. Some major issues and developments in the philosophy of science of logical empiricism. In H. Feigl and M. Scriven, eds., *Minnesota Studies in the Philosophy of Science*, vol. 1: *The Foundations of Science in the Concepts of Psychology and Psychoanalysis*. Minneapolis: University of Minnesota Press.

Flourens, P. 1842. *Recherches expérimentales sur les propriétés et les fonctions du système nerveux dans les animaux vertébrés*. 2nd ed. Paris: Baillière.

Foley, R. 1986. *The Theory of Epistemic Rationality*. Cambridge: Harvard University Press.

Freedman, J. L. 1984. Effect of television violence on aggressiveness. *Psychological Bulletin* 96:227–246.

Frege, G. 1892. Uber Sinn und Bedeutung. *Zeitschrift fur Philosophie und philosophische Kritik* 100:25–56. (In P. Geach and M. Black, eds., *Translations from the Philosophical Writings of Gottlob Frege*, pp. 56–78. Oxford: Basil Blackwell, 1960.)

———— 1979. *Posthumous Writings*. Chicago: University of Chicago Press.

Hayakawa, S. I. 1941. *Language in Thought and Action*. New York: Harcourt Brace.

Henderson, N. D. 1967. Prior treatment effects on open field behavior of mice—a genetic analysis. *Animal Behavior* 15:364–376.

Hoffman, H. S., L. A. Eiserer, A. M. Ratner, and V. L. Pickering. 1974. Development of distress vocalization during withdrawal of an imprinting stimulus. *Journal of Comparative and Physiological Psychology* 86:563–568.

Holton, G. 1973. *Thematic Origins of Scientific Thought*. Cambridge: Harvard University Press.

Hubner, K. 1983. *Critique of Scientific Reason*. Trans. by P. R. Dixon and H. M. Dixon. Chicago: University of Chicago Press.

Kagan J. 1984. *The Nature of the Child*. New York: Basic Books.

Kagan, J., S. Hans, A. Markowitz, D. Lopez, and H. Sigal. 1982. Validity of children's self-reports of psychological qualities. In B. A. Maher and W. B. Maher, eds., *Progress in Experimental Personality Research*, vol. 11. New York: Academic Press.

Kagan, J., J. S. Reznick, C. Clarke, N. Snidman, and C. Garcia-Coll. 1984. Behavioral inhibition to the unfamiliar. *Child Development* 55:2212–2225.

Knight, M. L., and R. T. Borden. 1979. Autonomic and affective reactions of high and low socially anxious individuals awaiting public performance. *Psychophysiology* 16:209–217.

Kraft, V. 1953. *The Vienna Circle.* New York: Philosophical Library.

Lang, P. J., D. N. Levin, G. A. Miller, and M. J. Kozak. 1983. Fear behavior, fear imagery, and the psychophysiology of emotion. *Journal of Abnormal Psychology* 92:276–306.

Le Douarain, N. 1982. *The Neural Crest.* Cambridge: Cambridge University Press.

Lowe, V. 1985. *Alfred North Whitehead: The Man and His Work.* Vol. 1. Baltimore: Johns Hopkins University Press.

MacCorquodale, K., and P. E. Meehl. 1948. On a distinction between hypothetical constructs and intervening variables. *Psychological Review* 55:95–107.

Mach, E. 1959. *The Analysis of Sensations.* New York: Dover.

Marsh, H. W., and J. W. Parker. 1984. Determinants of student self-concept. *Journal of Personality and Social Psychology* 47:213–231.

Nisbett, R. E., and T. D. Wilson. 1977. Telling more than we can know: verbal reports on mental processes. *Psychological Review* 84:231–259.

Ortony, A. 1979. Beyond literal similarity. *Psychological Review* 86:161–180.

Pears, D. 1984. *Motivated Irrationality.* Oxford: Clarendon Press.

Petersen, A. 1985. *The Philosophy of Niels Bohr.* In A. P. French and P. J. Kennedy, eds., *Niels Bohr: A Centenary Volume.* Cambridge: Harvard University Press.

Plomin, R., and T. T. Foch. 1980. A twin study of objectively assessed personality in childhood. *Journal of Personality and Social Psychology* 39:680–688.

Popper, K. R. 1972. *Objective Knowledge: An Evolutionary Approach.* Oxford: Clarendon Press.

Putnam, H. 1975. *Mind, Language, and Reality.* In *Philosophical Papers,* vol. 2. New York: Cambridge University Press.

——— 1983. *Realism and Reason.* In *Philosophical Papers,* vol. 3. New York: Cambridge University Press.

Reznick, J. S., and J. Kagan. 1982. Category detection in infancy. In L. Lipsitt, ed., *Advances in Infancy Research,* vol. 2. Norwood, N.J.: Ablex.

Rothbart, M. K., and D. Derryberry. 1981. Development of individual differences in temperament. In M. E. Lamb and A. L. Brown, eds.,

Advances in Developmental Psychology, vol. 1, pp. 37–86. Hillsdale, N.J.: L. Erlbaum.

Russell, B. 1962. *An Inquiry into Meaning and Truth.* Baltimore: Penguin.

Sackett, G. P., G. C. Ruppenthal, C. H. Fahrenbruch, R. A. Holm, and W. T. Greenough. 1981. Social isolation rearing effects in monkeys vary with genotype. *Developmental Psychology* 17:313–318.

Schlick, M. 1979. *Philosophical Papers: Volume II (1925–1936),* ed. H. L. Mulder and B. van de Velde-Schlick. Dordrecht: D. Reidel. (Rpt. in O. Hanfling, ed., *Essential Readings in Logical Positivism.* Oxford: Blackwell, 1981.)

Schneider-Rosen, K. 1984. Quality of attachment and the development of the self system. Ph.D. diss., Harvard University.

Sewitch, D. E. 1984. The perceptual uncertainty of having slept: the inability to discriminate electroencephalographic sleep from wakefulness. *Psychophysiology* 21:243–259.

Smith, T. W., B. K. Houston, and R. M. Zurawski. 1984. Finger pulse volume as a measure of anxiety in response to evaluative threat. *Psychophysiology* 21:260–264.

Stich, S. P. 1983. *From Folk Psychology to Cognitive Science: The Case against Belief.* Cambridge: MIT Press.

Strawson, P. F. 1985. *Skepticism and Naturalism: Some Varieties.* New York: Columbia University Press.

Thomas, D. 1979. *Naturalism and Social Science.* Cambridge: Cambridge University Press.

Tversky, A. 1977. Features of similarity. *Psychological Review* 84:327–352.

Waldrop, M. M. 1984. New light on dark matter. *Science* 224:971–973.

Wall, P. D. 1974. "My foot hurts me": an analysis of a sentence. In R. Bellairs and E. G. Gray, eds., *Essays on the Nervous System,* pp. 391–406. Oxford: Clarendon Press.

Washburn, S. L., and P. L. Dolhinow. 1983. Comparison of human behaviors. In D. W. Rajecki, ed., *Comparing Behavior: Studying Man, Studying Animals,* pp. 27–42. Hillsdale, N.J.: L. Erlbaum.

Watson, D., and L. E. Clark. 1984. Negative affectivity: the disposition to experience aversive emotional states. *Psychological Bulletin* 96:465–490.

Weisblat, D. A., and G. S. Stent. 1982. Cell lineage analysis by intracellular injection of tracer substances. In A. A. Moscona and P. Monroy, eds., *Current Topics in Developmental Biology,* vol. 17, pp. 1–31. New York: Academic Press.

Whitehead, A. N. 1928. *Science and the Modern World.* New York: Macmillan.

Wilson, E. O. 1975. *Sociobiology*. Cambridge: Harvard University Press.

Wittgenstein, L. 1922. *Tractatus Logico-Philosophicus*. London: Routledge and Kegan Paul.

—— 1953. *Philosophical Investigations*. New York: Macmillan.

Zubin, J., and B. Spring. 1977. Vulnerability—a new view of schizophrenia. *Journal of Abnormal Psychology* 86:103–126.

Chapter 2: Twentieth-Century Trends

Ainsworth, M. D. S., M. C. Blehar, E. Waters, and S. Wall. 1978. *Patterns of Attachment*. Hillsdale, N.J.: L. Erlbaum.

Arend, R., F. L. Gove, and L. A. Sroufe. 1979. Continuity of individual adaptation from infancy to kindergarten. *Child Development* 50: 950–959.

Baldwin, J. M. 1895. *Mental Development in the Child and the Race*. New York: Macmillan.

Belsky, J., and M. J. Rovine. 1988. Nonmaternal care in the first year of life and the security of infant–parent attachment. *Child Development* 59:157–167.

Bowlby, J. 1980. *Attachment and Loss*. Vol. 3, *Loss*. New York: Basic Books.

Bretherton, I., and E. Waters, eds. 1985. Growing points of attachment theory and research. *Monographs of the Society for Research in Child Development* 50:1–2.

Bridges, L. J., J. P. Connell, and J. Belsky. 1988. Similarities and differences in infant–mother and infant–father interaction in the Strange Situation: a component process analysis. *Developmental Psychology* 24:92–100.

Chen, S., and K. Miyake. 1982–1983. Japanese versus United States comparison of mother–infant interaction and infant development. In K. Miyake, ed., *Annual Report of the Research and Clinical Center for Child Development*. Hokkaido, Japan: Faculty of Education, Hokkaido University.

Compayre, G. 1914. *Development of the Child in Later Infancy*, pt. 2. New York: D. Appleton.

Cravens, H. 1978. *The Triumph of Evolution*. Philadelphia: University of Pennsylvania Press.

Dollard, J., and N. E. Miller 1950. *Personality and Psychotherapy*. New York: McGraw-Hill.

Donaldson, M. 1978. *Childrens' Minds*. New York: W. W. Norton.

Easterbrooks, M. A., and M. E. Lamb. 1979. The relationship between quality of infant–mother attachment and infant competence in initial encounters with a peer. *Child Development* 50:380–387.

Erickson, M. F., L. A. Sroufe, and B. Egeland. 1985. The relationship between quality of attachment and behavior problems in preschool in a high risk sample. In Bretherton and Waters, 1985.

Evans, E. E. 1975. *The Abuse of Maternity.* New York: Arno Press. 1st publication, Philadelphia: Lippincott, 1875.

Ferguson, G. O. 1916. The psychology of the negro. *Archives of Psychology* 36.

Fiske, J. 1909. *The Meaning of Infancy.* Boston: Houghton-Mifflin. 1st publication 1883.

Gesell, A., and E. E. Lord. 1927. A psychological comparison of nursery school children from homes of low and high economic status. *Pedagogical Seminary* 34:339–356.

Grossmann, K., K. Grossmann, F. Huber, and U. Wartner. 1981. German children's behavior toward their mothers at 12 months and their fathers at 18 months in Ainsworth's Strange Situation. *International Journal of Behavioral Development* 4:157–181.

Gulick, L. 1920. *A Philosophy of Play.* New York: Scribner's.

Gunnar, M. R., S. Mangelsdorf, R. Kestenbaum, S. Lang, M. Larson, and D. Andreas. 1988. Temperament, attachment and reactivity. In D. Cicchetti, ed., *Process and Psychopathology.* New York: Cambridge University Press.

Hock, E., and J. B. Clinger. 1981. Infant coping behaviors. *Journal of Genetic Psychology* 138:231–243.

Humphrey, G. G. 1921. Imitation and the conditioned reflex. *Pedagogical Seminary* 28:1–21.

Kagan, J. 1984. *The Nature of the Child.* New York: Basic Books.

Kagan, J., J. S. Reznick, and N. Snidman. 1988. Biological bases of childhood shyness. *Science* 240:167–171.

LaGasse, L., C. P. Gruber, and L. P. Lipsitt. 1989. The infantile expression of avidity in relation to later assessments of inhibition and attachment. In J. S. Reznick, ed., *Perspectives on Behavioral Inhibition.* Chicago: University Chicago Press.

Lewis, M., C. Feiring, C. McGuffog, and J. Jaskir. 1984. Predicting psychopathology in six-year-olds from early social relations. *Child Development* 55:123–136.

Link, H. C. 1923. What is intelligence? *Atlantic Monthly* 132:374–381.

Locke, J. 1892. *Some Thoughts Concerning Education.* Cambridge: Cambridge University Press. 1st published 1693.

MacArthur, C. G., and C. B. MacArthur. 1916. The menace of academic distinctions. *Scientific Monthly* 2:460–466.

Main, M., and J. Cassidy. 1988. Categories of response to reunion with the parent at age six: predictable from infant attachment classifications and stable over a one month period. *Developmental Psychology* 24:415–426.

Marquis, D. R. 1931. Can conditioned responses be established in the newborn infant? *Pedagogical Seminary* 39:479–492.

May, H. 1959. *The End of American Innocence*. New York: Knopf.

Miyake, K., S. Chen, and J. J. Campos. 1985. Infant temperament, mother's mode of interaction, and attachment in Japan: an interim report. In Bretherton and Waters, 1985.

Muller, H. 1933. The dominance of economics over eugenics. *Scientific Monthly* 37:40–47.

Naslund, B., I. Persson-Blennow, T. McNeil, L. Kaij, and A. Malmquist-Larsson. 1984. Offspring of women with nonorganic psychosis: infant attachment to the mother at one-year-of-age. *Acta Psychiatrica Scandinavia* 69:231–241.

Owen, M. T., M. A. Easterbrooks, L. Chase-Landsdale, and W. A. Goldberg. 1984. The relation between maternal employment status and the stability of attachments to mother and father. *Child Development* 55:1894–1901.

Pastore, N. 1949. *The Nature–Nurture Controversy*. New York: King's Crown Press.

Pearson, K. 1925. Problem of alien immigration into Great Britain. *Annals of Eugenics* 1:5–127.

Piaget, J. 1951. *Play, Dreams, and Imitation in Childhood*. Trans. by C. Gattegno and F. M. Hodgson. London: Routledge and Kegan Paul.

Plunkett, J. W., T. Klein, and S. J. Meisels. 1988. The relationship of preterm infant–mother attachment to stranger sociability at 3 years. *Infant Behavior and Development* 11:83–96.

Richardson, F. H. 1926. *Parenthood and the Newer Psychology*. New York: G. P. Putnam.

Schneider-Rosen, K. 1984. Quality of attachment and the development of the self system. Ph.D. diss., Harvard University.

Schneider-Rosen, K., K. G. Braunwald, V. Carlson, and D. Cicchetti. 1985. Current perspectives in attachment theory: illustration from the study of maltreated infants. In Bretherton and Waters, 1985.

Shinn, M. 1907. *Notes on the Development of a Child*. Vols. 1 and 2, University of California Series, 1893 to 1899. University of California Publications in Education.

Sroufe, L. A. 1985. Attachment classification from the perspective of infant–caregiver relationships and infant temperament. *Child Development* 56:1–14.

Stern, W. 1930. *Psychology of Early Childhood up to the Sixth Year of Age*. Trans. by A. Barwell. New York: Holt Rinehart.

Stevenson-Hinde, J., and A. Shouldice. Unpublished. Fear and attachment in 2.5 year olds.

Sully, J. 1896. *Studies of Childhood*. New York: D. Appleton.

Terman, L. 1916. *The Measurement of Intelligence.* Boston: Houghton Mifflin.

Thompson, R. A., M. E. Lamb, and D. Estes. 1982. Stability of infant–mother attachment and its relationship to changing life circumstances in an unselected middle-class sample. *Child Development* 53:144–148.

van IJzendoorn, M. H., R. van der Vier, and S. V. Vliet-Visser. 1987. Attachment three years later. In L. W. C. Tavecchio and M. H. van IJzendoorn, eds., *Attachment in Social Networks,* pp. 185–224. Amsterdam: North Holland.

Waters, E., J. Wippman, and L. A. Sroufe. 1979. Attachment, positive affect, and competence in the peer group. *Child Development* 50:821–829.

Watson, J. B. 1913. Psychology as the behaviorist views it. *Psychological Review* 20:158–177.

———— 1928. *Psychological Care of Infant and Child.* New York: Norton.

Yerkes, R. M. 1921. *Psychological Examining in the United States Army.* Memoirs of the National Academy of Sciences, vol. 15. Washington, D.C.: National Academy of Sciences.

Chapter 3: The Idea of Temperamental Types

Bain, A. 1861. *On the Study of Character Including an Estimate of Phrenology.* London: Parker.

Breuer, J., and Freud, S. 1956. *Studies in Hysteria.* Trans. by J. and A. Strachey. London: Hogarth Press.

Buss, A. H., and R. Plomin. 1975. *A Temperament Theory of Personality Development.* New York: Wiley.

———— 1984. *Temperament: Early Developing Personality Traits.* Hillsdale, N.J.: L. Erlbaum.

Carmichael, L. 1926. The development of behavior in vertebrates experimentally removed from the influence of external stimulation. *Psychological Review* 33:51–58.

———— 1927. The further study of the development of behavior in vertebrates experimentally removed from the influence of external conditions. *Psychological Review* 34:34–37.

Catsch, A. 1941. Korrelationspathologische Untersuchungen 4. Habitus und Krankheitdisposition Zugleich ein Beitrag zur Frage der Korperbautypologie. *Z. Menschl Vererb-u Konstitut-Lehre* 25:94–127.

Clarke, A. S., W. A. Mason, and G. P. Moberg. 1988. Differential behavioral and adrenocortical responses to stress among three macaque species. *American Journal of Primatology* 14:37–52.

Clarke, E. 1873. *Sex in Education: Or, a Fair Chance for the Girls.* Boston: James Osgood.

Cleland, J. 1882. *The Relation of Brain to Mind.* Glasgow: James Maclehose.

Combe, G. 1829. *The Constitution of Man.* Boston: Carter and Hendee.

Descartes, R. 1980. *Discourse on Method and Meditations on First Philosophy.* Trans. by D. A. Kress. Indianapolis, Indiana: Hackett. 1st published 1637/1641.

Draper, G. 1924. *Human Constitution.* Philadelphia: W. B. Saunders.

Eysenck, H. J. 1953. *The Structure of Human Personality.* London: Methuen.

────── 1957. *The Dynamics of Anxiety and Hysteria.* London: Routledge and Kegan Paul.

Fildes, V. A. 1986. *Breast, Bottles and Babies.* Edinburgh: University of Edinburgh Press.

Fowler, J. A. 1897. *A Manual of Mental Science for Teachers and Students.* New York: Fowler and Walls.

Gall, F. J. 1835. *On the Organ of the Moral Qualities and Intellectual Faculties and the Plurality of the Cerebral Organs.* Trans. by W. Lewis, 6 vols. Boston: Marsh, Copen, and Lyon.

Goldsmith, H. H., and J. J. Campos. 1982. Toward a theory of infant temperament. In R. N. Emde and R. Harmon, eds., *The Development of Attachment and Affiliative Systems,* pp. 161–212. New York: Plenum.

Harrington, A. 1987. *Medicine, Mind and the Double Brain.* Princeton: Princeton University Press.

Hinde, R. A., and A. Dennis. 1986. Categorizing individuals, an alternative to linear analysis. *International Journal of Behavioral Development* 9:105–119.

Hooton, E. A. 1939. *Crime and the Man.* Cambridge: Harvard University Press.

Janet, P. 1901. *The Mental State of Hystericals.* Trans. by C. R. Korson. New York: G. P. Putnam.

Jung, C. G. 1924. *Psychological Types.* New York: Harcourt Brace.

Kagan, J. 1966. Body build and conceptual impulsivity in children. *Journal of Personality* 34:118–128.

Kagan, J., J. S. Reznick, and N. Snidman. 1987. The physiology and psychology of behavioral inhibition in children. *Child Development* 58:1459–1473.

Klineberg, O., S. E. Asch, and H. Block. 1934. An experimental study of constitutional types. *Genetic Psychology Monographs* 16:141–221.

Kretschmer, E. 1926. *Physique and Character.* 2nd ed. Trans. by W. J. H. Sprott. New York: Harcourt Brace.

Kuo, Z. Y. 1924. Psychology without heredity. *Psychological Review* 31:427–448.

Lewis, M., and J. Brooks-Gunn. 1979. *Social Cognition and the Acquisition of Self*. New York: Plenum.

Lombroso, C. 1911. *Crime and Its Causes*. Boston: Little, Brown.

Magnusson, D. 1988. *Individual Development from an Interactional Perspective: A Longitudinal Study*. Hillsdale, N.J.: L. Erlbaum.

Mantegazzo, P. 1904. *Physigonomy and Expression*. 3rd ed. New York: Scribner's.

Myrtek, M. 1984. *Constitutional Psychophysiology*. Trans. by M. W. Greenlee. New York: Academic Press.

Paterson, D. G. 1930. *Physique and Intellect*. New York: Century.

Piaget, J. 1951. *Play Dreams and Imitation in Childhood*. London: Routledge and Kegan Paul.

Plomin, R. 1986. *Development, Genetics, and Psychology*. Hillsdale, N.J.: L. Erlbaum.

Preyer, W. 1888. *The Mind of the Child: Part 1, The Senses and the Will*. New York: D. Appleton.

—— 1889. *The Mind of the Child: Part 2, The Development of Intellect*. New York: D. Appleton.

Rothbart, M. K., and D. Derryberry. 1981. Development of individual differences in temperament. In M. E. Lamb, ed., *Advances in Developmental Psychology,* vol. 1. Hillsdale, N.J.: L. Erlbaum.

Russett, C. Unpublished. The scientific construction of womanhood in the late nineteenth century.

Sanford, R. N., M. M. Adkins, R. B. Miller, and E. A. Cobb. 1943. Physique, personality and scholarship. *Monograph of the Society for Research in Child Development* 8:1-705.

Sheldon, W. H. 1940. *The Varieties of Human Physique*. New York: Harper.

Simms, J. 1887. *Physiognomy Illustrated or Nature's Revelations of Character*. 8th ed. New York: Murray Hill.

Sperry, R. W. 1977. Bridging Science and Values. *American Psychologist* 32:237–245

Spurzheim, J. G. 1834. *Phrenology*. Boston: Marsh, Copen, and Lyon.

Stewart, B. 1881. *Conservation of Energy*. New York: D. Appleton.

Thomas, A., and S. Chess. 1977. *Temperament and Development*. New York: Brunner Mazel.

Walker, R. N. 1962. Body build and behavior in young children. I. Body build and nursery school teachers' ratings. *Monograph of the Society for Research in Child Development* 27:1–94.

Watson, J. B. 1928. *Psychological Care of Infant and Child*. New York: Norton.

Whitehead, A. N. 1925. *Science and the Modern World.* Cambridge: Cambridge University Press.

Chapter 4: Inhibited and Uninhibited Children

Adamec, R. E., and C. Stark-Adamec. 1986. Limbic hyperfunction, limbic epilepsy, and interictal behavior. In B. K. Doane and K. E. Livingston, eds., *The Limbic System,* pp. 129–145. New York: Raven.

Armario, A., A. Lopez-Calderon, T. Jolin, and J. Balasch. 1986. Response of anterior pituitary hormones to chronic stress: the specificity of adaptation. *Neuroscience and Biobehavioral Reviews* 10: 245–250.

Aston-Jones, G. 1985. Behavioral functions of locus coeruleus derived from cellular attributes. *Physiological Psychology* 13:118–126.

Bagnara, J. T., and M. E. Hadley. 1973. *Chromatophores and Color Change.* Englewood: Prentice Hall.

Blanchard, R. T., K. J. Flannelly, and D. C. Blanchard. 1986. Defensive behaviors of laboratory and wild *Rattus norvegicus. Journal of Comparative Psychology* 100:101–107.

Clarke, A. S., and W. A. Mason. In press. Differences between three macaque species in responsiveness to an observer. *International Journal of Primatology.*

Cohen, D. H. 1987. Some organizational principles of a vertebrate conditioning pathway. In N. W. Weinberger, J. L. McGaugh, and G. Lynch, eds., *Memory Systems of the Brain,* pp. 27–48. New York: Guilford.

Conley, J. J. 1985. Longitudinal stability of personality traits: a multi-trait multi-method multi-occasion analysis. *Journal of Personality and Social Psychology* 49:1266–1282.

Cooper, D. O., D. E. Schmidt, and R. J. Barrett. 1983. Strain specific cholinergic changes in response to stress. *Pharmacology, Biochemistry and Behavior* 19:457–462.

Coster, W. 1986. Aspects of voice and conversation in behaviorally inhibited and uninhibited children. Ph.D. diss., Harvard University.

Cranach, B. V., R. Grote-Dham, U. Huffner, F. Marte, G. Reisbeck, and M. Mittelstadt. 1978. Das social Gehemmte im Kindergarten. *Praxis der Kinderpsychologie und Kinderpsychiatrie* 27:167–179.

Csanyi, V., and J. Gervai. 1986. Behavior-genetic analysis of the paradise fish (macropodus opercularis). II. Passive avoidance learning in inbred strains. *Behavior Genetics* 16:553–557.

Cubicciotti, D. D., S. P. Mendoza, W. A. Mason, and E. N. Sassenrath. 1986. Differences between *Saimiri sciureus* and *Callicebus moloch* in physiological responsiveness. *Journal of Comparative Psychology* 100:385–391.

Dantzer, R., and P. Mormede. 1985. Stress in domestic animals. In G. P. Moberg, ed., *Animal Stress*, pp. 81–95. Bethesda: American Physiological Society.

Dargassies, S. S. 1986. *The Neuromotor and Psycho-Affective Development of the Infant*. Amsterdam: Elsevier.

Davidson, R. J., and N. A. Fox. In press. Frontal brain asymmetry predicts infants response to maternal separation.

Davis, M. 1986. Pharmacological and anatomical analysis of fear conditioning using the fear-potentiated startle paradigm. *Behavioral Neuroscience* 100:814–824.

Doerr, H. O., and J. E. Hokanson. 1965. The relation between heart rate and performance in children. *Journal of Personality and Social Psychology* 2:70–76.

Dunn, L. T., and B. J. Everitt. 1988. Double dissociations of the effects of amygdala and insular cortex lesions on conditioned taste aversion, passive avoidance, and neophobia in the rat using the excitotoxin Ibotenic acid. *Behavioral Neuroscience* 102:3–23.

Dunnette, J., and R. Weinshilboum. 1982. Family studies of plasma dopamine-beta hydroxylase. *American Journal of Human Genetics* 34:84–99.

Floderus-Myrhed, B., N. Pedersen, and I. Rasmuson. 1980. Assessment of heritability for personality based on a short form of the Eysenck Personality Inventory. *Behavior Genetics* 10:153–162.

Fox, N. A., and R. J. Davidson. 1988. Patterns of brain electrical activity during the expression of discrete emotions in ten month old infants. *Developmental Psychology* 24:230–236.

———— 1987. EEG asymmetry in ten month old infants in response to approach of a stranger and maternal separation. *Developmental Psychology* 23:233–240.

Garcia-Coll, C., J. Kagan, and J. S. Reznick. 1984. Behavioral inhibition in young children. *Child Development* 55:1005–1019.

Gellhorn, E. 1967. *Principles of Autonomic Somatic Integration*. Minneapolis: University of Minnesota Press.

Gersten, M. 1986. The contribution of temperament to behavior in natural contexts. Ed.D. diss., Harvard Graduate School of Education.

Goddard, M. E., and R. G. Beilharz. 1985. A multi-variate analysis of the genetics of fearfulness in potential guide dogs. *Behavior Genetics* 15:69–89.

Gray, J. A. 1982. *The Neuropsychology of Anxiety*. Oxford: Oxford University Press.

———— 1988. The neuropsychological basis of anxiety. In C. G. Last and

M. Hersen, eds., *The Handbook of Anxiety Disorders*, pp. 10–37. New York: Pergamon.

Henke, P. G. 1988. Electrophysiological activity in the central nucleus of the amygdala: emotionality and stress ulcers in rats. *Behavioral Neuroscience* 102:77–83.

Hockey, R. 1986. Temperament differences in vigilance performance as a function of variations in the suitability of ambient noise level. In J. Strelau, F. H. Farley, and A. Gale, eds., *The Biological Basis of Personality and Behavior*, vol. 2, pp. 163–171. Washington, D.C.: Hemisphere Publishing.

Jahr, C. E., and R. A. Nicoll. 1982. Noradrenergic modulation of dendrodendritic inhibition in the olfactory bulb. *Nature* 297:227–229.

Jung, C. G. 1924. *Psychological Types*. New York: Harcourt Brace.

Kagan, J., and H. A. Moss. 1962. *Birth to Maturity*. New York: John Wiley.

Kagan, J., R. Kearsley, and P. Zelazo. 1978. *Infancy: Its Place in Human Development*. Cambridge: Harvard University Press.

Kagan, J., J. S. Reznick, C. Clarke, N. Snidman, and C. Garcia-Coll. 1984. Behavioral inhibition to the unfamiliar. *Child Development* 55:2212–2225.

Kagan, J., J. S. Reznick, and N. Snidman 1987. The physiology and psychology of behavioral inhibition in children. *Child Development* 58:1459–1473.

——— 1988. Biological bases of childhood shyness. *Science* 240:167–171.

Kling, A. S., R. L. Lloyd, and K. M. Perryman. 1987. Slow wave changes in amygdala to visual, auditory, and social stimuli following lesions of inferior temporal cortex in squirrel monkey *(Saimiri sciureus)*. *Behavioral and Neural Biology* 47:54–72.

Loehlin, J. C. 1982. Are personality traits differentially heritable? *Behavior Genetics* 12:417–428.

McDonald, K. 1983. Stability of individual differences in behavior in a litter of wolf cubs. *Journal of Comparative Psychology* 97:99–106.

Messer, S. B. 1968. The effect of anxiety over intellectual performance on reflective and impulsive children. Ph.D. diss., Harvard University.

Millodot, M. 1975. Do blue-eyed people have more sensitive corneas than brown-eyed people? *Nature* 255:151–152.

Murphey, R. M., F. A. M. Duarte, and M. C. T. Penendo. 1980. Approachability of Bovine cattle in pastures: breed comparisons and a breed X treatment analysis. *Behavior Genetics* 10:170–181.

Nesse, R. M., G. C. Curtis, B. A. Thyer, D. S. McCann, M. Huber-Smith, and R. F. Knopf. 1985. Endocrine and cardiovascular responses during phobic anxiety. *Psychosomatic Medicine* 47:320–332.

Plomin, R. 1986. *Development, Genetics and Psychology.* Hillsdale, N.J.: L. Erlbaum.

Plomin, R., and D. C. Rowe. 1979. Genetic and environmental etiology of social behavior in infancy. *Developmental Psychology* 15:62–72.

Post, R. M., D. R. Rubinow, and J. C. Ballenger. 1986. Conditioning and sensitization in the longitudinal course of affective illness. *British Journal of Psychiatry* 149:191–201.

Redmond, D. E. 1986. The possible role of locus coeruleus noradrenergic activity in anxiety-panic. In W. E. Bunney, E. Costa, and S. G. Potkin, eds., *Proceedings of the 15th Collegium Internationale Neuro-Psychopharamacologicum Congress,* pp. 40–42. New York: Raven Press.

Reznick, J. S., J. Kagan, N. Snidman, M. Gersten, K. Baak, and A. Rosenberg. 1986. Inhibited and uninhibited behavior: a follow-up study. *Child Development* 51:660–680.

Rosenberg, A. A. 1987. Eye color and behavioral inhibition. Ph.D. diss., Harvard University.

Rosenberg, A. A., and J. Kagan. 1987. Iris pigmentation and behavioral inhibition. *Developmental Psychobiology* 20:377–392.

Royce, J. R. 1955. A factorial study of emotionality in the dog. *Psychological Monographs* 69, no. 22, whole no. 407.

Schneirla, T. C. 1965. Aspects of stimulation and organization in approach-withdrawal processes underlying vertebrate development. In D. S. Lehrman, R. A. Hinde, and E. Shaw, eds., *Advances in the Study of Behavior,* vol. 1., pp. 1–74. New York: Academic Press.

Scott, J. P., and J. L. Fuller. 1974. *Dog Behavior: The Genetic Basis.* 1st published as *Genetics and the Social Behavior of the Dog.* Chicago: University of Chicago Press, 1965.

Segal, M. 1985. Mechanisms of action of noradrenaline in the brain. *Physiological Psychology* 13:172–178.

Snidman, N. 1984. Behavioral restraint and the central nervous system. Ph.D. diss., University of California, Los Angeles.

Stacey, P. B., and D. Chiszar. 1978. Body color pattern and the aggressive behavior of male pumpkinseed sun fish *(Leomis Gibbosus)* during the reproductive season. *Behavior* 64:271–297.

Stelmack, R. M., E. Achorn, and A. Michaud. 1977. Extraversion and individual differences in auditory evoked response. *Psychophysiology* 14:368–374.

Stelmack, R. M., and K. B. Campbell. 1974. Extraversion and auditory sensitivity to high and low frequencies. *Perceptual and Motor Skills* 38:875–879.

Stevenson-Hinde, J., R. Stillwell-Barnes, and M. Zunz. 1980. Subjective assessment of rhesus monkeys over four successive years. *Primates* 21:66–82.

Strelau, J. 1985. Temperament and personality: Pavlov and beyond. In J. Strelau, F. H. Farley, and A. Gale, eds., *The Biological Bases of Personality and Behavior,* vol. 1., pp. 25–44. Washington, D.C.: Hemisphere Publishing.

Suomi, S. J. 1987. Genetic and maternal contributions to individual differences in rhesus monkey biobehavioral development. In N. A. Krasnegor, E. M. Blass, M. A. Hofer, and W. P. Smotherman, eds., *Perinatal Development: A Psychobiological Perspective,* pp. 397–420. New York: Academic Press.

Thomas, A., and S. Chess. 1977. *Temperament and Development.* New York: Brunner Mazel.

Thompson, R. F., N. H. Donegan, G. A. Clark, D. G. Lavond, J. S. Lincoln, J. Madden, L. A. Mamoulas, M. D. Monk, and D. A. McCormick. 1987. Neural substrates of discrete defensive conditioned reflexes, conditioned fear states and their interaction in the rabbit. In I. Gormezano, W. F. Prokasy, and R. F. Thompson, eds., *Classical Conditioning,* 3rd ed., pp. 371–399. Hillsdale, N.J.: L. Erlbaum.

Torgersen, S. 1988. *Genetics.* In C. G. Last and M. Hersen, eds., *Handbook of Anxiety Disorders,* pp. 159–170. New York: Pergamon.

Weinshilboum, R. M. 1979. Catecholamine biochemical genetics in human populations. In X. O. Breakefield, ed., *Neurogenetics,* pp. 257–282. New York: Elsevier.

Chapter 5: On Cognitive Development

Boysen, S. T., G. G. Bernston, and J. Prentice. 1987. Simian scribbles. *Journal of Comparative Psychology* 101:82–89.

Churchland, P. S. 1986. *Neurophilosophy.* Cambridge: M.I.T. Press.

Diamond, A. Unpublished. Differences between adult and infant competences. Presented at Fyssen Symposium on "Thought without Language," April 1987.

Duhem, P. 1906. *La Théorie Physique.* Paris.

Eimas, P. D., and J. L. Miller. 1980. Contextual effects in infant speech perception. *Science* 209:1140–1141.

Fischer, K. W., and L. Silvern. 1985. Stages and individual differences in cognitive development. In M. R. Rosenzweig and L. W. Porter, eds., *Annual Reviews of Psychology,* pp. 613–648. Palo Alto: Annual Reviews.

Flavell, J. H., J. R. Speer, F. L. Green, and D. L. August. 1981. The development of comprehension monitoring and knowledge about communication. *Monograph of the Society for Research in Child Development,* vol. 46, no. 5.

Frege, G. 1979. *Posthumous Writings.* Chicago: University of Chicago Press.

Kagan, J. 1981. *The Second Year.* Cambridge: Harvard University Press.

——— 1984. *The Nature of the Child.* New York: Basic Books.

Kagan, J., and R. E. Klein. 1973. Cross-cultural perspectives on early development. *American Psychologist* 28:947–961.

Kagan, J., R. E. Klein, G. E. Finley, B. Rogoff, and E. Nolan. 1979. A cross-cultural study of cognitive development. *Monographs of the Society for Research in Child Development,* vol. 44, no. 5.

Kuhl, P. K., and A. N. Meltzoff. 1982. The bi-modal perception of speech in infancy. *Science* 218:1138–1141.

Miller, J. L., and P. D. Eimas. 1983. Studies on the categorization of speech by infants. *Cognition* 13:135–165.

Mishkin, M., and T. Appenzeller. 1987. The ontogeny of memory. *Scientific American* 256:80–89.

Moore, D., J. Benenson, J. S. Reznick, M. Peters, and J. Kagan. 1987. The effect of numerical information on infant's looking behavior: contradictory evidence. *Developmental Psychology* 23:665–670.

Moore, M. J., J. Kagan, M. Sahl, and S. Grant. 1982. Cognitive profiles and reading ability. *Genetic Psychology Monographs* 105:41–93.

Oden, G. C. 1987. Concept, knowledge and thought. In M. R. Rosenzweig and L. W. Porter, eds., *Annual Review of Psychology,* pp. 203–228. Palo Alto: Annual Reviews.

Rumelhart, D. E., J. L. McClelland, and PDP research group. 1986. *Parallel Distributed Processing.* Cambridge: MIT Press.

Smith, J. M. 1985. *Science and Complexity.* Northwood, Eng.: Science Reviews.

Starkey, P., E. S. Spelke, and R. Gelman. 1983. Detection of intermodal numeral correspondence by human infants. *Science* 222:175–181.

Stent, G. S. 1987. The mind–body problem. *Science* 236:990–992.

Winner, E. 1988. *The Point of Words.* Cambridge: Harvard University Press.

Chapter 6: Creativity in Science

Axelrod, J. 1981. Biochemical pharmacology. In W. Shropshire, ed., *The Joys of Research,* pp. 25–37. Washington, D.C.: Smithsonian Institution Press.

Bronowski, J. 1958. *Science and Human Values.* New York: J. Messner.

French, A. P. 1979. *Einstein: A Centenary Volume.* Cambridge: Harvard University Press.

Hodges, A. 1983. *Alan Turing: The Enigma.* New York: Simon and Schuster.

Holton, G. 1988. *Thematic Origins of Scientific Thought.* Rev. ed. Cambridge: Harvard University Press.

Jacob, F. 1988. *The Statue Within.* New York: Basic Books.

Levi-Montalcini, R. 1988. *In Search of Imperfection.* New York: Basic Books.

Lowe, V. 1985. *Alfred North Whitehead: The Man and His Work,* vol. 1. Baltimore: Johns Hopkins University Press.

Rigden, J. S. 1987. *Rabi.* New York: Basic Books.

Russell, B. 1963. *Portraits from Memory and Other Essays.* New York: Simon and Schuster.

Chapter 7: The Emergence of Self-Awareness

Amsterdam, B. K. 1972. Mirror self image reactions before age two. *Developmental Psychology* 5:297–305.

Bloom, L., P. Lightbown, and L. Hood. 1975. Structure and variation in child language. *Monographs of the Society for Research in Child Development,* vol. 40, no. 1.

Bretherton, I., S. McNew, and M. Beeghly-Smith. 1981. Early person knowledge as expressed in gestural and verbal communications. In M. E. Lamb and L. R. Sherrod, eds., *Infant Social Cognition,* pp. 333–377. Hillsdale, N.J.: Erlbaum.

Bridgman, P. W. 1958. Determinism in modern science. In *Determinism and Freedom in the Age of Modern Science,* ed. S. Hook, pp. 43–63. New York: New York University Press.

Briggs, J. L. 1970. *Never in Anger.* Cambridge: Harvard University Press.

Buhler, C. 1975. *The First Year of Life.* New York: Arno. 1st published New York: John Day, 1930.

Cooley, C. H. 1902. *Human Nature and the Social Order.* New York: Scribner's.

Crook, J. H. 1980. *The Evolution of Human Consciousness.* Oxford: Clarendon Press.

Cummings, E. M., C. Zahn-Waxler, and M. Radke-Yarrow. 1981. Young children's responses to expressions of anger and affection by others in the family. *Child Development* 52:1274–1282.

Delcomyn, F. 1980. Neural bases of rhythmic behavior in animals. *Science* 210:492–498.

Eldredge, N., and S. J. Gould. 1972. Punctuated equilibria. In T. J. N. Schopf, ed., *Models in Paleobiology,* pp. 82–115. San Francisco: Freeman.

Gellerman, R. L. 1981. Psychological development of the Vietnamese child in the second year of life. Ph.D. diss., Harvard University.

Gould, S. J. 1980. *The Panda's Thumb*. New York: W. W. Norton.

Guillaume, P. 1971. *Imitation in Children*. Transl. by E. D. Halperin. Chicago: University of Chicago Press. 1st published Paris, 1926.

Jackowitz, E. R., and M. W. Watson. 1980. Development of object transformations in early pretend play. *Developmental Psychology* 16:543–549.

Kagan, J. 1971. *Change and Continuity in Infancy*. New York: John Wiley.

——. 1981. *The Second Year*. Cambridge: Harvard University Press.

Kagan, J., and H. A. Moss. 1962. *Birth to Maturity*. New York: John Wiley.

Kagan, J., R. B. Kearsley, and P. R. Zelazo. 1978. *Infancy: Its Place in Human Development*. Cambridge: Harvard University Press.

Katz, M. M. W. 1981. Gaining sense at age two in the outer Fiji Islands. Ph.D. diss., Harvard Graduate School of Education.

Lewis, M., and J. Brooks-Gunn. 1979. *Social Cognition and the Acquisition of Self*. New York: Plenum.

Mahler, M. S. 1968. *Human Symbiosis and the Vicissitudes of Individuation*. Vol. 1: *Infantile Psychosis*. New York: International University Press.

Mason, W. A. 1978. Social experience in primate cognitive development. In G. H. Burghardt and M. Bekoff, eds., *The Development of Behavior*, pp. 233–251. New York: Garland.

Mead, G. H. 1934. *Mind, Self, and Society*. Chicago: University of Chicago Press.

Newman, S. A., and H. L. Frisch. 1979. Dynamics of skeletal pattern formation in developing chick limb. *Science* 205:662–668.

Novey, M. S. 1975. The development of knowledge of others' ability to see. Ph.D. diss., Harvard University.

Piaget, J. 1976. *The Grasp of Consciousness*. Cambridge: Harvard University Press.

Preyer, W. 1888. *The Mind of the Child*. Part 1: *The Senses and the Will*. New York: Appleton.

Rabinowicz, T. 1979. The differentiate maturation of the human cerebral cortex. In *Human Growth*, ed. F. Falkner and J. M. Tanner, vol. 3, pp. 97–123. New York: Plenum.

Sackett, G. P., G. C. Ruppenthal, C. E. Fahrenbruch, R. A. Holm, and W. T. Greenough. 1981. Social isolation rearing effects in monkeys vary with genotype. *Developmental Psychology* 17:313–318.

Stanley, S. M. 1981. *The New Evolutionary Timetable*. New York: Basic Books.

Stern, C., and W. Stern. 1928. *Die Kindersprache: Eine Psychologische und Sprachtheoritische Untersuchwag*. 4th ed. Liepzig: Barth.

Sully, J. 1896. *Studies of Childhood.* New York: Appleton.

Tiedemann, D. 1787. *Beobachtungen uber die Entwicklung der Seelen-fahigkeiten.* Altenburg: Oskar Bonde.

Tracy, F., and J. Stimpfl. 1909. *The Psychology of Childhood.* 7th ed. Boston: D. C. Heath.

Weiskrantz, L. 1977. Trying to bridge some neuropsychological gaps between monkey and man. *British Journal of Psychology* 68:431–445.

Weiss, P. A. 1968. *Dynamics of Development.* New York: Academic Press.

Chapter 8: Measuring the Concept of Self

Bachman, J. G., and P. M. O'Malley. 1977. Self-esteem in young men. *Journal of Personality and Social Psychology* 35:365–380.

Baldwin, J. M. 1895. *Mental Development in the Child and the Race.* New York: Macmillan.

Bandura, A. 1977. Self efficacy: toward a unifying theory of behavioral change. *Psychological Review* 84:191–215.

Barker, R. G. 1968. *Ecological Psychology.* Stanford: Stanford University Press.

Brim, O. G., and J. Kagan. 1980. *Constancy and Change in Human Development.* Cambridge: Harvard University Press.

Bugental, J. F. T., and S. L. Zelen. 1950. Investigations into the "self-concept." I. The W-A-Y technique. *Journal of Personality* 18:483–498.

Burton, M. L., and S. B. Nerlove. 1976. Balanced designs for triad tests: two examples from English. *Social Science Research* 5:247–267.

Cliff, N., and F. W. Young. 1968. On the relation between unidimensional judgments and multidimensional scaling. *Organizational Behavior and Human Performance* 3:269–285.

Cooley, C. H. 1902. *Human Nature and the Social Order.* New York: Scribner's.

Coopersmith, S. 1967. *The Antecedents of Self-Esteem.* San Francisco: Freeman.

Ekman, P., W. V. Friesen, and P. Ellsworth. 1972. *Emotion in the Human Face.* Oxford: Pergamon.

Festinger, L. 1954. A theory of social comparison processes. *Human Relations* 7:117–140.

Fukutake, T. 1982. *The Japanese Social Structure.* Trans. by R. P. Dore. Tokyo: University of Tokyo Press.

Funk, S. G., A. D. Horowitz, R. Lipshitz, and F. W. Young. 1976. The perceived structure of American ethnic groups: the use of multi-dimensional scaling in stereotype research. *Sociometry* 39:116–130.

Harter, S. 1979. *Perceived Competence Scale for Children.* Denver: University of Denver.

Hogan, L. E. 1898. *A Study of a Child.* New York: Harper.

Hua, J., Z. We, and A. Zhang. 1983. *Contemporary Chinese Paintings.* Beijing: New World Press.

Izard, C. E. 1971. *The Face of Emotion.* New York: Appleton.

Kagan, J. 1958. The concept of identification. *Psychological Review* 65:296–305.

——— 1981. *The Second Year.* Cambridge: Harvard University Press.

——— and W. Phillips. 1964. Measurement of identification. *Journal of Abnormal and Social Psychology* 69:442–444.

Lewin, K. 1951. *Field Theory and Social Science: Selected Theoretical Papers.* New York: Harper.

Lewis, M., and J. Brooks-Gunn. 1979. *Social Cognition and the Acquisition of Self.* New York: Plenum.

Livesley, W. J., and D. B. Bromley. 1973. *Person Perception in Childhood and Adolescence.* New York: Wiley.

Maccoby, E. E., and W. C. Wilson. 1957. Identification and observational learning from films. *Journal of Abnormal and Social Psychology* 55:76–87.

McGuire, W. J. 1978. The spontaneous self-concept as affected by personal distinctiveness. Presented at Self-Concept Symposium, Boston, Massachusetts.

McGuire, W. J., C. V. McGuire, P. Child, and T. Fujioka. 1978. Salience of ethnicity in the spontaneous self-concept as a function of one's ethnic distinctiveness in a social environment. *Journal of Personality and Social Psychology* 36:511–520.

McGuire, W. J., and A. Padawer-Singer. 1976. Trait salience in a spontaneous self-concept. *Journal of Personality and Social Psychology* 33:743–754.

Mead, G. H. 1934. *Mind, Self and Society.* Chicago: University of Chicago Press.

Mischel, W. 1977. On the future of personality measurement. *American Psychologist* 32:246–254.

Murray, H. A. 1938. *Explorations in Personality.* London and New York: Oxford University Press.

Piers, E. V., and D. B. Harris. 1964. Age and other correlates of self-concept in children. *Journal of Educational Psychology* 55:91–95.

Preyer, W. 1889. *The Mind of a Child.* Part 2. New York: Appleton.

Pye, L. W. 1985. *Asian Power and Politics.* Cambridge: Harvard University Press.

Rabinowitz, G. B. 1975. An introduction to nonmetric multidimensional scaling. *American Journal of Political Science* 19:343–390.

Rosenberg, M. 1979. *Conceiving the Self.* New York: Basic Books.

Rosenberg, S., and R. Jones. 1972. A method for investigating and representing a person's implicit theory of personality: Theodore Dreiser's view of people. *Journal of Personality and Social Psychology* 22:372–386.

Shepard, R. N., A. K. Romney, and S. B. Nerlove, eds. 1972. *Multidimensional Scaling: Theory.* New York: Seminar Press.

Shrauger, J. S., and S. Schoeneman. 1979. Symbolic interactionist view of self-concept: through the looking-glass darkly. *Psychological Bulletin* 86:549–573.

Smith, M. B. 1979. Attitudes, values and selfhood. In W. J. Arnold and D. Levine, eds., *Nebraska Symposium on Motivation,* vol. 27. Lincoln: University of Nebraska Press.

Stern, W. 1930. *Psychology of Early Childhood up to the 6th Year of Life.* 6th ed. New York: Holt.

Stotland, E., and R. E. Dunn. 1963. Empathy, self-esteem, and birth order. *Journal of Abnormal and Social Psychology* 66:532–540.

Wells, L. E., and G. Marwell. 1976. *Self-Esteem: Its Conceptualization and Measurement.* Beverly Hills: Sage Publications.

Wylie, R. *The Self-Concept.* 1961. Lincoln: University of Nebraska Press.

—— 1974. *The Self-Concept: A Review of Methodological Considerations and Measuring Instruments.* Vol. 1. Lincoln: University of Nebraska Press.

—— 1979. *The Self-Concept.* Vol. 2. Rev. ed. Lincoln: University of Nebraska Press.

Young, F. W. 1974. *Conjoint Scaling.* Chapel Hill: University of North Carolina.

Acknowledgments

Parts of the Introduction first appeared in Jerome Kagan, Richard B. Kearsley, and Philip R. Zelazo, *Infancy* (Cambridge: Harvard University Press, 1978), and in "Perspectives on Infancy," in *Handbook of Infant Development,* 2nd ed., edited by Joy Osofsky (New York: Wiley, 1987). Sections of Chapter 1 were first published in "The Meanings of Personality Predicates," *American Psychologist* 43 (1988):614–620. Chapter 2 represents an extension of a shorter essay of the same title which appeared in *Fifty Years of Psychology,* edited by Ernest R. Hilgard (Glenville, Ill.: Scott, Foresman and Co., 1988).

J. Steven Reznick and Nancy Snidman have been continuous collaborators on the research on temperament that is summarized in Chapters 3 and 4. I am deeply appreciative of their friendship and constructive wisdom. Chapter 4 expands upon ideas that also appear in "The Concept of Behavioral Inhibition" in *Perspectives on Behavioral Inhibition,* edited by J. Steven Reznick (Chicago: University of Chicago Press, 1989).

Chapter 5 represents an elaboration of a paper delivered at a conference on cognitive development held at Rutgers University in 1987. The original paper appears in *Cognition and Education,* edited by Charles A. Maher, Milton Schwebel, and Nancy Fagley (New Brunswick, N.J.: Rutgers University Press, 1989). Some of the ideas in Chapter 6 were first presented at a conference on creativity at the Smithsonian Institution, Washington, D.C., in April 1988. Chapter 7 is an abridgment of "The Emergence of Self," *Journal of Child Psychology and Psychiatry* 23 (1982):363–381. Chapter 8 is a summary

Acknowledgments

of research that was first published in Jerome Kagan, Sydney Hans, Alice Markowitz, Diane Lopez, and Heidi Sigal, "Validity of Children's Self Reports of Psychological Qualities," in *Progress in Experimental Personality Research*, vol. 11, edited by B. A. Maher and W. B. Maher (New York: Academic Press; copyright © 1982 by Academic Press).

I have benefited from the loyalty and intelligence of the many students who have worked in our laboratory over the past twenty-five years. A special debt of thanks is owed to Marshall Haith for his comments on Chapter 1 and to Jack Hilgard for his critique of Chapter 2. For creative editing of this volume I am grateful to Susan Wallace of Harvard University Press.

The research described in these chapters was supported by grants from the Foundation for Child Development, National Institute of Mental Health, and the John D. and Catherine T. MacArthur Foundation.

Index

Abortion, 23, 24
Achorn, E., 168
Ackermann, R. J., 62
Adamec, R. E., 147, 173n
Adolescence, 92, 193–194, 208, 209–210, 212
Aggression, 8, 13, 21, 25, 26, 43, 225, 226, 228; and morality, 20, 72; and studies of brain, 27, 110; and TV violence, 54
Ainsworth, Mary, 81, 82, 89
Ainsworth Strange Situation, 60, 81–89, 95
Alexander, Secretary of the Army, 70
Allport, Gordon, 38, 213
Alvarez, Luis, 211
Amsterdam, B. K., 234
Anger, 9, 11, 25–26, 101, 278
Animal studies, 4, 6, 42, 43, 74, 102, 145–147, 283–284; use of animal models in, 50–51, 54, 67
Anxiety, 46, 83, 97, 98, 99, 127, 141, 190, 228–230. *See also* Ainsworth Strange Situation; Fear
Aquinas, Thomas, 20, 45
Aries, Phillipe, 262
Aristotle, 14
Artificial intelligence, 5, 17, 60n, 167, 200, 201, 203
Asch, Solomon, 115
Attachment theory, 79–83, 95, 174
Avery, Oswald, 206
Axelrod, Julius, 216

Bacon, Francis, 180, 222; *Novum Organum*, 110
Bain, A., 110
Baldwin, J. M., 76, 243
Beach, F. A.: "The Snark is a Boojum," 67
Behavioral Neuroscience, 65
Behaviorism, 69–74, 89, 90, 144
Beilharz, R. G., 146
Biology, 5–12, 13, 17, 20–21, 61; and behavior, 7–9, 21–22, 97, 109–110, 222–223; and environment, 13, 111, 125, 127; and meaning, 37, 39, 40, 47; molecular, 68; and racism, 70–74; and psychology, 73, 94, 115, 122, 131–132, 133, 134–136, 137, 139, 142, 194, 195, 200, 241; and cognitive functions, 93–94, 180, 182, 185, 186, evolutionary, 127, 202, 240, 241, 242; and inhibition, 156–160, 163, 169
Birth to Maturity (Kagan), 1, 13
Block, Helen, 115
Bloom, Lois, 233
Boaz, Franz, 71
Bohr, Niels, 41, 47, 48, 49, 50, 57, 102, 130, 184, 211
Boltzmann, Ludwig, 25
Bowlby, John, 10, 11, 80, 82, 89, 95
Brenner, Jeffrey, 237
Breuer, Joseph, 117, 118
Bridgman, P. W., 38, 44, 60, 61
Briggs, Jean, 25
Bronowski, J., 204
Brooks-Gunn, J., 124, 233, 239